Anita Stewart's
CANADA

Anita Stewart's CANADA

THE FOOD | THE RECIPES | THE STORIES

HarperCollins*PublishersLtd*

Anita Stewart's Canada
© 2008 by Anita Stewart.
Foreword © 2008 by Jean-Daniel Lafond, C.C.
All rights reserved.

Published by HarperCollins Publishers Ltd

First Edition

HarperCollins books may be purchased for educational, business,
or sales promotional use through our Special Markets Department.

HarperCollins Publishers Ltd
2 Bloor Street East, 20th Floor
Toronto, Ontario, Canada
M4W 1A8

www.harpercollins.ca

Library and Archives Canada Cataloguing in Publication

Stewart, Anita
Anita Stewart's Canada: the food, the recipes, the stories.

ISBN 978-1-55468-231-7

1. Cookery, Canadian. I. Title.

TX715.6.S737 2008   641.5971   C2007-906573-2

PP 9 8 7 6 5 4 3 2 1

Th author wishes to gratefully acknowledge the following source for information
relating to immigrants to Canada used in sidebars throughout this book:
The Encyclopedia of Canada's Peoples, Paul Robert Magocsi, Ed. Published for the
Multicultural History Society of Toronto, University of Toronto Press, Toronto, 1999

Photographs on pages 8, 26, 35, 48, 72, 98, 112, 116, 140, 174,
200, 218, 244, 276, 284, 294 and 304 by Robert Wigington
Food styling by Olga Truchan and Wendy Bowen
Prop styling by Susan Florian
Photo assistance by Mark Paré

All other photographs by Anita Stewart

Text and layout by Sharon Kish
Printed and bound in China

Page ii: To me, this sign, at a crossroads in Nova Scotia, is a symbol of the cultural diversity of Canada.
Page vi: In her 90th year, Mom set out on her first fishing expedition. On a day when few other fish
were being caught, and with her grandson Mark's help, she proudly landed this 12.3 kilogram halibut.
Page viii: On Grand Manan Island in the Bay of Fundy, herring are smoked over a smouldering fire
on the floor of a barn. Upper doors are opened to release some of the smoke.
Page x: The eagle exists in the myths of the Northwest coast as a symbol of power and prestige.
This magnificent dance mask, carved by Dick Joseph in the late 1980s, hung for years in the April Point Lodge.
It now lives in Eagle View, one of the Peterson family homes on Quadra Island.
Page xiii: Winter in Wellington County, Ontario.
Page xiv: Floating peacefully just before dawn near the shore at Bella Bella (Waglisla), B.C., these canoes
were part of a gathering to celebrate the canoe, an extraordinary part of First Nations' culture.

"The state of nations depends upon how they eat."

—Jean Anthèlme Brillat-Savarin, *The Physiology of Taste* (1825)

To Mom, Anne MacDonald, for teaching
by example and never, ever, putting
a limit on my dreams.

To my sons, Jeff, Brad, Mark & Paul,
those feisty guys who, spread
out across the land, love and
honour Canadian food like I do.

To my many friends here at home
in my village and all over the
nation. You've forgiven my
long absences with such
understanding.

It's time to celebrate!

Contents

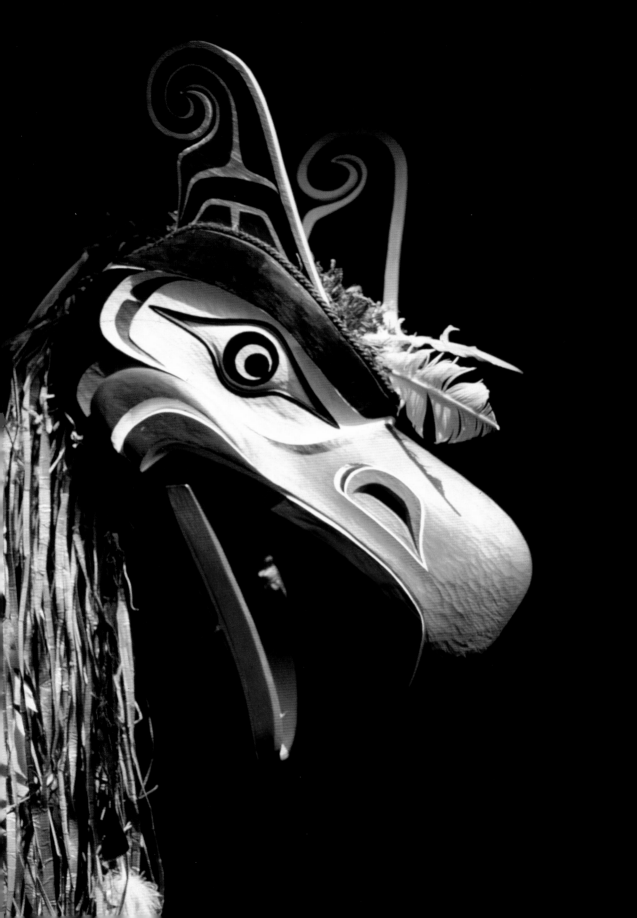

FOREWORD

The purpose of food is not simply to nourish the body. It is also to celebrate what makes a country unique, something that Anita Stewart's beautiful book illustrates perfectly: her tremendous knowledge about Canadian cuisine, about its traditions and diversity, and her insatiable curiosity about new flavours, have enabled her to share her passion by bringing together recipes from a bygone era and the latest food trends. She pays tribute to the home cooking of our grandmothers while celebrating the exoticism and richness of cultural diversity. She showcases regional products as culinary explorations and flavourful discoveries that will delight gourmets and gourmands.

This is no mere cookbook. It is a travel guide, brimming with adventure and wisdom. It takes us on a pan-Canadian journey to sample meat and fish delicacies and to explore enchanted gardens bursting with fruits and vegetables. It introduces us to the men and women who live across this land and gives us a taste of their passion for the art of cooking by sharing recipes that invite us to travel through time and across our country.

I must admit that I love how Anita Stewart invites us to visit "her" Canada by blending old and new traditions, by being at once true to ourselves and open to others. This is what good cooking is all about: openness and integration, maintaining yet shaping the identity of a country. We must celebrate it for what it is. This is what I take away from this book, which offers us a glimpse of what it means to belong.

It is in this spirit that I proposed the creation of an award for the culinary arts to my wife, the Governor General of Canada, so that we might celebrate the work and talent of those who, from the field to the table, are proof positive that the poets were not mistaken in singing the praises of good food and wine. They represent our gift for happiness and joyful living: in short, what is best about culture and humankind, and—as Anita Stewart's book confirms—a Canadian virtue.

His Excellency Jean-Daniel Lafond, C.C.
Rideau Hall, Ottawa
January 2008

His Excellency Jean-Daniel Lafond is also a filmmaker and writer. At Rideau Hall, alongside his spouse, the Right Honourable Michaëlle Jean, Governor General of Canada, he spearheads the programs examining the arts and culture in Canada. He created the Art Matters/Le point des arts forum and the Citizen Voices/À l'écoute des citoyens website. He is also the patron of The Cuvée, a red carpet celebration of the best of Ontario wine and food in the heart of Niagara wine country.

Canada is a menu of stories—a land of ultimate culinary possibilities! The richness and biodiversity of the indigenous harvest, our Original Palate, is the foundation of it all. Built solidly upon that base are our iconic ingredients—wheat, beef, apples—enriching and embroidering the culinary traditions of a multitude of immigrant groups who have gathered together from the four corners of the globe, men and women with a passion for this land which they now call "home."

After five centuries or so, the real food of Canada is still largely found in the home kitchens scattered across the land, in our beautiful rural communities and in our ever-expanding vibrant cities. Likewise, our food producers are spread from ocean to ocean. Our collective challenge is to build and nurture the connection between those producers and consumers, urban and rural.

Thankfully, we're experiencing a sea change. Local ingredients are becoming sexy, and we're beginning to recognize that seasonally harvested food actually tastes better. It's causing a massive repositioning of our entire culinary economy—and it's just beginning. By being attentive to our food sources, not only do we keep the cash flowing for our producers, but we also enable them to maintain and nurture diversity, creating a fabulous edible shopping list for us now and, even more important, for future generations.

This is a book about pride and tenacity—and it's about the pure sensual pleasure of tasting the richness of Canada on every level, from the physical to the intellectual.

So join the party! Head to a market, buy local, go home and cook with the rhythms of the seasons. Be true to your own culinary story. It's really that simple.

Anita Stewart

The late-afternoon air smelled good—of the ocean and Douglas fir—as we prepared a feast of wild sockeye at April Point Lodge in 1988. The fire was built, the cobble stones would be used to cook other seafood in bentwood boxes and the salmon was rubbed, rather non-traditionally, with brown sugar and sea salt, to roast to utter perfection.

"So much forest, so little time!" With this loud, verging-on-strident exclamation, geologist, mycologist and expert forager chef Bill Jones jumped out of his well-used Ford 4x4 and into mushroom heaven, disappearing into the brush beside the logging road a few kilometres from his home in Vancouver Island's Cowichan River Valley. This is coastal British Columbia, incised with deep valleys that cut their way high into the hills and rivers that flow fast with salmon and steelhead. It's where trees are draped with moss, and dampness invades every pore. It's a soft, forgiving climate. Being a plant here is far easier than anywhere else in Canada, and harvesting the wild has been going on for millennia.

I had arrived early, and while the sun was just beginning to slant across his gardens, Bill gave me a good overview of the local mushroom terrain. There are three climatic zones in that valley. The first is the temperate rainforest with its huge Douglas fir trees, red cedar and hemlock. This is pine mushroom territory, but there are many, many other mushrooms, including white morels, like the one-pound specimen he found several years ago. The second is the plateau where we would find Zellers boletes and "likely lots of chanterelles." The third is the hillside areas where again there'd be more chanterelles and birch boletes. He failed to mention a fourth: out his back door. Before heading off, we wandered the woods beside his driveway and collected a motherlode of scarlet lobster mushrooms and utterly enormous white chanterelles. After just 10 minutes, we had to return to the porch of his home and to drop off our cache, part of which would last me for the duration of my stay in B.C.

The logging roads we followed into the Cowichan hills were so rough my notes are smeared and illegible. We climbed into the low-hanging mist and began the trek to equal all treks. Within three metres of the road, I asked my first dumb question: "What's this one?" Bill went into paroxysms of laughter and joyfully announced that he'd never before seen a pine mushroom here. And it was a big one! Carefully, I removed it from its bed of natural mulch and deposited it with reverence into a recycled grocery bag. As we wove and climbed and tramped through the softest of forest floors, we were rewarded with dozens of other varieties, from slippery Jacks to birch boletes to more gorgeous white chanterelles. Bill's voice echoed: "Wait till you see *this!* Over *here, over here!*" In a small basin-like depression on the forest floor, he'd found a large perfect cluster of boletes, which Europeans know as cèpes, or porcini. The bags overflowed, filling the back of his truck and infusing the air with the smell of our earthy harvest for the entire ride home.

When one collects such treasure, it's essential to admire it and smile a lot. So for at least 30 minutes, Bill spread our cache all over his back porch table, arranging and rearranging as we just gazed and chatted about life—and mushrooms. Then, after this mycological beauty contest, he chose a few choice specimens and headed into his kitchen. And we tasted! For a food person, it hardly gets any better.

I have been blessed to enjoy similar experiences all across Canada with creative, generous, curious men and women. I have gone over the sides of various icebreakers and onto islands to visit lightkeepers whose survival depends on knowing what grows there. I have visited the Cree in northern Quebec in the dead of winter to watch them roast beavers and wild geese around a glowing stove in a tent on a trap line as the snow blew sideways and the temperature plummeted. I have fished, batting off deer flies, for pike in northern Manitoba, where unless you know how to cook these rather feisty fish, you just might starve. I have walked the coastal forests of Vancouver Island with the great ethno-botanist Nancy Turner while she thoughtfully explained what she calls the "earth's blanket," native plant foods that form the web of life, which sustained the First Nations for centuries.

Food in all its wild forms is Canada's reality. It is our original palate, a natural wonder, and we are blessed to be one of the few nations on earth where wild food still exists. We have not spoiled the landscape with roads and canals and factory farms. We have not invaded its hidden corners.

Humans have occupied North America for only 10,000 to 12,000 years. In the beginning, long before mankind dragged packs across the prairies or paddled the St. Lawrence, there was food. In Kamloops Lake, salmon fossils have been dated as ancient at 18,000 years old. The Northwest was so rich that diverse cultures flourished and the need for a nomadic life was minimized. Trading routes stretched like gigantic webs across the land mass, creating the culinary supply lines of pre-history that, after European settlement and the partitioning of our various national and provincial jurisdictions, we have yet to duplicate. There were no borders save linguistic ones, no boundaries save geographic ones.

Unlike most nations on earth whose lands have been settled for centuries,

THE POTLATCH TRADITION

The potlatches of the northwest coast were an intricate way of distributing wealth. The feasts and celebrations went on for days. They marked initiations, the mourning of the dead and investitures of new chiefs. Whole communities would bear witness to them as a confirmation of social structures within native society. The host family would give away blankets and clothing, sometimes even canoes. But among the most important treasures was food, from gallons of freshly salted herring roe to the liquid gold known as eulachon grease. The potlatch celebrated the bounty of the land and the ocean. It was a system of economics that worked and the attendant redistribution of wealth was critical to the various bands. However, this system was so foreign to the way of thinking of the Canadian government that officials banned the potlatch from 1884 to 1951.

Planning the food for a potlatch, particularly on a remote island, is a monumental task. Hundreds sit down to be fed for three evening meals, not to mention midnight lunches, which are a mere break in the ceremonial dancing and drumming. During the previous season, berries are gathered and preserved. Venison from B.C.'s coastal forests finds its way into a rich stew, while local razor and butter clams are fried in fritters. Fresh eulachon is baked in layers or battered and fried. There are dozens of fish soups and baked seafood. Salmon are often roasted en masse, splayed open on cedar strips, beside a bonfire. Guests never leave hungry or empty handed!

Canada is spacious and largely unspoiled. To understand the food of our country, though, it is first imperative to understand Canada, the land.

Canada's land mass is roughly 9,976,128 square kilometres, and we boast the longest coastline on earth bordering on three oceans and measuring 243,000 kilometres. This is a staggering figure when held up against Europe. It would take nine regions the size of Italy, which measures a mere 116,303 square kilometres, to fill the space occupied by the province of Ontario alone. There are 1.4 hectares of arable land for each living Canadian.

From the boreal forest to the tundra, from the Prairie grasslands to Ontario's Carolinian woodlands, Canada is stunningly rich with flora and fauna. Biodiversity is our most valuable heritage. With 71,000 species that have been scientifically described and another estimated 69,000 species yet to be named and classified, it becomes crystal clear to all but the most foolish that the protection of our ecological heritage is absolutely paramount. These raw materials are the building blocks of future crops, both food and medicinal. As plant breeders head to the original cradles for the landraces of the particular crops with which they are working, so too will future biologists come to Canada.

For the First Nations, the rhythm of life was in the harvest and the attitudes toward it. The notion of "oneness" with the earth and its gifts was embedded in Aboriginal belief long before contact with the white man, predating the modern concept of ecosystems by millennia. For the Nuu-chah-nulth people of coastal British Columbia, physical reality was transposed into their culture. They believe all things are related and interconnected; all things are sacred.

The polar opposite was the European belief that the land must be conquered. And who could blame the first settlers when they arrived with virtually nothing and faced the brutality of winter? The new immigrants hunkered down, felled some trees or dug some prairie sod, built their cabins or earthy shelters, planted some seeds they understood how to cultivate and, if they were lucky, survived. No fancy brochures could have ever prepared *les colons* in New France or the first settlers in English Canada for the ferocity of wind that drove snow through each tiny crack in the wall and isolated entire communities for weeks at a time. But before Samuel de Champlain and Cartier and the voyageurs, the continent did have a population that harvested and, in many cases, husbanded the land.

Throughout pre-contact times, agriculture seemed to develop in a parallel fashion across the nation, although in widely diverging patterns. On the northwest coast, indigenous peoples named over 300 plants; among them, more than 100 were used as food sources, many harvested from particular places within specific regions. The concept of ownership of these sites is coupled with growing evidence of plant management—what we might loosely term "farming." All along the coast, small plots of land were sowed, weeded, tilled, transplanted and burned to encourage growth. "Northwest Coast Aboriginal peoples were not passive occupants and opportunistic users of the environment," Dr. Turner observes. They managed clam beds, moved tiny salmon, or even the eggs, to streams that needed what we now call enhancing. They burned meadows, much as our own farmers burn off the stubble, so that the precious, widely traded camas lilies could flourish and other plants would grow in order to attract deer and elk. They patiently harvested such foods as herring roe by suspending hemlock boughs into the water; the boughs would become coated with the foamy spawn and the roe dried for use year round. But when Europeans arrived, with their concept of fenced, geometrical fields, their perception was that no management practices were in place.

In central Canada, the three sisters—corn, beans and squash—provided the explorers with a more understandable picture. By the time they arrived, the three crops were being grown together very successfully in companion plantings, and their range of cultivation extended from what is now Windsor to Eastern Ontario and up to Georgian Bay. About 23,000 acres were under cultivation, while another 175 plants were gathered specifically for food and at least 52 others were collected for beverages.

Today's agricultural landscape is multi-layered and so complex that few truly understand more than a small segment. However, much of the original palate remains: flora and fauna that populate the wild and semi-urban areas of Canada with edible possibilities. From wapato and cattails to nodding onions and seaweed, they deserve our attention and much wider acceptance on our tables.

Canada's boreal region, which covers 58 percent of our national land mass, is filled with such treasures. From Newfoundland to the Yukon, Canada is one of the last places on earth that has entire ecosystems still intact. It teems with life—and with food.

This food is Canada's first natural wonder, rivalling any on earth. Hand in hand, we are privileged to bear witness to the extraordinary story of Canadian cuisine, its history and how it came to be. As a people, we are so young that our collective memory is intact.

Restaurants may set benchmarks of excellence and, at times, even inspiration, but it is the dishes in this book, from generations of home kitchens, that define us as a culinary nation. Canada, the second-largest nation on earth, was built on a foundation of honest, generous cooking.

Dancing before a salmon feast on Quadra Island, B.C.

While inside the tent game was roasting, outside the north winds howled.

The north wind blows hard in a Cree hunt camp in northern Quebec near Mistassini.

Our reality is that we use very few truly indigenous foods. Food, like humankind, is on the move. It was always so. Ingredients, techniques and customs travel, and as they cross geographic and national boundaries, they are absorbed from one cultural group into another. In the Old World, the roots are hidden from view; food customs are more static and often very entrenched. But here, in the New World, we are part of a dramatic culinary evolution. We are busy creating a new national food culture. Canada, because of its youth and immensity, is less of a melting pot than it is one long smorgasbord of global tradition. Here we can taste the world, but we do it on our own terms, and with our own ingredients, ingredients whose origins are often hidden in ancient lands but which we now joyously claim and grow as our own. Even the First Nations brought corn, beans and squash from the south about a millennium ago. Conversely, Basque and Portuguese sailors harvested the Grand Banks and took shore-salted cod home to France, Spain and Portugal in the 1500s, allowing those nations to have regional specialties that one still can taste today. In the 1800s, our cheddar cheeses and Westphalian-style hams went back to Great Britain. Today, our mustard makes Dijon, our flour travels to Italy, and our oils head to Southeast Asia. The first wheat known to humankind was black einkorn. It's now being harvested in southern Saskatchewan and was recently tested for brewing in Ontario. The first apple may have been picked in Eden or the Caucasus, depending on one's interpretation, but across the land we have heritage orchards with hundreds of varieties. While my Anglo traditions and tastes demand that I use the spices of the islands in my Christmas baking and on barbecued chicken, a Moroccan mother will use salted lemons and pomegranate paste. While my family considered the potato a full partner to the meat from their farm, Chinese cooks regard potatoes as stir-fried vegetables to be served atop rice. We have *frites* from France and *spätzle* from Germany, *pulla* from Finland and *laska* from Southeast Asia.

Language has supported these food ways and is one of the best determinants of what early cuisine was cooked where: Gaelic in Scottish Cape Breton, Nova Scotia; Acadian across the once isolated regions in the Maritimes; German in Kitchener, Ontario; Ukrainian throughout the Prairies—all tossed in with Chinese, Japanese and Korean, not to mention English and French. Being able to retain language identity made the preservation of a homeland cuisine more possible. In this culinary New World, geography was an enforcer, as was the other Canadian reality, winter.

As villages swelled into towns and then cities, traditions transposed themselves into farmers markets, community suppers and, in some cases, restaurants. Our agricultural research stations, established in 1886, were linked across the land, allowing newly developed crops to be introduced from coast to coast. Our national parks system was created in 1887 to ensure the protection of both our wild spaces and, inadvertently, our wild food sources.

There is not one just Canadian cuisine; there are hundreds, depending upon ethnicity, climate and history. Our national cuisine is ultimately based in the land and the sea. It is defined by a mindset, a philosophy, an attitude, and it uses ingredients that speak volumes about the glorious culinary history of Canada. The world is truly richer for it.

PRESERVING OUR FUTURE

The protection of Canada's biodiversity is one of our greatest opportunities as a nation. Canada's Gene Bank, officially known as Plant Gene Resources Canada (PGRC), is based in Saskatoon. Its goal is to conserve and protect germplasm while allowing it to be used by plant breeders in Canada and globally. Other collections are scattered across the country, but PGRC is the central repository for over 110,000 seed samples, which include world base collections of barley and oats. The collection of native plant material is a work in progress. Holding rare and threatened Canadian plants protects them from extinction.

An extraordinary public organization that is quietly doing its part to preserve our national biodiversity is The Nature Conservancy of Canada. Largely a volunteer organization, it conducts flora and fauna inventories as actively as resources allow. Since 1962, The Nature Conservancy has preserved 1.9 million acres of land—from rolling grasslands and tall grass prairie to wetlands and seashores.

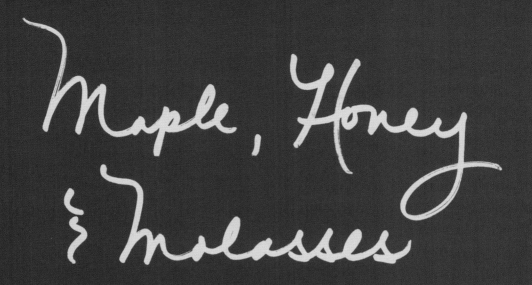

Maple, Honey & Molasses

The coverlet was crocheted beside the sugar kettle by my grandmother, the late Jessie Rogers. The fruit nappy was from a set that my grandparents received as an incentive to buy chewing gum for their restaurant in Mount Forest after they moved off the farm. For as long as I can remember, Grandpa ate his syrup from one of these nappies.

Early March was the time when my grandfather Albert Ovens would have what he would call his annual "feed" of first-run maple syrup in a fruit nappy filled to overflowing. It was pure gold, and he spooned it onto thick slices of buttered homemade white bread to soak up every last drop. One of my most treasured heirlooms is a coverlet, crocheted by my paternal grandmother, Jessie Rogers, while she sat beside the sugar kettle waiting for the sap to boil down.

Wherever you live in eastern Canada, spring really begins when narrow streams of smoke spiral from the forests. It's the unmistakable signal, as it has been for centuries, that sugaring-off time has begun. The only sweetener available to the early settlers was maple syrup.

The tradition of collecting maple sap and boiling it down—it takes 40 litres of sap to make one litre of syrup—spans eastern Canada. But nowhere is it better understood and more embedded in the culture than in Quebec, which produces 77 percent of the entire world supply, over 32,000 metric tonnes.

The First Nations taught the early French to use the sap. Maple sugar making was an important social activity for the indigenous peoples. Families and small groups gathered in temporary camps in early March, staying for about a month in order to make their yearly supply. Diagonal cuts were made in the base of the sugar maple trees (*Acer saccharum*) with an axe, and the sap that flowed out was gathered in shallow containers. Originally, the syrup was boiled by plunging hot stones into the sap in large wooden troughs.

The settlers quickly adapted this ancient knowledge using more "modern" methods, tapping the trees with metal spigots and collecting the sap in pails. It was hard work, usually done on snowshoes when the snow was deep. Rather than wooden troughs, they had large metal cauldrons.

In the maple forests, *les cabanes* were the quarters for those harvesting the sap. There was a wood stove for cooking and keeping warm. With cast-iron frying pans, the traditional foods of *les cabanes à sucre* evolved to satisfy the enormous appetites. Fèves au lard (pork and beans), liberally sweetened with maple syrup, simmered on the stove-top. Potatoes were fire-roasted, and eggs were poached in syrup. There were thin crêpes made from sarrazin (buckwheat flour). Ham and bacon, both requiring little refrigeration, were fried, and omelettes were cooked to go with them. Syrup was poured over everything. And the workers didn't just make syrup—they boiled down sugar, fermented partially boiled sap into maple vinegar and even made maple wine.

Today, the tradition continues. From Easter on, Quebeckers flock to the countryside to visit their favourite *cabane à sucre*. There are more than 400 *cabanes* located near the province's major urban centres. The translation of *cabane à sucre* as "sugar shack" hardly does it justice. The *cabanes* are not shacks. They're warm wooden buildings that are filled with grand aromas and the foods of old Quebec, all ready to be doused with the season's first nearly transparent syrup. Tourtière has been added to the list of foods served, as has a myriad of good pickles: ketchup *rouge*, which in English might be called chow chow or chili sauce; pickled beets; and sometimes green tomato pickles. The meal is accompanied not only by entertainment but also by an unbelievably potent drink called cariboo—red wine spiked with white alcohol. After the meal, it's time for *le tire*, or the taffy pull. Syrup is boiled to the candy stage and poured upon the snow.

As homespun as maple syrup may be, it remains one of Canada's iconic crops, and is used in everything from tarts to curing salmon. Our largest export market is the United States, which imports 73 percent of the value of our production. Japan is the next largest consumer of Canadian maple products.

Across Canada, maple is celebrated with festivals and at pancake houses. The Elmira Maple Syrup Festival in early April is the most venerable. Held in the heart of Ontario's Mennonite community, the festival has been listed in *The Guinness Book of World Records* as the largest one-day maple syrup festival on earth. Attendees can visit a buggy factory or watch the pancake-flipping contest. There's also an annual Quilt Block Challenge. Quilting in this region is a very important pastime, and there are many skilled quilters in the community. About 680 litres of syrup are consumed over 15,000 servings of pancakes.

In New Brunswick, the springtime tradition has been kept alive at the Loyalist village of Kings Landing Historical Settlement near Fredericton. Every year in late March, there's a Sugar Bush Weekend, showcasing how New Brunswick maple syrup was produced 150 years ago by early pioneers, using horse-drawn collectors and iron cauldrons to boil down the sap from grand old maple trees.

Molasses—which comes from the Greek word *mellas*—was a trade good, along with rum, from the Caribbean. It's embedded in the food history of Atlantic Canada and was familiar to the earliest of settlers. However, many

WHITE SUGAR PRODUCTION

Canada's answer to white cane sugar, sugar beets *(Beta vulgaris)* are a biennial root vegetable grown primarily in the temperate climates of North America. In Canada, 92 percent of domestic white sugar production and co-products are refined from *imported* raw cane sugar, while the remaining 8 percent are processed from Canadian-grown sugar beets, all produced in southern Alberta, where the first sugar beet–refining factory was built in the very early 1900s in Lethbridge. The ongoing challenge for this production is water; beets need lots of it, and irrigation is essential.

CANADA'S MAPLE YIELD

Canada manufactures 84 percent of the world's maple syrup. According to Dave Chapeskie of the Ontario Ministry of Agriculture, Food and Rural Affairs, there are over "30,000,000 taps, with roughly 15 million trees tapped in Canada." He says "there is approximately one tap, or spile or spout, for each Canadian." Each tap yields about 0.8 litres on average.

people couldn't get it, so they did without or made their own from the forest. Maple molasses was what historian Mary Williamson calls "a standby on every pioneer table. Thicker than maple syrup, the molasses was the residue left to drain out of sugar casks or moulds after the hot syrup was made into soft sugar or cakes. It was also sometimes called maple honey."

Catharine Parr Traill included instructions on how to make the viscous liquid, suggesting that it be used to preserve small wild red plums and to sweeten pies.

Real cane sugar molasses, along with rum and sugar, began to arrive in Atlantic Canada in the late 1600s and early 1700s, when the British set up serious trading with the Caribbean. In 1879, young Lorenzo George Crosby established his trading company in Yarmouth, Nova Scotia. At the age of 20, he founded an institution that is now over 125 years old. Crosby's Molasses, which moved to Saint John, New Brunswick, in 1897 in order to be closer to American markets and central Canada, is still a staple in virtually every Maritime kitchen.

One time when I was sitting on the rocks in Gros Morne National Park with a group of hikers, a young interpreter poured steaming mugs of tea and suggested that we sweeten it with some good Crosby's molasses. I did and the chill of the evening air completely evaporated. Try as I might, I've never been able to replicate that very real Newfoundland experience here in Ontario. That shot of molasses tasted so right at that particular moment in time. The sweetener is simply part of the Atlantic Canadian culture, and a real kitchen essential.

Surprisingly, honey is a much later arrival. Honey bees (*Apis* species) are not native to North America. They came originally from the Old World to the 13 colonies in 1621 but did not arrive in Canada until the early 1800s.

The impact that bees have on Canadian crops through pollination is immense. It is extraordinarily important to the food chain. Bees pollinate over 30 percent of the plant-based foods that appear on our dinner table. In Ontario, apiarists load their hives onto trailers and strategically place them in orchards and fields where everything from strawberries to apples to cucumbers have been planted. The main concern of researchers like Dr. Peter Kevan of the University of Guelph is whether there will be enough bees to do the job.

Canada is the world's sixth-largest producer of honey, and it comes in a magnificent array of colours and flavours, from crystalline, almost white fireweed to dark, pungent buckwheat. Good apiarists can tell you precisely which flowers the bees have visited and when. The earliest honeys are the lightest; the later ones, dark and pungent. Purple loosestrife is a perfect

example of a later honey; it's greenish in colour and extraordinarily strong. Beekeepers often purposefully set hives in particular locations, like cranberry bogs, pumpkin patches or turnip fields, in order to extract a particular flavour. Borage and canola honeys are harvested in Saskatchewan. Every farmers market seems to have at least one honey vendor, often quite specialized. As pure, unadulterated comfort food, I don't think anything quite rivals a spoonful of fragrant local honey on warm, buttered toast. My current favourite is a combination of goldenrod and other wildflowers from along the Grand River, close to where I live.

A bee hangs tenaciously on a borage blossom. To harvest one kilogram of drippingly delicious honey, a bee flies 180,000 kilometres at about 25 kilometres per hour. While it may not break any speed limits, it is in a hurry because it has to visit 4 million blossoms.

The Reverend F. W. Clarke gave the first lectures on beekeeping at Ontario's University of Guelph in the late 1800s. The university's Bee Lab was also established around that time. Besides offering undergraduate, graduate and post-graduate courses, the lab monitors about 300 hives in eight locations near the city. The honey produced there ranges from basswood and clover to goldenrod and alfalfa. Some buckthorn and hawthorn honey is also produced.

Caryn Colman's Cabbage Rolls (Halupches)

Caryn Colman of Temagami's Smoothwater Eco-Lodge in Northern Ontario is a natural cook, and she loves to return to her roots to perfect traditional Russian-Jewish recipes. Caryn writes: "My family always said that a dish like halupches (pronounced hul'upsees) is a 'putchka' to make. Translation: it's a lot of work. But the results are amazing and if you make lots and freeze a few cooked dishes, it's really worth the time." Caryn always recommends going big.

"I adored my grandmother Min's cabbage rolls," says Caryn. "She made two kinds so she could please everyone. One type was with ground beef, the other vegetarian. But Min had a secret ingredient—the leftovers of her honey cake" (see page 16). "I've also used crushed gingersnaps. The cabbage rolls must be served with sour cream.

"The only time my grandmother made honey cake was in preparation for the high holidays in the fall," says Caryn. "So I can deduce that the only time she made cabbage rolls was in the late fall when the honey cake was crumbled and, heaven forbid, on the stale side. Fall is also the time when cabbages are harvested. Cabbage is a mainstay in the root cellar over the winter in both the Old Country and the Canadian north."

Because she lives in a region rich in local ingredients, Caryn uses as many as possible. The lamb and the beef for her cabbage rolls come from just up the road, near New Liskeard.

YIELD: 8 servings

In the early morning, the forest is mirrored in James Lake beside Smoothwater Ecolodge.

1 cabbage

2 lb (1 kg) each ground beef and lamb

1 large onion, finely minced

1 tbsp (15 mL) minced garlic

½ cup (125 mL) uncooked white or brown rice

2 tsp (10 mL) salt

1 tsp (5 mL) freshly ground pepper

½ cup (125 mL) raisins (optional)

1½ cups (375 mL) crumbled leftover Min Biback's Honey Cake (page 16)
   or crushed gingersnaps

2 cans (each 28 oz/796 mL) crushed tomatoes or tomato sauce

1 cup (250 mL) water, beer or wine

¼ cup (60 mL) lemon juice

½ cup (125 mL) maple syrup

Sour cream

As an experienced guide and canoe tripper, Caryn Colman offers her years of knowledge to novices and experts alike. With her trusty dog, Sasha, Caryn took me on out onto James Lake for a paddling lesson.

With a sharp knife, remove the cabbage core. Fill a large pot with water; submerge the cabbage, cover and bring to a boil. Reduce heat and simmer for 10 minutes. Remove the cabbage, reserving the boiling water. Let the cabbage cool enough that you can peel off the pliable outer leaves. When you cannot peel off any more, re-submerge the cabbage in the hot water and bring to a boil again. Repeat the process until all the larger leaves have been removed.

Combine meat, onion, garlic and rice. Season with 1 tsp (5 mL) of the salt and half of the pepper. Stir in raisins (if using) and 1 cup (250 mL) of the crumbled honey cake.

Place about 2 tbsp (30 mL) of the filling at the stem end of one cabbage leaf. Fold over the sides of the leaf; roll up. Place in a casserole dish, leaf end down. You can stack the rolls 2 or 3 high, depending on the depth of your dish, but be sure the top layer is partially submerged in liquid.

Stir together tomatoes, water, lemon juice, maple syrup, remaining honey cake, and remaining salt and pepper. Pour over the cabbage rolls; cover and bake in a preheated 325°F (160°C) oven for 3 hours, checking occasionally that the liquid has not evaporated, adding water if needed. It will be rich and saucy. Serve with sour cream.

Min Biback's Honey Cake

Caryn Colman says that her grandmother Min's cake gets better with age. It's great with tea or for dessert, although I suspect I could be cajoled into eating it for breakfast, too. She uses buckwheat honey from Temiskaming, Ontario, and stone-ground, locally grown flour from Terza Farms. When she can get it, she substitutes buckwheat flour for 1 cup (250 mL) of the all-purpose flour in the batter.

YIELD: One 10-inch (25 cm) honey cake, about 16 servings

4 cups (1 L) all-purpose flour

2½ tsp (12 mL) baking powder

½ tsp (2 mL) salt

¼ tsp (1 mL) ground cloves

½ tsp (2 mL) ground ginger

1 tsp (5 mL) cinnamon

1 cup (250 mL) granulated sugar

2 cups (500 mL) buckwheat honey

5 eggs, separated

½ cup (125 mL) corn oil

1 tsp (5 mL) baking soda

1½ cups (375 mL) warm strong coffee

½ tsp (2 mL) cream of tartar

Sift the flour, baking powder, salt, cloves, ginger, cinnamon and sugar into a large mixing bowl. Stir together honey, egg yolks and oil. Make a well in the centre of the dry ingredients and beat in the honey mixture. Stir the baking soda into the warm coffee and add to the batter, mixing well so that no dry spots remain.

In a separate bowl, beat the egg whites with the cream of tartar until stiff peaks form. Gently fold into the cake batter.

Pour into a greased and floured tube pan. Bake at 325°F (160°C) for 1½ hours or until the top looks spongy and the cake is a rich brown.

Store in a tightly covered container or wrap well in plastic wrap.

Don Oliver's Classic Crêpes with Maple Syrup and Fresh Nova Scotia Fruit

These basic crêpes can be served for breakfast with maple syrup or for dessert at dinnertime. After cooking, the crêpes can be refrigerated or packed with parchment in between and frozen.

In Nova Scotia, my friend Don Oliver fills them with summer preserves he makes from his own garden, folds them over and dollops them with whipped cream, strewing some Annapolis Valley raspberries and blueberries on top.

YIELD: About 18 crêpes

1½ cups (375 mL) all-purpose flour
2 tbsp (30 mL) granulated sugar
½ tsp (2 mL) salt
2 cups (500 mL) milk
4 eggs
¼ cup (60 mL) melted butter
1 cup (250 mL) fruit preserves
Whipped cream (optional)
Lots of fresh berries
Maple syrup, preferably Nova Scotian

Senator Don Oliver in his Nova Scotia garden.

In a large bowl, whisk together the flour, sugar and salt. Vigorously whisk in the milk, eggs and butter. Let batter stand for 30 minutes before using.

Heat a lightly greased crêpe pan or non-stick skillet over medium heat. Pour in about 3 tbsp (45 mL) of batter for each crêpe. Tilt and swirl the pan to spread batter evenly. Cook for 1 to 2 minutes or until bottom is golden and edges begin to lift. Flip and cook for 10 to 15 seconds. Remove and stack until ready to use.

Fill each crêpe with 1 tbsp (15 mL) preserves, fold over, spoon on the cream (if using) and strew with fruit. Pass the maple syrup.

Fat Archies

I first met my friend Kevin MacLeod, or as he likes to refer to himself, MacLeod of MacLeod, in 2000 at the Canadian Pavilion at the World's Fair in Hanover, Germany, where we were both working for the Department of Canadian Heritage. This man understands "heritage," and he is as proud of and knowledgeable about Canada as anyone I know. So much so that in 1992, Her Majesty the Queen invested him as a Member of the Royal Victorian Order (M.V.O.) for personal service to the Sovereign. A decade later, she promoted him to the rank of Lieutenant (L.V.O.) during the highly successful Golden Jubilee visit that he masterminded and, in 2005, to Commander (C.V.O.)—the highest level available to Canadians. Kevin is the only Canadian to have been promoted through all three ranks.

But even though he lives and works in Ottawa as the chief of state protocol for the Department of Canadian Heritage, his heart is in the highlands of Cape Breton where his roots run deep and where his parents live on Boularderie Island in the middle of Bras d'Or Lake. His recently published book, *A Stone on Their Cairn/Clach air An Càrn* (Glen Margaret Publishing, 2007), is a Celtic saga of tenacity and perseverance during a time when the Gaelic language and indeed the entire Scottish tradition were disappearing.

Ask Kevin about his family's food traditions and it's a bit like a dam bursting. But of all the traditions, there are two that he says are quintessential—maragan sausage (page 146) and Fat Archies.

Kevin's parents, Norma and John MacLeod, grew up on the island, too. Their ancestors came from the Outer Hebrides of Scotland during the last of the Clearances in the 1830s. They recall the days of the grist mills, which have gradually disappeared. Norma's father and sometimes Norma herself would use a flail ("two big sticks with a leather strap in between") to thresh wheat on the barn floor before they'd fan the chaff away and send the grain to the grist mill. They picked wild strawberries and blackberries to make jam "to die for."

Fat Archies are puffy spice cookies (Kevin thinks of them as "biscuits") that are best "spread with butter while they're hot." While they're baking, people hover around the house—the smell is fabulous. When they're cold, they're great with tea. Norma makes them from memory but, with some coaxing, she shared this recipe.

YIELD: 12 cookies

3 cups (750 mL) all-purpose flour
1 tsp (5 mL) salt
1 tsp (5 mL) cinnamon
1 tsp (5 mL) ground ginger
½ tsp (2 mL) nutmeg
½ cup (125 mL) butter, softened
½ cup (125 mL) packed brown sugar
½ cup (125 mL) granulated sugar
1 egg
½ cup (125 mL) molasses
½ cup (125 mL) boiling water
2 tsp (10 mL) baking soda

Sift together the flour, salt, cinnamon, ginger and nutmeg. Set aside.

Cream the butter with the brown sugar, granulated sugar and egg. Beat in the molasses. Add the flour mixture.

Combine the boiling water with the baking soda and mix into the cookie batter to make a soft dough. Roll out on a floured surface and cut into 3-inch (7.5 cm) rounds. Place on a well-oiled or parchment-lined baking sheet. Bake in a preheated 350°F (180°C) oven for 15 to 20 minutes or until puffed and browned.

Pain Perdu on the Restigouche

Paddling 90 kilometres on the Restigouche, one of North America's legendary salmon rivers, we ate like royalty because the entire trip was organized by culinary perfectionist David O'Brien. He brought the finest ingredients and a huge cooler of great wine and even had us hauling top-of-the-line Paderno cookware. We journeyed in style, through rapids and even into the tail end of a hurricane. We paddled past clusters of fishermen fly-casting in private pools. I secretly smirked—no lodge I know allows guests to dine in the style we did every night, at the Brogan-O'Briens camps along that river. This recipe was great on the expedition because it requires less-than-fresh bread.

YIELD: 4 servings

> 3 eggs
> 1 tbsp (15 mL) icing sugar
> ¼ tsp (1 mL) salt
> ¾ cup (175 mL) milk
> Grated rind of half a lemon or orange
> Thick slices of French bread
> Unsalted butter, for frying

Whisk together the eggs, icing sugar, salt, milk and lemon rind. Dip bread into the mixture, soaking it well on both sides.

Fry in plenty of unsalted butter until golden brown and crisp on both sides. Serve immediately with maple syrup or honey.

At a bend in the Restigouche River, the Brogan-O'Brien family gets ready for one of our feasts. The menu? Fire-toasted bagels and thick slices of smoked salmon!

Oatmeal and Whole Wheat Waffles

Dorothy Grove is one of the finest Mennonite cooks in my village. Her maiden name was Bechtel. The family, German speaking and of Swiss heritage, immigrated to Upper Canada from Pennsylvania in the late 1700s or early 1800s, because land was inexpensive and available. They settled at the confluence of the Speed and Grand Rivers, where the city of Cambridge now sprawls. Many Mennonites came to Canada via Russia and, as Dorothy says, it's possible to tell them from the others just by their names. Rather than Weber, Martin and Brubacher, Mennonites of Russian origin have names like Thiessen, Friesen and Nafziger.

Dorothy grew up on a farm at the edge of what was once Hespeler. Her family's food traditions were similar to many in the area, but her mother planted unusual vegetables like kale and kohlrabi in the garden, which was ringed with a huge perennial border.

The fruit cellar was the mainstay of the winter diet, and the many desserts that graced the Mennonite table were a result of a summer's worth of very hard work. Canned raspberries, gooseberries and cherries would be served as is ("just so") or with custards and milk pudding.

As Dorothy matured, she leaned toward the ethical, tasty cooking that she found in the *More with Less Cookbook,* published by the Mennonite Central Committee and one of the most ragged and well-used volumes in my own collection.

For years, she owned a bed and breakfast, where she perfected her morning offerings. With these delicious waffles, she'd serve Wellington (or Waterloo) County maple syrup, strawberries she'd frozen from her friends' summer harvest and unsweetened whipped cream.

If you don't have a waffle iron, heat a griddle and make golden, nutty-flavoured pancakes using this batter.

YIELD: 4 to 6 servings

1½ cups (375 mL) rolled oats
2 cups (500 mL) milk
½ cup (125 mL) whole wheat flour
½ cup (125 mL) all-purpose flour
1 tbsp (15 mL) packed brown sugar
1 tbsp (15 mL) baking powder
1 tsp (5 mL) salt
½ tsp (2 mL) cinnamon
2 eggs, beaten
¼ cup (60 mL) canola oil

In a large bowl, stir together the oats and milk. Let stand for 5 to 10 minutes. In a separate bowl, sift together the whole wheat and all-purpose flours, brown sugar, baking powder, salt and cinnamon. Add to the rolled oat mixture along with the eggs and oil, stirring until no dry spots remain.

For each waffle, pour ⅓ to ½ cup (75 to 125 mL) batter onto a hot, lightly oiled waffle iron, cooking until golden on both sides.

The Mennonites who came to Canada brought their solid husbandry and a huge, delicious food tradition. Here, sweet and sour preserves made from garden produce, cabbages wrapped in newspapers, and summer sausages hanging from the rafters crowd the Wideman cellar in Wellington County.

Maple Pouding Chomeur

This delicious self-saucing pudding from the Laurentians in Quebec is laced with maple syrup and is a perfect winter dessert served with a bit of table cream. The translation of the name is "Lazy Cook's Pudding," and, in fact, it is very easy to make. When my son Mark's in-laws were visiting from Kyoto, Japan, I added extra syrup and made it in a casserole, then inverted it onto a big glass plate to let the sauce ooze down over the warm pudding. You can add nuts or almost any other dried fruit to the batter to make it your own.

YIELD: 6 servings

PUDDING BASE:
   1 cup (250 mL) granulated sugar
   2 cups (500 mL) all-purpose flour
   2 tsp (10 mL) baking powder
   ¼ tsp (1 mL) salt
   1 cup (250 mL) milk
   ¼ cup (60 mL) melted butter

SAUCE:
   ¾ cup (175 mL) maple syrup
   ¾ cup (175 mL) packed brown sugar
   1 cup (250 mL) water
   ¼ cup (60 mL) butter
   1 tsp (5 mL) vanilla or maple extract

PUDDING BASE: In a bowl, stir or sift together the sugar, flour, baking powder and salt. Add the milk and melted butter, stirring to make a thick batter. Transfer to a lightly oiled 8-cup (2 L) glass casserole.

SAUCE: In a saucepan, stir together the maple syrup, brown sugar, water, butter and vanilla extract. Bring to a boil, stirring to dissolve the sugar. Pour over the pudding base. Bake in a preheated 350°F (180°C) oven for 35 to 45 minutes or until bubbling and golden.

MAPLE SYRUP GRADES

When using maple syrup, decide which of the various grades is best. First run is just that—the finest and freshest you'll find. Pour it on and treat it like the treasure it is. As the season warms, the syrup becomes darker but no less flavourful; since it's not as crystal clear it's less expensive. The amber grades are the ones to use in cooking. I find that the best way to preserve amber syrup is to freeze it in Mason jars. Fill the jars to within about 1 inch (2.5 cm) of the top and seal loosely. Store it on a shelf in your freezer, then when frozen (it never fully freezes), tighten the lid so it won't leak if tipped. I've also frozen syrup in the plastic jugs they're sold in, but with a cup or so removed to allow for expansion.

Buttermilk Biscuits with Molasses Mousseline

This recipe is adapted from one that the Losier family in the Acadian region of New Brunswick shared with me in the mid-'80s, when I was writing my first *Country Inns Cookbook* (Stoddart, 1987). Familial roots in that region are deep, and years ago, when there was a family reunion planned, some 3,000 people would gather to celebrate their connection.

Originally, these biscuits were made with the surplus quarts of buttermilk from the Losiers' dairy herd. The biscuits are served with the sweet mousseline after a meal of salt fish and with a cup of New Brunswick's King Cole Tea. Any of Canada's great syrups can be substituted for the mousseline: maple, apple, saskatoon berry or wild elderberry (page 278).

YIELD: 12 biscuits and 1 cup (250 mL) mousseline

BISCUITS:

2 cups (500 mL) all-purpose flour
1 tbsp (15 mL) baking powder
½ tsp (2 mL) cream of tartar
½ tsp (2 mL) salt
1 tbsp (15 mL) granulated sugar
¼ tsp (1 mL) baking soda
½ cup (125 mL) cold butter
1 cup (250 mL) buttermilk

MOUSSELINE:

¾ cup (175 mL) molasses, preferably Crosby's
½ cup (125 mL) packed brown sugar
1 tbsp (15 mL) butter
Additional butter, softened

BISCUITS: In a large bowl, sift together flour, baking powder, cream of tartar, salt, sugar and soda. Cut in the butter until the mixture resembles coarse crumbs. Add the buttermilk, stirring lightly with a fork to make a soft dough.

On a floured board, knead the dough gently to form a round ball. Roll or pat out to ½-inch (1 cm) thickness. Cut with a floured cookie cutter or thin-rimmed drinking glass. Place on a greased or parchment-lined baking sheet. Re-roll the trimmings and cut more biscuits. Bake in a preheated 375°F (190°C) oven for 15 to 20 minutes or until golden.

MOUSSELINE: In a small saucepan, combine the molasses, brown sugar and butter. Cook, stirring over low heat, until the mixture comes to a boil. Simmer gently for 5 minutes.

To serve, split and butter the biscuits. Drizzle with hot syrup directly from the saucepan.

The Red Shoe's Gingerbread

Craig Flinn, a particularly talented chef who has cooked in many of the best kitchens in Atlantic Canada, created this recipe for The Red Shoe Pub in Mabou, Cape Breton. The Shoe, as it's called locally, is owned by the Rankin sisters of the renowned family of recording artists. Music pervades the village, and people line up, often in their lawn chairs, waiting to go inside to partake.

Gingerbread is classic in the Maritimes. Up and down the St. John River, I've tasted it at inns and in homes, but this is the best I've ever sampled—period! While it's baking, the house smells of spice. Serve it with whipped cream or, as Craig does, with a scoop of good vanilla ice cream topped with grated fresh ginger and a spoonful of applesauce, if you like.

YIELD: 8 to 12 servings

½ cup (125 mL) butter, softened
½ cup (125 mL) packed brown sugar
2 eggs
1 cup (250 mL) molasses
1 tbsp (15 mL) grated fresh ginger
2 cups (500 mL) all-purpose flour
2 tsp (10 mL) baking powder
1 tsp (5 mL) baking soda
½ tsp (2 mL) salt
2 tsp (10 mL) cinnamon
1 tsp (5 mL) ground ginger
½ tsp (2 mL) ground cloves
1 cup (250 mL) boiling water

Filled with good food and music, the Red Shoe Pub is considered by some the heart of Mabou, Nova Scotia.

In a large bowl, cream the butter with the sugar until light in colour. Add eggs, one at a time, and continue beating until fluffy. Beat in molasses and grated ginger.

In a separate bowl, sift together the flour, baking powder, soda, salt, cinnamon, ginger and cloves. Add to the creamed mixture along with the boiling water. Pour into a parchment-lined 9- x 13-inch (3.5 L) baking pan. Bake in a preheated 325°F (160°C) oven for 45 to 50 minutes or until a tester comes out clean.

Let cool. Cut into large squares and serve directly from the pan.

Corn, Beans & Squash

The three sisters—corn, beans and squash—simmer in a soup over a fire at a powwow near Brantford, Ontario. The kettle is like the one my grandmother would have used to make maple syrup and her hand-blistering lye soap.

Drumming and chanting echoed through the Six Nations forest near Brantford, Ontario. The annual powwow was in full swing. Under a huge maple tree, a giant cauldron of golden Three Sisters soup bubbled and steamed. Among the First Nations in what was to become eastern Canada, this soup of corn, beans and squash is steeped in tradition and it has been a staple for centuries in one variation or another, depending on the cook.

These "three sisters" were the foundation plants of First Nations agriculture. Canadians have embraced them all—corn on the cob dripping with butter, creamy polenta, pots of beans laced with maple syrup and made smoky with bacon, and autumnal squash baked into harvest pies or stuffed into perfect ravioli. While corn, beans and squash didn't arrive in Canada as a trio, they travelled up similar, likely watery, pathways from their native Mesoamerica within only a few hundred years of each other.

Corn is the most important indigenous grain to the Americas and the second-largest grain crop on earth. From Mesoamerica, it was introduced along the trading routes northward until, around 500 AD, it arrived in the region that was to become Canada. By 1000 AD, the crop was being actively cultivated as a food source in eastern Canada, including Cape Breton and the St. Lawrence River Valley. Called maize, it was first taken to Europe by the Portuguese where it quickly became an essential ingredient in dishes like polenta and cornbread. When Jacques Cartier and Samuel de Champlain chronicled their voyages, they noted how it was heavily relied upon as a food source and that there were many types of corn under cultivation: dent, flint, flour, sweet and even popcorn.

Dr. Peter Kevan of the Bee Lab at Ontario's University of Guelph describes the symbiotic relationship between the hoary squash bee (*Peponapis pruinosa*) and its host plants, squash and pumpkins. This particular bee specializes in pollinating them. Both the bee and its attendant crops now range from the Great Lakes to Mexico, and Kevan postulates that these particular vegetables, foundation blocks of early Canadian agriculture, travelled north, up the trading routes, together.

The cultivation of the three sisters is a great example of companion planting. Ethnobotanist Nancy Turner of the University of Victoria describes it:

> Corn, beans and squash . . . were planted each year with great ceremony by the women. The seeds were planted in rows, and various types of hoes or digging implements were used. Before planting, the corn grains were soaked in herbal solutions made from reed grass and other types of plants. Seeds of beans and squash, and sometimes sunflower, were planted together with the corn; beans would grow up the cornstalks. Prayers were offered and ceremonies performed throughout the growing season. . . . The ripened ears were harvested into baskets, then shelled, except for a few husks, which were left on for braiding the ears into long strings for drying. The dried corn was stored in large bins or cribs, or in underground caches.

Corn was eaten green and was used for making bread, and in soups and puddings; it was roasted for travelling and to make a coffee-like drink. For immigrants to Canada, corn soon became a staple, used in everything from cooked desserts, often dubbed "Indian pudding," to the fabulous golden breads of the Loyalists and later the Portuguese and Italian communities, who brought their well-practised corn-based recipes with them.

The second "sister" is the bean—both the common bean and the lima bean. Their ancestry is even more venerable than that of corn. The common bean was brought in from the wild, along with peppers, sunflowers and squash, in a number of locations that range from the Andes and into Argentina and even North America. They spread northward to arrive above the Great Lakes sometime after corn, fixing the nitrogen content in the soil for the corn plants, which are particularly heavy feeders, thereby allowing its sister to flourish.

Beans were so widely used that in 1916 Waugh, in *Iroquois Foods and Food Preparation,* named and illustrated 27 varieties. Ripe beans were cooked and eaten whole or mashed or made into a type of bread. The twin staples of beans and corn were used in another very important dish we know today as succotash. The name comes from the Narragansett word *m'sickquatash,* meaning "many fragments."

Settlers from the Old World also brought beans. From the early references to the planting of "beanes," it is not possible to determine whether they were the large, flat faba, fava or broad beans with which European explorers were likely more familiar or if they were in fact the beans of the First Nations. Certainly, when the Loyalists arrived from the United States, they brought with them many of the latter. When perusing old seed catalogues and listings,

INDIAN PUDDING

Catharine Parr Traill used cornmeal, calling it "Indian meal." Here are two recipes for Indian pudding from her 1854 book *The Female Emigrant's Guide.*

Baked Indian Meal Pudding
Scald a quart of milk, and stir in seven or eight tablespoonfuls of Indian meal, a little salt, sugar or molasses to sweeten it, a cup of beef or veal suet, nicely shred, a teaspoonful of ginger or any spice you prefer, a tea-cupful of currants or chopped apples, and four eggs beaten to froth; sprinkle a little fine suet on the top and grate a little nutmeg.

Plain Indian Pudding
The same as above, only omitting the eggs and fruit. The same pudding may be boiled instead of baked, but the cloth must be tied so as to allow of the meal swelling, and requires to be boiled two or three hours.

it's striking how many varieties were known and named. Seeds of Diversity has close to 4,000 beans in its heritage plants database; names include Black Coco and Blue Lake, Dragon's Tongue, Hopi Black, Mostoller, Wild Goose, Ozark Heirloom and Scarlett Runner.

Canadian beans come in an extraordinary array of shapes, sizes and colours. Under the heading "white beans," there are white pea beans and navy beans. Coloured beans include Great Northern, Black Turtle, Pink, Dark Red Kidney, Light Red Kidney, White Kidney, Dutch Brown, Cranberry and Small Red. I met Dr. Tom Michaels in 1997, when he was working at the University of Guelph. He was the first bean researcher I'd ever connected with, and he has a sense of humour. He hybridized and released what he named OAC (Ontario Agricultural College) "Thunder," which has become the bean used in most recipes for canned beans in tomato sauce. Michaels is attempting to develop a sweeter bean for snack foods. Better still is his idea to create a popping bean—as in popped corn. Sadly, neither will be on the market soon. It can take 15 years from the genesis of an idea to the final release of a new variety.

When Europeans arrived in the new land, the third sister, squash, was also being widely used. Explorers noted how delicious it was. Besides squash, they also learned about its culinary twin, pumpkin, and its cousins, cucumbers and melons.

Squash and pumpkins had many traditional uses. They were eaten fresh and also dried for winter storage. The Iroquois boiled them or baked them in ashes. Squash was often mixed with deer fat and maple syrup to make a dish similar to the one we still find on Thanksgiving tables that has been mashed with brown sugar and butter. The early settlers baked them into pies, made soups with them and, according to Marie Nightingale in her landmark book *Out of Old Nova Scotia Kitchens,* even cooked them into jam. For many Canadians, squash is a staple in the colder months. Simply mashed with butter; roasted with herbs as Alex Sgroi does it for his Perfect Pasta (page 158) or puréed for soups or pies, squash is a spectacular winter vegetable.

Jean Soulard (right) from Quebec City's Château Frontenac was one of the first "big name" chefs to shop from local growers. He's shown here with one of his favourite farmers, Robert LaBlond in Les Eboulements.

Paddling Pumpkins

Likely one of the most adventurous, and decidedly non-culinary, uses of pumpkins occurs every autumn in Windsor, Nova Scotia, on the first Saturday in October. This is the home of both the Atlantic Giant Squash and the Atlantic Giant Pumpkin. Since Canada is renowned for its paddling experiences, in 1999 a group of somewhat wacky business people decided to have a pumpkin race!

The goal is to grow, hollow out, customize and decorate a pumpkin boat; participants climb into it barefoot and paddle furiously across Lake Pesaquid with great good humour and sometimes even fireworks. The pumpkins used need a lot of tender loving care. And they need space—at least 230 square metres per plant. Several of the flowers are hand-pollinated; each grower has his or her own favourites and often experiments every year with different cultivars. Because pumpkin skin is very tender, the big pumpkins are often set on a bed of Styrofoam or sawdust to grow to the fullest size. After the September sun has swelled the fruit, racers make the decision about which pumpkin will become their racing vessel. When the time comes to lift the one selected, a number of strong friends are also needed to raise it onto a wooden pallet.

The really big specimens—that is, those over 350 kilograms—are kept for showpieces. Some folks deem perfect the specimens that weigh in at about 200 or 250 kilograms. While the larger ones might be more stable in the water, competitors still have to propel the huge weight from start to finish without sinking or tipping or simply splitting the pumpkin apart, as one did when its captain, a local bank manager, forgot to take his carving knife out of the "hull" of his craft!

Two or three days before the race, the top must be cut off the pumpkin and the seeds removed. The flesh can easily be 13 to 18 centimetres, so this is a laborious, messy job. At least 45 kilograms of innards are taken out, and removal is an art form; if too much is discarded, you risk springing a leak, but if too little is carved out, weight becomes a factor. Pumpkins are blunt-ended dead weight and require considerable strength to keep moving forward.

Like the bank manager, many of the 30 or so competitors capsize or sink and don't make it; hence the need for the local fire department to be present both off the water and in it. It's a wet, wild race to the finish.

Roasted Winter Squash Ravioli with Sage Browned-Butter Sauce

Switzerland-born chef Alex Sgroi never skimps on the cheese or butter. He built his culinary reputation over many years in Canada (see page 158). This is one of his signature dishes, a real favourite with vegetarians and carnivores alike.

Any winter squash is fabulous in this filling—buttercup, butternut or my favourite, Sweet Mama. If you wish, make the filling ahead of time and refrigerate it until needed. The only caveat is that it must be cool when used to fill the ravioli.

This amount will fill about 50 to 60 large ravioli, enough for 12 servings, and uses the full batch of the pasta dough. It's easy, however, to halve or even quarter the filling recipe if you wish to serve four to six and reserve the remaining dough for linguine or some other recipe.

The cheese can be any pungent Canadian variety that is hard enough to grate. I once used a little-known surface-ripened sheep's milk cheese called Allegretto, which I picked up directly from the cheesemakers when I was in northern Quebec. It was splendid.

YIELD: 50 to 60 large ravioli

4 cups (1 L) chopped peeled winter squash
¼ cup (60 mL) canola oil
4 whole cloves garlic (peeled)
1 onion, coarsely chopped
3 sprigs fresh thyme
½ tsp (2 mL) salt
2 eggs
2 cups (500 mL) grated hard cheese
½ tsp (2 mL) freshly grated nutmeg
1 batch Alex's Perfect Pasta (page 158)
Freshly ground or cracked pepper (optional)

EGG WASH:
1 egg
1 tbsp (15 mL) milk

SAGE BROWNED-BUTTER SAUCE:
½ cup (125 mL) unsalted butter
¼ cup (60 mL) shredded fresh sage

Place the squash chunks in a 9- x 13-inch (3.5 L) shallow pan. Drizzle with all but 1 tbsp (15 mL) of the oil. In a skillet, heat the remaining oil over medium-high heat; sauté the garlic and onion until beginning to brown. Add to the squash along with the thyme. Sprinkle with the salt.

Roast in a preheated 375°F (190°C) oven, stirring several times, until tender and beginning to brown, 35 to 40 minutes. Remove from the oven and let cool to room temperature.

When cool, remove the leaves from the thyme sprigs, discarding the stems. Mash the roasted vegetables together. Stir or whisk in the eggs until thoroughly blended. Add the cheese and nutmeg. Use immediately or chill until needed, up to 2 days.

EGG WASH: Whisk together the egg and milk. Set aside.

Roll one piece of pasta dough as per instructions on page 159. Lay the sheet on a floured surface. Brush half with the egg wash and place 1 tbsp (15 mL) filling at 2-inch (5 cm) intervals along the egg-washed half. Fold the unwashed pasta over; with your fingertips, press the edges together. Press gently between each mound of filling; using a pasta wheel, cut into squares. This seals the ravioli. Reuse any trimmings.

Transfer the ravioli to a floured parchment-lined pan. Dust ravioli with a little additional flour; cover lightly. Continue the process until all the pasta is used. If there is any left over, roll it out and cut it into linguine or gather up into a ball; wrap well in plastic wrap and freeze until needed.

SAGE BROWNED-BUTTER SAUCE: Melt and stir the butter in a large heavy skillet until it is just beginning to brown. Stir in the sage and cook until just wilted.

Bring a large pot of water to a boil. (Remember the ratio of water to pasta is 7:1.) When boiling, add about ½ tsp (2 mL) salt per 4 cups (1 L) water. Add the ravioli and cook for 2 to 3 minutes or until they float to top and are al dente (just barely tender).

With a slotted spoon, transfer the ravioli to the skillet, tossing in the sauce to coat evenly. To serve, arrange on a heated platter or individual serving plates (allow 5 to 6 ravioli per person). If desired, grind a bit of pepper to taste over top.

Nettie Stanoyev's Fabulous Fresh Bean Soup

Candice Stanoyev and I met in Vancouver's Tamarind Restaurant, where she was doing some recipe development. Her Yugoslavian grandmother, Nettie, was one of many good cooks in the family, which settled in Saskatchewan in the 1920s. Candice reminisces: "Nettie was my step-grandmother; my paternal grandmother, who was Croatian, had died of cancer in 1949, seven years before I was born. Sometime thereafter, my grandfather remarried. Nettie was a widow from the Yugoslavian community in Regina. She was truly a grandmother to me and my sisters, and we all loved her immensely. My grandparents' house was always full of love and fabulous food. After my family moved to Delta, B.C., my grandparents followed from Regina and settled in Chilliwack. In my teens, Sundays meant driving 1½ hours to and from my grandparents' house for wonderful family dinners. As we all got older, our respective boyfriends would even drive all the way out to take part in the fabulous ritual. And, of course, we were always sent home with something—a bottle of preserves or the most coveted item of all, a pan of Nettie's homemade strudel."

Candice characterizes the foods of their homeland as being similar to those of northern Greece and Macedonia, with melted lard rather than butter being used for making stews and strudels. Dill was one of the herbs of choice, and Nettie canned many jars of tomatoes and tomato juice, which Candice wistfully remembers when she makes this excellent soup.

"The amount of dill depends on how fresh and intense it is," says Candice. "The dill I used recently wasn't very intense, so I used the ½-cup measure and it was great. However, fresh dill in the summer would probably be more intense; you would want to use less so it doesn't overwhelm the soup."

This soup won *The Toronto Star*'s Golden Whisk Award for being one of the top 10 recipes of 2006. Serve it hot or cold but always with a generous dollop ("at least a tablespoon") of full-fat sour cream on top. Candice calls it "a taste of summers past." Shown here with Portuguese Cornbread (page 42).

YIELD: 6 to 8 servings

2 tbsp (30 mL) canola oil
1 cooking onion, finely diced
1 clove garlic, crushed
4 cups (1 L) sliced (1-inch/2.5 cm pieces) green and/or
    yellow string beans
¼ to ½ cup (60 to 125 mL) chopped fresh dill
1 tsp (5 mL) crushed dried basil
1 can (28 oz/796 mL) diced tomatoes
3 cups (750 mL) tomato juice
1 tbsp (15 mL) granulated sugar
1½ tsp (7 mL) salt
1 tsp (5 mL) freshly ground pepper
Sour cream and additional dill

Heat oil in heavy-bottomed stainless steel stockpot over medium-low heat; sauté onion until transparent. Stir in garlic and cook for 2 minutes. Add beans and sauté for 1 minute longer.

Add the dill, basil, tomatoes, tomato juice, sugar, salt and pepper. Cover and bring to a boil. Reduce heat and simmer for 30 minutes to allow flavours to blend.

Ladle into warm soup bowls and serve immediately garnished with sour cream and additional dill (if using). Or let cool slightly and refrigerate until thoroughly chilled before serving.

Mark Mitchell's Spicy Squash, Cauliflower and Fresh Ginger Soup

This soup is light and has tons of flavour. From his downtown Vancouver home, Mark Mitchell, a real natural in the kitchen, suggests serving it with crusty bread. Dollop it with good plain yogurt or a swirl of buttermilk. Cooking it on an October day perfumes the house with the fragrance of autumn. You can use any of the dark yellow winter squash varieties or local sweet potatoes.

YIELD: 6 to 8 servings

1 tbsp (15 mL) canola oil
1 large cooking onion, chopped
3 cloves garlic, coarsely chopped
½ to 1 tsp (2 to 5 mL) hot pepper flakes
2 inches (5 cm) fresh ginger, chopped
3 cups (750 mL) cubed peeled winter squash
3 cups (750 mL) chopped cauliflower
3 cups (750 mL) chicken or vegetable stock
Salt and freshly ground pepper
Plain yogurt or buttermilk (optional)

In a large saucepan, heat the oil over medium heat; cook the onion until transparent. Stir in the garlic and hot pepper flakes and continue to cook until garlic is just beginning to brown. Add the ginger and cook, stirring constantly, for 1 minute longer. Add the squash and cauliflower, tossing to coat with the onion mixture. Pour in the stock, cover and bring to a boil. Reduce heat to medium-low and simmer until vegetables are tender. Remove from heat and let cool for 15 minutes. Purée with a hand blender or in a food processor. Season with salt and pepper to taste. Reheat before serving. Pass yogurt or buttermilk (if using).

A delicate squash blossom at Kings Landing Historic Village, New Brunswick.

Tony's Pasta with Beans (Pasta e fagioli)

This is classic Italian vegetarian fare. Fresh beans are best, but the dish is easily made with dried beans in the wintertime. Tony Garaffa came to Guelph from southern Italy in the 1960s, during the time in Ontario when "the footballs weren't round and olive oil came in tiny bottles," he says. His mother, now in her early 80s, still bakes bread every Wednesday and grows her own romano beans, garlic, basil and tomatoes for this dish. The family freezes the beans by simply popping the shelled beans directly into bags and putting them in the freezer with no additional processing. Tony says that to use the fresh or frozen beans, barely cover them with water, bring them to a boil and simmer until tender, about 10 minutes. Then proceed with the recipe by adding the salt, garlic and so on.

YIELD: 6 servings

1 cup (250 mL) dried romano beans
3 cups (750 mL) water
1 tsp (5 mL) salt
2 to 3 cloves garlic, minced
1 large sprig fresh basil
1 can (5½ oz/156 mL) tomato paste
1 can (28 oz/796 mL) Roma tomatoes
2 tbsp (30 mL) olive oil
2 cups (500 mL) pasta (such as penne, fusilli or macaroni)
Olive oil, crushed dried hot peppers, chopped fresh basil and freshly grated Parmesan cheese, for garnish

If using dried beans, rinse them well and soak them in the water overnight. The next day, transfer the beans and soaking liquid to a small heavy saucepan. Cover, bring to a boil and cook over low heat until the beans are tender and begin to absorb the liquid, about 1½ hours.

Add the salt, garlic and basil; bring to a boil. Reduce heat and cook, uncovered, for 10 to 15 minutes. Add the tomato paste and an equal amount of water. Chop the tomatoes and add them along with their juice. Stir in the oil. Continue to simmer until the sauce thickens.

In a separate saucepan, cook the pasta in boiling salted water until barely tender. Drain and serve immediately in soup bowls with the beans ladled on top. Let each diner add olive oil, crushed hot peppers, chopped fresh basil and grated Parmesan to their taste.

BEANS AND HEALTH
The humble bean is already rich in protein, carbohydrates, folate, calcium and fibre, and we can now add anthocyanins to this list. Gram for gram, dry black beans have more antioxidant activity than any other coloured bean. The darker the skin, the higher the flavonoids and anthocyanins. According to a statement released in 2003 by researcher Clifford Beninger of the department of environmental biology at the University of Guelph, these antioxidants destroy free radicals, which, when found in excess, are linked to heart disease and cancer.

Karen's Brazilian Black Bean and Chickpea Salad

Expat Brazilian Karen Gerlinger-Baxter loves black beans; they're part of her heritage. (For more of her story, see page 160.)

Known in Brazil as *feijão preto,* they are the basis of the national dish *feijoada,* an elaborate black bean stew filled with an array of pork products. Brazilians love their meat. This salad is great as part of a barbecue.

YIELD: 6 to 8 servings

1 can (19 oz/540 mL) black beans
1 can (19 oz/540 mL) chickpeas
1 large sweet red pepper, finely chopped
1 large cooking onion, finely chopped
½ cup (125 mL) packed minced fresh coriander
¼ cup (60 mL) cider vinegar
¼ cup (60 mL) olive oil
½ cup (125 mL) canola oil
Juice of 1 lime
Salt and freshly ground pepper

Drain and rinse the beans and chickpeas and combine in a large bowl. Add the red pepper, onion, coriander, vinegar and olive and canola oils. Combine thoroughly; stir in the lime juice. Add salt and pepper to taste. Cover and refrigerate for a few hours before serving.

Marie Nightingale's Baked Jacob's Cattle Beans

Halifax-based author Marie Nightingale was writing an article on beans and found this great recipe on the back of the package from Webster's Farms in Cambridge, Nova Scotia. When she called the family to ask their permission to publish it, she was greeted with a laugh. It turned out that the recipe was one of her own that they'd used because it was so delicious.

Jacob's Cattle Beans are the prettiest beans I've ever seen. They're an old variety that seems, until recently, to have been specific to the Maritimes and New England. They most certainly migrated north with the Loyalists and, like many beans, have a biblical reference.

YIELD: 6 servings

> 1 pkg (1 lb/454 g) dried Jacob's Cattle Beans
> 2 tsp (10 mL) dry mustard
> ⅓ cup (75 mL) packed brown sugar
> ⅔ cup (150 mL) molasses
> 1 tsp (5 mL) salt
> ¼ tsp (1 mL) freshly ground pepper
> 4 oz (115 g) salt pork or bacon
> 1 tsp (5 mL) white vinegar
> 1 onion, diced

Cover the beans with cold water and soak overnight. Alternatively, place the beans in a large pot with 6 cups (1.5 L) water, cover and bring to a boil. Boil for 5 minutes, remove from heat and let stand for 1 hour. Drain and discard water; rinse.

Place drained beans in a large pot with 6 cups (1.5 L) water; bring to a boil and boil for 5 minutes. Reduce heat and simmer until beans are tender, about 30 minutes. To check whether a bean is tender, remove it from the boiling water and blow on it; if the skin cracks and peels back, it's ready. Drain, reserving 1 cup (250 mL) of the liquid. Transfer to a slow cooker, bean pot or casserole with a lid. Combine the reserved water with mustard, brown sugar, molasses, salt, pepper, pork or bacon and vinegar. Stir in the onion.

Cook on high in the slow cooker for about 6 hours or in a preheated 300°F (150°C) oven for 4 to 6 hours, adding water as needed to keep beans moist.

LOYALISTS IN CANADA

At the beginning of the War of Independence in 1775, Loyalists fled their homeland. The largest wave of immigrants occurred in the years 1781 to 1790. They spilled north through towns like Shelburne, Nova Scotia, and settled in western Quebec (Lower Canada), expanding the number of English-speaking settlers. By 1812, Americans represented 80 percent of the entire population of Upper Canada.

Hearty Italian Vegetable and Bean Soup (Minestrone)

Guelph would not be the same city without the incredible Italian presence. Much of the vibrant, largely southern Italian community came to Canada in the early 1900s. The community included the hard-working labourers who built the Welland Canal and many of Toronto's heritage buildings.

This is a very forgiving recipe reminiscent of one from Abruzzi, the region in southern Italy to which many of Guelph's Italians trace their ancestry. There, as here, it is a seasonally inspired soup. If you wish, add extra vegetables, such as sweet red peppers, celery root (celeriac) and drained chickpeas, and top with other cheeses. It's great with a splash of hot pepper oil at the end.

YIELD: 8 servings

2 tbsp (30 mL) unsalted butter

2 onions, minced

2 cloves garlic, minced

2 to 3 potatoes, peeled and diced

2 to 3 carrots, peeled and finely diced

1 celery stalk, chopped

4 cups (1 L) chicken stock

1 cup (250 mL) fresh or canned (undrained) chopped plum tomatoes

Salt and freshly ground pepper

½ cup (125 mL) diced green beans

1 can (19 oz/540 mL) romano beans, drained

1 cup (250 mL) small pasta shells or macaroni

¼ cup (60 mL) chopped fresh basil

¼ cup (60 mL) finely chopped fresh Italian parsley

Freshly grated hard cheese, such as Parmesan or Romano

Hot pepper oil (optional)

Melt the butter in a large saucepan over medium heat; sauté the onions and garlic until tender. Toss in the potatoes, carrots and celery. Stir and cook for 2 to 3 minutes just to coat the vegetables with the butter and to soften slightly. Add the stock and tomatoes; cover and bring to a boil. Reduce heat and simmer for 20 to 25 minutes or until the vegetables are barely tender. Stir in the green beans, romano beans, pasta, basil and parsley. Simmer until pasta is tender, about 30 minutes.

To serve, ladle into hot soup bowls and pass the cheeses to sprinkle generously onto each serving. Drizzle with hot pepper oil (if using).

New Vegetable Hodgepodge

This very traditional Maritime recipe is reminiscent of the early springtime stew from Quebec known as *bouilli*—a one-pot meal that has meat added. Hodgepodge, on the other hand, relies solely on the freshest vegetables and lashings of butter and cream. The ingredient list is altered by every cook, depending on what is in his or her garden.

In her classic book, *Out of Old Nova Scotia Gardens,* Marie Nightingale describes hodgepodge:

> It's a traditional way to welcome the harvest from Nova Scotia gardens. Farmers dig up tiny new potatoes and sell them as "hodgepodge potatoes." Finger-length carrots are pulled and scrubbed to accompany the first pickings of peas and beans into the pot. Snow peas are a new, delicious and crunchy addition. Tiny beets, cauliflower, and broccoli florets can be cooked separately and added to the pot just before serving. Ten minutes total cooking time is usually sufficient for new spring vegetables. Drain only if a lot of liquid remains, but it's best to keep any water-leached nutrients in the pot.

YIELD: 6 to 8 servings

2 cups (500 mL) tiny new potatoes, scrubbed
2 cups (500 mL) new baby carrots, scrubbed
2 cups (500 mL) green beans, trimmed
2 cups (500 mL) yellow beans, trimmed
2 cups (500 mL) snow peas, trimmed
2 cups (500 mL) shelled peas
2 to 3 green onions, chopped, or 1 onion, chopped
2 cups (500 mL) light cream (5%) or milk
2 tbsp (30 mL) butter
Salt and freshly ground pepper
2 tbsp (30 mL) chopped fresh parsley

Place the potatoes in a large pot with about 1 inch (2.5 cm) boiling water. Cover and boil gently for 2 to 3 minutes before adding the carrots. Cook for another 1 to 2 minutes, then add the green and yellow beans. Cook, uncovered (so the green beans retain their bright colour) for 2 minutes more. Add the snow peas, shelled peas and green onions; cook gently until all the vegetables are tender.

Drain only if necessary. Add the cream and butter; season to taste with salt and pepper. Sprinkle with parsley and serve.

Portuguese Cornbread

In 2006, I tasted an almost perfect rendition of this bread on San Jorge, an island in the Azores. But I first encountered it in the late 1980s at a now automated light station on remote Pointer Island, off the coast of British Columbia. When I first met the lightkeepers, Dan and Fil (short for Filamena) McMurray, they were grinding their own flour in a small mill that Dan had artfully enclosed in a yew wood case. They baked all their own bread using grain shipped from Winnipeg. This is a classic Portuguese recipe from Fil's files. Although our cornmeal is yellow, in Portugal the cornmeal used in bread is white. You can use either in this recipe. (Pictured with Nettie's Soup on page 35.)

YIELD: 2 loaves

> 1 cup (250 mL) milk
> 2 tsp (10 mL) salt
> ⅓ cup (75 mL) granulated sugar
> ½ cup (125 mL) butter
> ½ cup (125 mL) warm water
> 2 tbsp (30 mL) active dry yeast
> 2 eggs, well beaten
> 3½ to 4 cups (875 mL to 1 L) all-purpose or bread flour
> 1¾ cups (425 mL) cornmeal

In a small heavy saucepan, warm the milk until it's steaming. Stir in the salt and sugar, reserving 1 tsp (5 mL) of sugar. Stir to dissolve. Add the butter and allow to melt. Remove from heat and let cool to lukewarm.

Combine the warm water and reserved sugar in a large mixing bowl. Sprinkle with the yeast and stir. Let stand for 3 to 4 minutes to puff. Pour in the lukewarm milk mixture, beaten eggs, half of the flour and the cornmeal. Beat by hand or with an electric mixer until a thick batter forms. Work in most of the remaining flour by hand until dough is no longer sticky. Dust a surface with the remaining flour, turn out dough and knead for 5 to 6 minutes or until the dough is elastic and smooth. Cover and let rise on the counter until doubled.

When doubled, punch down, divide in half and shape into 2 round loaves. Place on a parchment-lined baking sheet dusted with cornmeal. Cover and let rise again until doubled in bulk, 45 to 50 minutes.

Bake in a preheated 375°F (190°C) oven until golden brown, about 45 minutes.

Buttermilk Maple Cornbread with Flax

This Loyalist quick bread was likely brought to Canada with the first wave of immigration in the late 1700s. More and more often, it's possible to find good locally grown and milled cornmeal. For this recipe, I've used a New Brunswick product from Speerville Mills and jazzed it up with a healthy dose of ground flax.

YIELD: 6 to 8 servings

2 cups (500 mL) cornmeal
1½ cups (375 mL) all-purpose flour
1½ tbsp (25 mL) baking powder
1 tsp (5 mL) salt
¾ cup (175 mL) ground flaxseed
2 eggs
⅔ cup (150 mL) maple syrup
2 tbsp (30 mL) canola oil
1 cup (250 mL) buttermilk
½ cup (125 mL) crisp cooked bacon pieces

Oil a 9-inch (23 cm) cast-iron skillet. Place in a preheated 400°F (200°C) oven. Meanwhile, sift together the cornmeal, flour, baking powder and salt. Stir in the flax. In a separate bowl, whisk together the eggs, maple syrup, canola oil and buttermilk. Combine with the dry ingredients, stirring just until no dry spots remain. Pour into the preheated skillet and sprinkle with bacon pieces.

Bake for 25 to 30 minutes or until browned. Cut into wedges to serve.

CORN HYBRIDIZATION

Like other iconic crops, corn has been widely researched. The process of hybridization is one that needs an explanation, particularly when so much interest, both negative and positive, has been focused on genetic modification. Hybridization has been going on in nature since plants first sprang forth from the earth's soil. Wind, insects and birds helped it along. Corn is particularly susceptible to cross-pollination. When farming first began, particular plants were selected for their apparent vigour, among other characteristics, and cultivated. It took years. More recently, scientists have developed a menu of methods to use when making such crosses. Corn was and is quite responsive. Hybrids, however, have a relatively short field life—their vigour and even some of their dominant characteristics diminish over the years. Whether it occurs in nature or in the field lab, hybridization is essential if the species is to survive. Although it would be ideal, farmers are not able to save the seed for more than a few years. Consequently, new varieties are constantly being bred.

FLYING PUMPKIN FEST

At McCully Farm, just outside Stratford, Ontario, pumpkins catapult high through the autumn air, landing with a thud and a squish onto the pasture below, all in the name of charity. Dave Pullen, the owner who dreamed up this use for his less-than-perfect pumpkins, oversees the loading and firing. For a toonie, visitors can launch a pumpkin, and Dave's livestock are eternally grateful for the delicious, split, ready-to-eat feast.

McCully Farm has been in the McCully family since 1847, and is one of Ontario's finest examples of agricultural tourism. The farm store overflows with homemade preserves, maple syrup—"from the bush over there"—and farm-raised meat.

Giant Pumpkin and Apricot Muffins with Sugary Nut Topping

There are lots of good muffin recipes, but this one is part of my own personal story. It was in an article I wrote for *Homemakers* magazine on the trend toward giant muffins in the late 1980s. It was in a later piece for that publication that a talented young photographer made my food look better than anything that had ever come out of my kitchen. His name was Robert Wigington. It's still a joy to watch what he and his team do with my creations. He just sees things differently.

If you have access to local walnuts, heart nuts or hazelnuts, use them for the topping. They'll make these mufins even even more special.

YIELD: 12 large muffins

½ cup (125 mL) butter, softened
1 cup (250 mL) packed brown sugar
3 eggs
1 cup (250 mL) puréed pumpkin
1 tsp (5 mL) vanilla extract
½ tsp (2 mL) almond extract
Grated rind and juice of 1 orange
2 cups (500 mL) all-purpose flour
1 tbsp (15 mL) baking powder
1 tsp (5 mL) cinnamon
½ tsp (2 mL) salt
½ tsp (2 mL) freshly grated nutmeg
1 cup (250 mL) slivered dried apricots
½ cup (125 mL) buttermilk

TOPPING:
2 tbsp (30 mL) packed brown sugar
2 tbsp (30 mL) chopped walnuts or slivered almonds

In a large mixing bowl, cream together the butter, brown sugar and eggs until light and fluffy. Stir in the pumpkin, vanilla, almond extract, orange rind and juice.

In a separate bowl, sift together the flour, baking powder, cinnamon, salt and nutmeg; add it to the creamed mixture along with the apricots. Stir in the buttermilk, mixing just until no dry spots remain.

Heap into 12 lined or well-oiled large muffin tins. Combine the brown sugar and nuts; sprinkle over the batter.

Bake in a preheated 375°F (190°C) oven for 30 to 35 minutes or until deep golden brown and firm to the touch. Let cool for 10 minutes before removing from the muffin pan.

Towering trees and freshly gathered hazelnuts at the historic Gellatly Nut Farm (now a regional park) near Kelowna, B.C., in the south Okanagan Valley.

Mom's Pumpkin Pie

While you can use canned pumpkin purée for this recipe, the wonderful squash that can be found all autumn long at our farmers markets work perfectly also. Simply steam or bake them, scoop out the flesh and purée or mash it. Any leftovers can be frozen for use as a vegetable or for another batch of this delicious pie. This is my mother's recipe, and I've not tasted better. Mind you, I *am* a tad biased.

YIELD: 6 servings

1½ cups (375 mL) puréed pumpkin or squash
¾ cup (175 mL) granulated sugar
1 tsp (5 mL) cinnamon
½ tsp (2 mL) ground ginger
3 eggs
1½ cups (375 mL) homogenized (3%) milk
2 tbsp (30 mL) melted butter
One unbaked 9-inch (23 cm) pie shell
Lightly sweetened whipped cream

In a large bowl, whisk together the pumpkin, sugar, cinnamon, ginger and eggs until thoroughly combined. Whisk in the milk and melted butter. Pour into the unbaked pie shell.

Bake in a preheated 350°F (180°C) oven until the centre is set, 35 to 40 minutes.

Serve at room temperature with lightly sweetened whipped cream. Refrigerate any leftovers.

Mom and my daughter-in-law, Kaori, harvesting the garden in Willow Point, near Campbell River, B.C.

Salmon

Iridescent salmon skin.

"The salmon are part of the country's character, as are the fishermen and the fishing settlements."
Roderick Haig-Brown

As the sun was setting over the Restigouche, the camp owner, André Arpin, came to our little log cabin with a gift, a pan of *cipâte* (a.k.a. cipaille or sea pie), the Acadian-style potato and chicken casserole hidden under a rich lard pastry. He announced that in the morning he would be serving *ployes,* the buckwheat pancakes for which this region of New Brunswick, known as the Republic of Madawaska, is famous. The following day, my friends, the O'Brien-Brogan family, and I were setting out on a 90-kilometre paddle down the legendary salmon river from Kedgewick, past fishers from all over the world, by the Million Dollar Pool, past wild forests, rock-strewn beaches and high bluffs, to finally pull out at the Rafting Grounds. We weren't going to fish; we were going to experience the river.

The Restigouche has always been a salmon river. Legend has it that it was named by a Mi'kmaq chief whose son, contrary to his father's wishes, led a party of warriors against the Mohawk, who were purportedly poaching the fish. The name Restigouche means "he who disobeys his father."

After the battle of 1760, which saw the destruction of the French fleet en route to Quebec City, British troops settled the region to protect Anglo fur traders. To their delight, they found a river rich in salmon, perfect for fly-fishing. But it was the Scotsmen who worked as boat pilots who saw the economic opportunity and encouraged their countrymen to come and take a look. By the 1800s, a thriving fishing industry was in full swing, and the Restigouche was considered to be the most productive river in North America. As seems to happen in our extractive culture, it was over-fished. Four million pounds of salmon were shipped away annually.

As early as 1824, fishing restrictions were established, becoming some of the first conservation laws on the continent. By 1858, the river had to be closed to commercial fishing, and it was then that private lodges, with their land access to the river and ownership of particular pools, started to spring up. The area became the property of the rich and often quite famous.

Today the Restigouche envelops the senses. You smell its freshness. You listen to layers of sounds—the water, the forest silence, the paddle dipping, the rapids in the distance. You feel the river's chill as you swim. Adrenalin rushes. Beneath, in the depths, shadowy outlines of sea-run trout slip by; above, eagles soar. Panicking flocks of tiny ducks skitter across the water like so many wildly flapping wind-up toys. And all the while, the water swiftly seeks the ocean as the salmon climb the riffles and rapids to reach their spawning pools.

Canada is bracketed with salmon in all its incarnations. It is *the* Canadian fish—a fish of legends and so delicious that it is served with pride in the kitchens of dozens of cultures. First Nations cooks splay it on cedar and fire-roast it; the Japanese-Canadians love it raw; those of Scandinavian descent make it into gravlax—the list is long.

Across eastern Canada, the Atlantic salmon is iconic. Twice within its Latin name, *Salmo salar,* is a reference to the root "leaper." This mighty fish can accelerate to 30 kilometres per hour to jump up to four metres. Until the late 1700s, rivers flowing into Lake Ontario supported an extremely large population of Atlantic salmon. Salmon still migrate great distances from their home rivers, some up to 4,000 kilometres. Like their distant cousins, the Pacific salmon in British Columbia, the salmon of the Atlantic return to their own pools to spawn. However, unlike B.C. salmon, they live to spend at least one or two more seasons at sea, punctuated by other spawning runs.

During their first return to their home river, Atlantic salmon usually weigh one to two kilograms. After that, they are considered adult salmon and can grow to 20 kilograms. The largest Atlantic salmon officially landed in North America was in 1939 on Quebec's Cascapedia River; it weighed 25 kilograms.

Today, not all is sweetness and light. The Atlantic Salmon Federation (ASF) has been ringing alarm bells and mobilizing volunteers for years. At the time of writing, the ASF had recorded that fewer than 200,000 two-sea-winter salmon return to North American rivers. Eight rivers in Maine and 32 rivers that flow into the Bay of Fundy have salmon populations that have been named "endangered." Rivers flowing into the St. Lawrence are in "somewhat better shape," according to the ASF. However, in Atlantic Canada the picture is bleak.

Once a seemingly inexhaustible resource in Lake Ontario, salmon were in trouble there by the early 1800s. The last record of the original stock of Atlantic salmon in Lake Ontario was one fish, netted in 1898. Since then, however, the Great Lakes have seen a tremendous amount of rehabilitation. Salmon have been re-established and, although it's doubtful there will ever again be a commercial fishery, the salmon sport fishery is very healthy.

Every autumn for millennia, the salmon of the Pacific have returned to the bronze-washed British Columbian coast. The kelp-filled coves and the

SALMON PRESERVATION PROGRAMS

River restoration and the preservation of salmon spawning habitat is critical and takes enormous investment, often far beyond the capabilities of the government. There's a perfect example of this salmon culture along B.C.'s Campbell River, where the Nature Conservancy of Canada is partnering with the community in a massive reconstruction of the 47-acre estuary where half of the river's salmon hatch. They are spurred on by the children and grandchildren of conservationist and author Roderick Haig-Brown.

Tons of industry-polluted soil have been removed; new creek beds have been designed and dredged, then reconstructed with truckloads of clean gravel so that water again flows fast and deep over the spawning beds. Salmon enhancement programs like the one at the hatchery on the Quinsam River, a tributary of the Campbell, ensure that there are enough fish to return. Quinsam River releases four million Chinook annually.

With local vision supported by such extraordinary generosity, Haig-Brown's salmon will be protected for generations of anglers to come, and perhaps my own grandchildren, like his, will ponder the mystery of this great fish and swim with them in his river.

Very happy guests of Sund's Lodge on Malcolm Island.

streams are full of spawning salmon in autumn—coho, pink, chum, sockeye, steelhead and the noble chinook. They sense their way and head to the pool in which they hatched. It might be in a small, woodsy stream like the creek that flows through Stanley Park or the Capilano River in downtown Vancouver. It could be hundreds of kilometres up the wild Fraser River into the Interior or up the newly created fish runs along the estuary of the legendary Campbell River of Vancouver Island.

For the natives of the northwest coast, the returning fish were held in such reverence that their images were adopted as clan crests to be emblazoned on dance robes and totems. Belief systems sprang up around the fish and its relationship to life. The natives watched for nature's seasonal signals—the blooming of the sagebrush buttercup announced one run, while the clicking noise of a certain grasshopper announced another.

In those times, the salmon came back in abundance. Weirs were placed at the mouths of rivers, nets were woven, sharp-pronged spears were made, and there were also the simple hooks and lines made from cedar or kelp. The native communities had the technology to catch entire runs, but they didn't. At least one band, the Nuxalk of Bella Coola, had river guardians who, through heredity, were charged with the responsibility to protect the waterway from pollution and over-fishing. Punishment was severe and could, in some cases, be death.

Fresh salmon were often simply butterflied, fastened on cedar sticks and roasted beside an open fire. The fish were layered with seaweed and cooked in large communal pits or stewed in bentwood boxes using hot rocks to bring the water to a furious boil—Canada's only indigenous cooking method (see page 70). Covered smokehouses were, and in many regions still are, part of the fish camp. In drier areas, wind dehydrated the catch. Salmon roe was smoked by hanging it in large clumps over a smouldering fire, most likely of alder wood. The tails and the backbone were dried for crisp snacks. The heads were cooked, and the nuggets of flesh in the cheeks and around the eyes were a particular delicacy.

By the mid- to late 1800s, a substantial commercial fishing industry had sprung up wrapped around the canneries and packing houses dotting the coast. Japanese, First Nations and fishers of European origin netted their catches all the way from the Strait of Juan de Fuca to the Alaskan border. It became such big business that *BCP 45,* the B.C. Packers fishing boat belonging to Harry Assu of Cape Mudge, a village just opposite Campbell River on Vancouver Island, was pictured on the back of Canada's old five-dollar bills.

Commercial salmon fishing has now become high tech and high stake. With GPS, sonar for tracking fish and satellite communication, the industry has evolved to the point where it's simply a regulated harvest.

But sport fishing remains a more elemental hunt, connecting the fisher with the circle and the cycle of the salmon, absolutely in tune with and dependent upon the environment. Two of the most persistent threats to the survival of the wild B.C. salmon population have been pollution and environmental degradation. Since sport fishing's value to the B.C. economy is estimated to be between $400 million and $600 million, whole communities are working hard to nurture it back to health. There are province-wide initiatives, including B.C. Rivers Day and, as on the Atlantic coast, river restoration and preservation are becoming high priorities for activists.

I cannot write about this species without mentioning salmon aquaculture and its current state. It is an enormous industry, with worldwide production of over one million tons. In our country, as I write this, only one company is Canadian owned. The head offices of the rest are tucked away in Chile and Norway. This industry has some serious documented

B.C. FISHING LODGES

Family-run fishing lodges are a wonderful long-standing tradition on the coast of British Columbia. Although many of the icons, like Painters Lodge in Campbell River and April Point on lush Quadra Island, are now corporately owned, there are still a few that offer guests a very personal experience. Food and fishing are at the core of places like Sund's Lodge on Malcolm Island. Dave and Sally Sund bought their lodge in 1984, relatively recently in coastal terms (April Point was founded in 1947, while the original Painters was built in 1948). Scott and Heather Sund are now the second generation to welcome guests. Under their care, this small lodge, which only accommodates 20 guests at a time, offers one of the finest fishing experiences on the British Columbian coast.

The days begin on the water, with guests landing everything from chinook to halibut or simply kayaking the hidden coves of the Inside Passage. Invariably, the days end somewhat languorously in the dining room where visitors enjoy barbecued salmon or roasted quail and swap fishy tales.

Because of the lodge's proximity to Sointula, the old Finnish village, dessert is frequently a version of Tuula Lewis's Whipped Wild Berry Pudding (page 257).

challenges. On the East Coast, salmon escapees mate with wild relatives, and the close proximity of cages to spawning rivers encourages the spread of disease. These are not insurmountable problems—we have the know-how to farm the finest fish on earth. However, to put such technology into place is very expensive and, at the moment, we seem to have reached an economic plateau where neither the political nor corporate will is present. Largely because of the activist lobby, British Columbia has one of the most highly regulated industries, with far tougher rules than those set by the jurisdictions of the parent companies. But, in my opinion, these rules are still not strict enough, mainly because British Columbia is so unique, its ecosystems so fragile. Nowhere else on earth are farmed salmon living side by side with significant wild stocks, and, surprisingly, the fish often share the same wild food resources. A legal harvest of 500 tons of krill, the tiny creatures that give the salmon flesh its red colour, is used as food on the salmon farms along the coast. It's well known among fishermen that herring is the main food of wild salmon, yet a full-scale herring roe harvest is allowed, which includes killing the adult fish.

Sockeye salmon, roasting on cedar stakes at Cape Mudge village, Quadra Island, B.C.

Is there a solution? Dramatically fewer fish per cage is certainly one option; another may be land-based aqua farms with proper water recirculation; and, finally, development and implementation of better feeding regimens. But until consumers of salmon are given the option of an environmentally sound product and green dollars are invested in research and development, real progress may be a long way off. Let's hope not, for as one of the early aquaculture industry leaders says, whether we're commercial or sport fishers or sea farmers, we must start thinking about what's best for the salmon.

Salmon was a culinary cornerstone for First Nations, and today, because it's so quick to cook, it has become a mainstay for many Canadians. I grew up on salmon loaf, made from the tinned fish that likely came from some far-away B.C. packing house; it's still comfort food for me. But I've also learned to love it pan-fried with fresh herbs and a splash of cider vinegar or, if I'm feeling particularly flush, a few drops of Minus 8, Niagara's stellar icewine vinegar. Across the nation, we eat salmon raw in sashimi or bake it with Japanese flavourings. We preserve it in salt for Scandinavian gravlax, and we can it or smoke it over wood chips. We may find it as the centrepiece of an upscale Vancouver barbecue or simply grilled over a beach fire in Atlantic Canada. Salmon is a luxurious food, a seasonal specialty, and is as much an icon of Canadian food as maple syrup and wheat.

Ode to the Salmon

It was on the banks of the Campbell River that author and regional magistrate Roderick Haig-Brown lived and wrote his journals and classic river stories. His family found this handwritten poem tucked into one journal, the only poetry the fabled author ever penned. The following passage has been reproduced with the kind permission of the Haig-Brown family.

Pacific Salmon

River-born fugitives, red muscled under sheathing silver,
Alive with lights of ocean's changing colors,
The range of deeps and distances through wild salt years
Has gathered the sea's plenty into your perfection.
Fullness is the long return from dark depths
Rendering toll of itself to the searching nets
Surging on to strife on brilliant gravel shallows
That opened long ago behind the failing ice.
In violence over the gravel, under the blaze of fall
Fullness spends itself, thrusting forth new life
To nurse in the stream's flow. The old life
Used utterly, yields itself among the river rocks of home.

Roderick Haig-Brown

Mark Mitchell's Grilled Salmon

Salmon is a brilliantly easy fish to barbecue. Vancouverite Mark Mitchell, an expert in fast, flavour-filled meals, is a free-form cook who likes to invent new combinations on the fly. He loves to eat, but he'd rather play tennis or go for a run.

YIELD: 3 to 4 servings

Brush or rub the salmon with one of the mixtures below. Preheat barbecue to medium and oil grill lightly. Lay fish on grill, skin side down; close the lid and cook for 7 to 10 minutes. There's no need to flip the fish. When the fish is done, the flesh lifts easily from the skin. The standard recommended cooking time is 10 minutes per inch (2.5 cm) of thickness. The following proportions work for 1 lb (500 g) of fish.

ASIAN MARINADE: Whisk together 2 tbsp (30 mL) sesame oil and 1 tbsp (15 mL) soy sauce. Brush or rub over the salmon. Let stand, flesh side down, in the marinade for 30 minutes at room temperature or for 60 minutes in the refrigerator. Remove from marinade and grill as above.

ISLAND FLAVOURS: Lightly sprinkle the fillet with about ½ tsp (2 mL) sea salt and a generous grinding of pepper. Grill as above. Serve with mango salsa: combine ½ red onion, finely chopped, 1 ripe mango, diced, 1 small cucumber, diced, 3 tbsp (45 mL) lime juice, 1 jalapeño pepper, seeded and finely minced, and 2 tbsp (30 mL) chopped fresh coriander.

INDIAN FLAVOURS: Combine ½ tsp (2 mL) cumin, ½ tsp (2 mL) ground coriander, ¼ tsp (1 mL) garlic powder, ¼ tsp (1 mL) turmeric and ¼ tsp (1 mL) cayenne. Rub into the surface of the salmon; sprinkle lightly with salt. Grill as above.

Washed with the gold of a Prince Edward Island dawn, a lobster fishing boat heads out from North Lake for its second run of the morning to pull the traps on the final day of fishing.

Crispy Potato Pancakes with Smoked Salmon

These multicultural homespun pancakes are also great with maple syrup.

YIELD: 4 to 5 servings

1 large onion, finely grated
6 large potatoes, peeled and grated
3 eggs, lightly beaten
¼ cup (60 mL) all-purpose flour
1 tsp (5 mL) salt
1 tsp (5 mL) baking powder
Melted butter or canola oil, for frying
Smoked salmon slices
Sour cream
Minced chives or green onions

In a large bowl, combine the onion, potatoes and eggs. Sift or stir together the flour, salt and baking powder; add to potato mixture, combining thoroughly.

Lightly butter or oil a heavy skillet; place over medium heat. Using about ¼ cup (60 mL) batter for each pancake, drop into the heated pan, pressing down lightly to spread for even cooking. Cook for 3 to 5 minutes total or until well browned on both sides.

Place pancakes on each serving plate. Heap on the smoked salmon and top with a dollop of sour cream and minced green onion or chives.

On Quadra Island, B.C. Need we say more?

Roger's Coho Salmon Gravlax with Salmon Mousse

The best recipes are often the simplest. But if there is one secret in the creation of a special dish it has to be the correlation between freshness and the final perfect result. Gravlax is such a dish. It can only be made with the freshest salmon. Thankfully, even in the land-locked regions of Canada, good wild-caught coho is available from time to time.

Roger Dufau's cooking reflects his belief in simplicity. He's also frugal. He uses a whole side of salmon, and after curing, he trims the thinner tail and belly portions of the fish because they absorb more of the "cure" than the thicker parts. He uses these pieces to make what he calls a salmon mousse; in reality, it's a whipped cream cheese mixture that's spiked with horseradish, a spoonful of prepared wasabi or even cayenne. Spread it on toast or, better still, on Crispy Potato Pancakes (page 57) that will be heaped with thin slices of the fish.

YIELD: 1¾ cups (425 mL)

1 side of coho salmon (about 2 lb/1 kg), bones removed, skin on
¾ cup (175 mL) salt
¾ cup (175 mL) granulated sugar

SALMON MOUSSE:
8 oz (250 g) plain cream cheese
4 oz (125 g) cured salmon trimmings
Juice of 1 lime
3 tbsp (45 mL) half-and-half cream (10%)
Grated horseradish, wasabi or cayenne pepper

W. W. Doak, like the Miramichi River itself, is central to the fishing life of New Brunswick. Although you can buy their gear on line, for serious anglers, this store is absolutely worth the trek to central New Brunswick.

A heap of fishing nets in the Campbell River harbour.

Lay the salmon, skin side down, in a large flat pan with sides. Stir together the salt and sugar and spread evenly over the fish. Cover tightly with plastic wrap; place another pan on top and weigh it down with tins or a large clean stone.

Refrigerate for 24 to 36 hours. Remove from pan, discard the collected juices and rinse the salmon under cold water. Pat dry.

Trim off the thin portions, setting aside to make the salmon mousse; wrap remaining fish and refrigerate until ready to serve.

SALMON MOUSSE: Place the cream cheese in a food processor along with the salmon trimmings. Process for a few seconds before adding the lime juice and cream. Add horseradish, wasabi or cayenne to taste. Process until smooth. Refrigerate until serving.

Salmon Spring Rolls with Sweet Plum Dipping Sauce

The Asian influence is clear in this fabulous British Columbian recipe. When I can't obtain sockeye, I substitute another lean salmon, coho.

YIELD: 10 to 12 spring rolls

3 tbsp (45 mL) drained capers
½ red onion, chopped
1 tbsp (15 mL) lemon juice
2 tbsp (30 mL) mayonnaise
¼ cup (60 mL) chopped fresh dill
½ tsp (2 mL) salt
½ tsp (2 mL) ground white pepper
1 fresh sockeye or coho salmon fillet (1 lb/500 g),
    skinned
10 to 12 spring roll wrappers
1 egg
1 tbsp (15 mL) water
Canola oil, for frying

In a food processor, combine capers, onion, lemon juice, mayonnaise, dill, salt and pepper. Process until finely ground. Chop salmon and add to the spice mixture. Pulse on and off to grind the salmon coarsely.

Lay spring roll wrappers on flat surface. Whisk together egg and water; brush over the edges of the wrappers. Place a spoonful of filling in the centre of each and roll up. Heat oil in 350°F (180°C) fryer; deep-fry spring rolls in batches until golden brown, 4 to 6 minutes. Drain on paper towels. Serve hot.

Sweet Plum Dipping Sauce

Half jalapeño pepper, seeded and coarsely chopped
2 large cloves garlic
2 tbsp (30 mL) chopped fresh ginger
2 tbsp (30 mL) dry mustard
3 tbsp (45 mL) apple cider vinegar
1½ tbsp (25 mL) soy sauce
2 cups (500 mL) plum jam
⅓ cup (75 mL) apple cider or apple juice

In a food processor, purée jalapeño, garlic, ginger, mustard, vinegar and soy sauce.

In a heavy saucepan, combine plum jam and apple juice; bring to a boil over medium heat. Stir in purée. Simmer for 3 minutes. Let cool.

My son Mark, chef and expert fishing guide, happily carrying my salmon. Dinner is less than an hour away, and one of these beautiful fish will be on the table. The rest he'll cure in brown sugar and coarse salt, then smoke over shaved bits of alder.

Keiko's Japanese-Style Baked Salmon

My friend Keiko Yakimo's mother, Yoshiko Takahashi, was born in Britannia Beach, British Columbia. Her father, Genji Yada, who was born in Japan, came to Vancouver and ran a small grocery store until the family was "evacuated" in 1941 to Bridge River, near Lillooet, in the B.C. Interior after Pearl Harbor was bombed. Keiko was born in that internment camp in 1943. When the family returned in 1949, all their assets, including their grocery store, had been taken. So they rolled up their sleeves and started over. Keiko's brother, Rickey, who was born in 1954, has become one of Canada's most respected food scientists, holding a prestigious Canada Research Chair at the University of Guelph in Ontario. Keiko now lives next door to where her parents ran their store, and it was there that I visited her. She is a gentle, pragmatic person and a great cook. Her recipes reflect the decades that her family has spent in Canada: they are Japanese in style but with fewer of the more exotic ingredients that show up in my daughter-in-law Kaori's cooking. When Keiko was a child, they just weren't available.

Keiko roasts salmon, after marinating it for about half an hour, at a very high temperature. Whereas Kaori bakes her salmon right in the teriyaki-style sauce, Keiko removes it, spreads it in a single layer on a baking sheet and paints it with mayonnaise or even Miracle Whip. She uses the entire side of the salmon, including the bones and the succulent belly flaps.

Keiko serves this salmon simply, with plain steamed rice. But before sitting down, she reverently fills a small bowl and places it prayerfully at the beautifully carved family shrine. Later she will eat it with no other food except Japanese pickles.

Japanese chili powder, a pungent combination of orange peel, red pepper, sesame and seaweed, can be purchased at most Asian markets. If it's unavailable, use hot pepper flakes.

YIELD: 4 servings

2 lb (1 kg) side of salmon
1 cup (250 mL) Japanese soy sauce
½ cup (125 mL) water
¼ cup (60 mL) mirin
2 tbsp (30 mL) grated fresh ginger
2 or 3 cloves garlic, grated
½ tsp (2 mL) Japanese chili powder
½ to ¾ cup (125 mL to 175 mL) mayonnaise

On display at the Pier Street Farmers Market, Campbell River, a mural of the legendary Japanese fishing boat Soyokaze, painted by Dan Richey. The Japanese have lived in this region of B.C. for over a century.

Cut the salmon into serving pieces and place in a 9- x 13-inch (3.5 L) baking dish lined with foil and lightly oiled. Stir together the soy sauce, water, mirin, ginger, garlic and chili powder. Spoon half of it over the fish, turning to coat. Cover and let stand for 20 to 30 minutes. Rearrange the fish so that it's skin side down. Spread the upper side with the mayonnaise.

Bake in a preheated 450°F (220°C) oven for 20 minutes or until the fish flakes easily and is beginning to brown slightly on top.

Meanwhile, heat the remaining marinade in a small saucepan over medium heat until boiling. Simmer, uncovered, until reduced to half the original volume and pass as a sauce. Serve salmon with steamed rice and Cucumber Seaweed Salad (page 65).

Seaweed Harvesting

The plant foods of our oceans have long been ignored. Diane Bernard, who lives near Sooke, B.C., has created a very successful enterprise by hand-harvesting sea vegetables from what she describes as "one of the richest seaweed floras in the world for the highest quality seaweed." Her seaweed "emerges clean from the cold Canadian Pacific, rich in vitamins (A1, B1, B2, B6, B12, C, E, K, pantothenic acid, folic acid and niacin), minerals and trace elements."

These are the types of seaweed Diane harvests:

Winged Kelp *(Alaria)*: This olive brown seaweed has a large frond, or blade, with a distinctive flattened mid-rib.

Feather Boa *(Egregia)*: This attractive brown kelp is fringed with rich chocolate brown blades. It actually looks like the once fashionable scarf made of feathers.

Nori *(Porphyra)*: Several varieties of this beautiful ruffled seaweed range from olive green to rose pink to purple. Historically, this plant was important to indigenous peoples. It has a sweet, meaty flavour pleasant to most palates.

Rainbow Seaweed *(Iridaea)*: This type of seaweed has broad, smooth blades that are dark bluish, purple and iridescent.

Rockweed *(Fucus gardneri)*: This grows on rocks in mid-intertidal zone in temperate water; it is olive green to dark green in colour and has a long history as a herbal remedy for headaches and indigestion.

Sea Cabbage *(Hedophylum)*: As this thick chocolate-coloured seaweed grows, it wraps around itself; hence the name sea cabbage. The blade can be lacerated, smooth form or undulated. The taste is sweet and the texture is pleasant.

Sea Lettuce *(Ulva lactuca)*: This bright green, tissue-like seaweed resembles leaf lettuce. When dried in the sun, it looks and feels like tissue paper. Japanese researchers have found Ulva to contain about 26 percent protein and 23 percent minerals by dry weight. It contains vitamins A, B1, B2, C, niacin, and a high amount of iron.

Cucumber Seaweed Salad

English cucumbers are now widely grown in greenhouses across Canada, thanks to Dr. Arthur Loughton, an agrologist from the Simcoe region in Ontario who perfected their greenhouse culture.

Although Canada is rich in a huge variety of seaweed, or "sea vegetables" as some call them, few cultures relish them as much as the Japanese and use them in so many dishes. This recipe uses dried wakame, which can be found in most Asian grocery stores. Vary the amount to your own taste.

YIELD: 4 servings

1 English cucumber, thinly sliced lengthwise or crosswise
½ tsp (2 mL) salt
1 to 2 tbsp (15 to 30 mL) dried wakame
2 tbsp (30 mL) mirin
2 tbsp (30 mL) seasoned rice wine vinegar
2 tsp (10 mL) sesame oil

In a medium bowl and using your hands, toss the cucumber with the salt, working the salt into the cucumber well. Let stand for 10 to 15 minutes to draw some of the moisture from the cucumber.

Soak the wakame in cold water for 15 minutes; drain and slice into thin strips.

When ready to serve, squeeze the sliced cucumber to remove excess liquid; toss it with the wakame, mirin and vinegar. Drizzle with oil. Serve at room temperature.

Seaweed lady Diane Bernard ships her fresh harvest from Sooke, B.C., across the continent. Throughout the summer, she leads hands-on tours along the rocky seashore at low tide.

Barbecued Salmon with Wild Red Huckleberry Butter Sauce

Red huckleberries *(Vaccinium parvifolium)* grow everywhere on the islands of British Columbia and are perfectly ripe when the chinook begin their late-spring run. The tartness of the berries is a perfect counterpoint for the richness of barbecued salmon. If you can't get huckleberries, substitute ½ cup (125 mL) fresh cranberries.

With this technique for barbecuing salmon, the skin becomes crisp and the cooked flesh is easily lifted off with a wide spatula.

YIELD: 6 to 8 servings

2 tbsp (30 mL) canola oil
¼ cup (60 mL) minced shallots or green onions
1 cup (250 mL) dry white wine
1 cup (250 mL) fish or chicken stock
1 tbsp (15 mL) grated fresh ginger
¼ tsp (1 mL) freshly ground pepper
1¼ cups (300 mL) fresh or frozen red huckleberries
1 tsp (5 mL) liquid honey
1 tbsp (15 mL) apple cider vinegar
1 cup (250 mL) unsalted butter, chilled and cut into small bits
Salt
6 to 8 salmon fillets (6 to 8 oz/175 to 250 g each), skin on

In a large skillet, heat oil over medium heat. Sauté the shallots until tender but not browned, about 3 minutes. Increase heat to high; add the wine, stock, ginger, pepper, 1 cup (250 mL) of the huckleberries, honey and vinegar. Bring to a boil and cook, stirring constantly, until reduced to almost syrupy. Remove from heat; press pulp through a strainer. Return sauce essence to skillet; bring to a rapid boil and reduce the volume by two-thirds. Remove from heat; whisk in butter a few bits at a time, until sauce is smooth and glossy. Add salt to taste. Stir in remaining huckleberries. Keep warm.

Meanwhile, heat barbecue to medium-high. Place fillets, skin side down, on grill. Salt lightly and close lid. Grill until firm to the touch, 6 to 8 minutes, or until done as desired.

Spoon half of the sauce onto heated plates. Slide a wide spatula between the flesh and the salmon skin; carefully transfer 1 salmon fillet onto the centre of each plate and drizzle with a little additional sauce. Garnish with fresh huckleberries.

Miso-Barbecued Spring Salmon with Roasted B.C. Hazelnuts

This was one of the recipes chef Michael Stadtländer created when he arrived on Quadra Island, B.C., for a visit. He used freshly fermented miso that his Japanese wife, Nobuyo, had brought with them from her home in Okinawa. The salmon was provided by my son Mark, who has guided on the British Columbian coast since 1988. The recipe honours the purity of the ingredients of both nations, Canada and Japan.

Since few in Canada have access to homemade miso, try the mildest form available, such as that made with sweet rice.

YIELD: 6 to 8 servings

¼ cup (60 mL) sweet rice miso
2 tbsp (30 mL) mirin
1 spring salmon fillet (2 lb/1 kg), boneless but with skin on
½ tsp (2 mL) crushed black pepper
⅓ to ½ cup (75 to 125 mL) chopped roasted hazelnuts

Clean the grill of the barbecue and wipe with canola oil. Preheat it to high for 7 to 10 minutes.

Combine the miso and the mirin and spread it over the top of the salmon. Sprinkle with pepper and hazelnuts.

Reduce heat to low. Transfer fillet to grill, skin side down; close lid and cook for 10 to 12 minutes or until opaque and beginning to flake. The secret is to leave the lid closed during cooking.

Carefully remove the salmon flesh from the skin, which will, by this time, have stuck to the grill. Serve immediately.

MISO

Making great miso is an intensive operation. Because of the long fermentation process, it takes months to get it just right and requires the very best ingredients, preferably organic. The first "locally grown/locally made" miso I was ever aware of in Canada came from a tiny B.C. company, Shinmeido Miso, on Denman Island. It was, and still is, excellent. In Ontario, purists Jerry Lewycky, one of the founders of Toronto's legendary Big Carrot health food store, and musician Suzanne Cardinal have teamed up to open Tradition Miso, just north of Toronto in Claremont. Tradition Miso is one of a small handful of companies in North America that processes miso. Its Barley and Brown Rice Miso are certified organic.

Traditional Maritime Fish Chowder

This family recipe from David O'Brien of Woodstock, New Brunswick, uses staples that were, and still are, often available in the kitchens of Atlantic Canada—canned evaporated milk and potatoes. Smoked cod or haddock is essential. Try to find strips of salmon belly flaps, the part of the fish that is so often discarded. They are the fattest and most delicious part of the salmon. David says the potatoes should be "three-quarters cooked" before adding the fish to the pot.

YIELD: 4 to 6 servings

> 3 lb (1.5 kg) fish, including at least 1 lb (500 g) salmon belly strips and ½ lb (250 g) smoked fish
> 5 cups (1.25 L) water
> 4 cups (1 L) cubed unpeeled potatoes
> 1 cup (250 mL) chopped onion
> 2 cans (each 385 mL) evaporated milk
> 2 tbsp (30 mL) granulated sugar
> Salt and hot sauce

Skin the salmon and cut the rest of the fish into large cubes. Set aside.

Bring water to a boil; add potatoes and onion and cook until potatoes are almost tender.

Add fish and cook for 4 to 6 minutes or until just beginning to flake. Do not overcook. Pour in milk and reheat. Add sugar; taste and add salt and hot sauce as desired.

Salmon Loaf

When one lives on a remote light station like Ivory Island in the middle of the Inside Passage on the British Columbia coast, self-sufficiency is a prerequisite. You garden, you bake and you catch your own fish. When Judy Schweers, an American who came north in the 1960s, lived there, she and her family hauled in both halibut and salmon. The last time I spoke with her she was still baking this loaf at Langara Point, on the uppermost reaches of the Queen Charlotte Islands. Home- or commercially canned salmon can also be used. This is almost identical to the salmon loaf my mother made, but she used the canned salmon that was available in post-war, land-locked Ontario. She didn't use cottage cheese and added crushed saltine crackers instead of the bread crumbs.

A lighthouse rises high above the water at the north tip of Langara Island, B.C.

YIELD: 4 to 6 servings

2 cups (500 mL) flaked cooked salmon
OR
2 cans (7½ oz/213 g each) sockeye salmon, undrained and flaked
1 cup (250 mL) cottage cheese
1 cup (250 mL) dry bread crumbs
1 tbsp (15 mL) butter
2 green onions, minced
1 egg, beaten
¾ cup (175 mL) milk
¼ tsp (1 mL) freshly ground pepper
¼ tsp (1 mL) cayenne pepper
1 tbsp (15 mL) minced fresh parsley
Melted butter (optional)

Place salmon in a bowl, removing or crushing any bones. Stir in the cheese and bread crumbs, mixing well.

In a small skillet, melt the butter over medium heat; sauté green onion until tender. Add to the salmon along with the egg, milk, pepper, cayenne and parsley.

Pack into a lightly oiled or parchment-lined 8½- x 4½-inch (1.5 L) loaf pan. Brush with a little melted butter, if desired. Bake in a preheated 350°F (180°C) oven for 35 to 45 minutes or until puffed and beginning to brown. Let stand for 5 minutes before removing from the pan with a wide spatula. Remove parchment and serve piping hot.

Bentwood Box Cooking

Bentwood box cooking, as it was done by the First Nations of coastal British Columbia, is the only method of cooking to originate in Canada. From pre-history, the boxes, skilfully made with planks of red cedar, were used for family meals or the most elaborate feasts. Often ornately decorated and of various sizes, they were also used for storage and even, at times, for burial.

When Captain James Cook first sailed to the wild western shores of Vancouver Island in 1777, his artist, John Webber, drew portraits of the Nootka people boiling their foods in just such a box, likely made of cedar.

In Northwest culture, the red cedar was a revered tree, often many storeys high. It was life giving, being used for a myriad of practical purposes, from canoe building to blanket weaving. When the cedar was used for cooking, planks were removed from the tree with yew wedges and a stone maul. They were scored and then placed in a pit lined with hot stones and seaweed. The steam started to rise, and more seaweed was piled on before the pit was covered with mats. Left for several days, the wood became pliable. The planks were removed and bent around a wooden base carved to fit perfectly into notched grooves that would tightly seal the bottom of the box. The boxes were then either pegged or sewn with strips of cedar taken from the long, graceful limbs of the tree.

Bentwood box cooking was the work of the women, and they took great pride in it. Depending on the size of the meal, at least two of these handmade boxes were filled with water to soak and tighten for three to four days before cooking. Four to five hours before cooking, a fire was lit on the shore, and potato-sized beach rocks were placed into it. The rocks absorbed the heat of the constantly tended fire. They had to be dense and compact. If not, they could fracture violently when placed in the box to heat cold sea water, blowing apart the painstakingly made cedar box. The rocks that did not split were precious and were saved in a cedar basket to be used over and over again.

Next the women cut a branch of alder, a soft, pliable tree that is often used today for smoking salmon. With a stone knife, it was split partway up one end, making a pair of rudimentary tongs. The hot rocks were then picked up with the split alder branch, washed in the first of two boxes and placed in the second with fresh water. Franz Boas, the anthropologist who studied the coastal First Nations from 1880 to 1920, described how, in the springtime, the tender shoots of the salmonberry bush were added to the water for flavouring. In mere moments, the water would foam and boil. Seafood was added—prawns, scallops, clams, chunks of salmon, cod or snowy white halibut—and a woven mat was placed over top to hold the steam. As the food was savoured, more was added, and the cooking continued until finally the delicious brothy liquid could be consumed. Within minutes, sweet tastes of the Pacific were retrieved from the box.

Over the centuries, other foods also have been cooked in the bentwood box, notably a wild berry "jam." Salal, a member of the heather family, with the Latin name *Gaultheria shallon,* was one of the most relished of these coastal fruits. Crushed salal berries were added to the box, then small, hot pebbles were arranged in a layer on top. More berries were added and the small stones were stirred into the liquid, bringing it to a boil and thickening it. While the contents of the box were cooking, a wooden rack was made and placed over a fire. Layers of skunk cabbage leaves *(Lysichitum americanum),* now sometimes called "Indian waxed paper," were arranged on top. The berry mixture, minus the stones, was then transferred to small four-sided cedar containers set on the leaves. There the fruit would dry to a leathery consistency before being stored in another bentwood box.

Fish & Shellfish

Returning to North Lake, P.E.I., loaded with lobster.

When I was a child, I'd stand on the third step of our back porch, and in the very early morning on the coldest winter days, I'd try to blow rings of steam as far as I could on that more-than-frosty air. It was on that sort of day that I met David Olson. His card read Commercial Fisherman. With leathery hands, he presented it to me with the pride that comes with being the fourth generation of his family to fish Lake Winnipeg, where lack of industrial pollution and sensible conservation efforts on the part of the provincial government have kept these waters full of fish. I was in Gimli, Manitoba, with Scot McTaggart, owner of Winnipeg's Fusion Grill, to go ice fishing with the Olsons. There's ice fishing—sitting in a hut dangling a line and drinking the odd frosty beverage—and there's *ice fishing*: in the open, on a snowdrifted, deeply frozen lake when it's -25°C and the north wind is blowing sideways. It is a profound test of one's mettle.

David Olson's heritage is Icelandic—his great-grandfather immigrated to Gimli in 1876. The demand for fresh pickerel and whitefish, particularly among the Jewish community of Winnipeg, then the third-largest in Canada, encouraged the Olson family and other Icelandic immigrants to develop a strong commercial fishery on the lake. It's been a rich relationship ever since, with Olsons and others providing the essential ingredients for gefilte fish. While David loves his pickerel simply pan-fried, other Icelanders still make their traditional sweet-and-sour fish soup, *fiskisúpa,* laced with vinegar and prunes, and *fiskbollur,* the round dumplings similar to the Danish *frikadeller* (page 128) in shape but made with fish rather than meat. They preserve it to make one of their oldest dishes, *harðfiskur,* or "hard fish."

After climbing into one of his two ancient Bombardiers, the hulking machines known as Snow Cats that one sees grooming ski hills, we set out onto the blue expanse. David "tuned it" with a hammer he uses to bash the ice away from the doors so they close. Grinding down the laneway and across what in summer are wetlands, we crossed masses of broken pack ice to reach two markers indicating each end of the nets that had been set a few days before. As we spilled out of the vehicle, the wind caught my face. I felt as though I'd been pierced by a thousand needles. The searing pain was extraordinary. Yet David worked with his bare hands. The Snow Cat had been retrofitted with an auger, and as he ground a hole through the 75 or so centimetres of ice, lake water gushed upwards. With a steel rod that looked like a giant crochet hook, he caught the end of the net and attached it firmly to the snow machine. Back we went to the other marker and repeated the process.

In this icy weather, he and his then 84-year-old dad, Paul, pulled in the gossamer nets, disentangling their catch and filling a bin with still squirming fish. The Olson catch goes directly to the Gimli Fish Market in Winnipeg, where David's sister, Karen, sells the fish the same day they're hauled from the lake. It's a family affair!

Across Canada, the wealth of freshwater and saltwater fish is being harvested as it has been for centuries by sport and commercial fishers alike. It may be romantic to think that the earliest Europeans came for furs to clothe the fashionistas of the day. They didn't; they came for fish. Although Basque galleons hunted whales, it was cod that began the story.

When entire nations were forbidden to eat meat on Fridays by the Catholic Church, the need for a good source of fish became an economic reality. Thousands of men and hundreds of ships crossed the Atlantic from Spain, France, Portugal and Britain to haul back tons of cod to feed the faithful. In the beginning, it was a migratory fishery, possibly pre-dating John Cabot's voyage in 1497, but by the 1600s there were land-based stations established to salt and dry the cod. At first, the fish were simply spread on the cobblestone beaches, but eventually they were split and dried on racks or flakes. The fishermen were poor European agricultural workers who chose this form of seasonal, quasi-indentured labour as a way to survive. It was hellishly hard work.

After eastern Newfoundland was staked out by the British in 1690, the French and, in particular, the Basques from St-Jean-de-Luz and Bayonne continued to fish along the western part of the island. A handful settled in Plaisance (Placentia) but were eventually forced to move to a nascent community that was to become the great fortress of Louisbourg on Île Royale (Cape Breton).

Cod was the foundation of the Maritime culture of the Acadians and all those who followed. The salty bounty was extraordinary. But with the decline in cod stocks, the fishery has diversified. Although herring is a memory-laden fish for many Atlantic Canadians, who grew up with preparations like the spiced pickled herring dish called Solomon Gundy, it's lobster, oysters, scallops, mussels and snow crab that really pay the bills today.

Lobster was the food of the poor until it became the pricey delicacy it is today. It's now the most valuable fishery for provinces like Prince Edward

COOKING UP A SUSTAINABLE PROGRAM

Established in 2005, Ocean Wise is a brilliant Vancouver Aquarium conservation program dedicated to raising awareness about sustainable seafood options. Local chefs and restaurant owners are encouraged to reduce the number of non-sustainable seafood items on their menus. Participating restaurants highlight sustainable seafood options on their menus, using the Ocean Wise logo.

In such a dynamic market, it's a bit like turning around the *Queen Mary*, but this program is becoming de rigueur for any restaurateur who wants to increase business. Restaurants commit to the removal from their menu of at least one unsustainable seafood choice every six months, until none of the listed species are offered.

Ocean Wise defines sustainable seafood as a species of seafood that is abundant and resilient to fishing pressures; well managed with a comprehensive management plan; and harvested in a way that limits habitat destruction.

Island and Nova Scotia. Scallops are number two in Nova Scotia, while on P.E.I. world-famous Malpeque oysters come in second. And it's those oysters that are celebrated for their quality and taste.

John Bil is Canada's 2006 oyster-shucking champion. "The first 20,000 are the hardest," he quips. Then Bil gets serious: "Oysters are the essence of the ocean, and they're environmentally very sensitive. So if there are any chemicals around, they die." He shucks Malpeques, the branded oyster of Prince Edward Island, which he refers to as "free range." They are the Eastern oyster, which actually flourishes from the Gulf of Mexico northward. But in the cold waters off P.E.I., they simply taste better, and that's the key to the Malpeque's success. These fabulous bivalves are firmer and saltier than their southern cousins, particularly in the summer after they spawn. By winter, as they fatten with glycogen, they're at their New Year's Eve best.

Another type of oyster that's grown in Atlantic Canada is the European flat. It has a slightly stronger flavour, often with a coppery taste. Unlike the Malpeque, which is great year-round, the European flat is most delicious when eaten in months containing an "r." From British Columbia come the smaller Pacific and the buttery deep-shelled Kumamoto. Bil says that the Pacific is the best for the neophyte oyster eater because of its size and its mild flavour.

From coast to coast, we fish in all seasons—whether it's breaking through the ice to pull in ropes of fat mussels on P.E.I. or landing perfect walleye when the lakes have become thick mirrors of ice. In the summer, Georgian Bay whitefish is harvested from water so pristine that cottagers are still able to run a line out into the limestone-filtered bay and use it, as is, for drinking.

There is a carefully monitored, limited sturgeon fishery in Northern Ontario and Quebec. Rainbow trout and Arctic char are grown in ponds, and tilapia is grown in closed-cycle farms across Canada.

Wild-caught fish from about 400 lakes scattered across northwestern Ontario, Manitoba, Saskatchewan, Alberta and the Northwest Territories are marketed by the Freshwater Fish Marketing Corporation, a Crown corporation based in Winnipeg. That company's fish menu includes walleye, whitefish, pike, lake trout and perch, harvested and sold to global markets.

In British Columbia, the historical range of seafood has been rich and diverse. The First Nations relished butter, horse and razor clams, blue and California mussels, Dungeness, Alaska King and box crab, goose-neck barnacles, octopus and squid. Some were pit-cooked for immediate consumption, while others were strung on sticks and dried. It's possible to locate ancient camping sites just by looking for the middens along the shore where shells were cast aside after consumption. They were, in effect, the garbage heaps, and as one travels throughout the Gulf Islands and up the coast, you can sometimes see them as streaks of white just above the high tide mark on a variety of beaches. Historically, the Aboriginal populace made careful use of resources. Clam "gardens" were tended and managed. Abalone, which for 15 years was in such short supply that its harvest was banned, was only gathered at the lowest tides.

A shift toward healthier eating patterns in Western societies has led to an increased demand for seafood. At the same time, we've seen plummeting fish stocks, with some dire global predictions that many species will be extinct in less than 50 years, and a notable increase in aquaculture, albeit with mixed reviews. Nonetheless, a number of our fisheries, such as those in Lake Winnipeg, are very well managed. The wild harvest records for British Columbia are like a culinary wish list. Of the groundfish, halibut and sablefish lead the way. Both have spectacular flavour. It is said by many connoisseurs that sablefish, which was once known as Alaskan black cod, is the finest fish we harvest in Canada. Off the coast of Vancouver Island, albacore tuna, another valuable resource, is being landed, while up and down that same coast of British Columbia wild shellfish is being harvested, including prawns, an array of clams, crab, and both green and red sea urchins.

It's still a dilemma though: what is the average, ethically inclined consumer to do if she happens to love a fishy feast? Chef and Slow Food proponent Mara Jernigan, founder of Vancouver Island's Feast of Fields, takes the most radical of stances. "Only eat non-carnivorous farmed seafood or that which has been fished in a sustainable fashion. Farmed shellfish is great—in fact shellfish aquaculture is among the most sustainable ways of growing seafood." On a more practical pan-Canadian level, consumers can make a difference, particularly if we attempt to adopt the balanced approach of the Vancouver Aquarium's Ocean Wise (see page 75) program and delete from our shopping lists one poorly managed species at a time. Being attentive to one's food supply is a very important step in environmentally conscious consumption. In fact, it's critical, because so much of our Canadian food culture—from the simplest cornmeal-coated, butter-fried fillets or Greek fish soup with dollops of garlic mayonnaise to peppery Portuguese fish stew or Kashmiri fish masala—is based on fish and shellfish.

The life of a fisherman—in this case Prince Edward Island's Edwin McKie—is a hard one. The names of the boats often reflect this reality.

Clams for sale beside the Bay de Chaleur, Caraquet, N.B.

Georgian Bay Whitefish Masala with Kashmiri Mint Chutney

Manjit Singh Bali and his wife, Jagjit, came to Canada with $100 in his pocket from his home in the Bararmulla district of Kashmir on October 16, 1972, when he was 33 years old. His brother was studying for his PhD in Crop Science at the University of Guelph, and Mr. Bali—that is how all his Elora, Ontario, neighbours know him—joined the aspiring scientist.

Mr. Bali already was a science and math teacher but, like so many immigrants, he left that career behind and started work in Brantford, Ontario, at the Massey Ferguson factory, where he stayed until 1988. He then moved his family to Elora, where I got to know him as the really kind man who owns a gas station on Mill Street. He was clearly more than a gas jockey. Behind his spotless home is a huge garden that puts most others to shame. Once we started to talk food, the ice was broken, and I began to learn bits of his story. "When you are born here in Canada," he told me one day, "you have every opportunity." He has five children—three boys and two girls. The girls are in medical school.

Both he and Jagjit are great cooks but when Mr. Bali is in the kitchen, she defers to him. He mixes and fries; she harvests the garden and chops. In their native Kashmir, the fish that's available is from fresh water. Here in Canada, he uses trout and his new favourite, magnificent Georgian Bay whitefish. This spicy recipe works with pickerel, splake and even trout. The bonus is that this method is also perfect with his Paneer (page 214) or firm tofu to make a great vegetarian main course. In order to speed things up, he fries the fish a few hours or even the day before and refrigerates it. In my own kitchen, I simply pan-grill it or barbecue it until it begins to flake, then spoon the masala over it. The Kashmiri Mint Chutney is the perfect condiment made with fresh mint and coriander leaves. The tiny green chilies can be found at most Indian grocery stores but Mr. Bali grows them himself in his sunny, spacious backyard and freezes them. This condiment is great with grilled meats. I've spooned it onto leftover chicken folded into soft pita bread.

The Balis serve this fish with rice or with roti that Mrs. Bali makes, but it would be great with steamed barley or even wheat berries. Lake whitefish is second only to Atlantic salmon in the amount of omega-3 fatty acids that are contained within its wild-caught flesh.

YIELD: 3 to 4 servings

1½ lb (750 g) whitefish or other freshwater fish, boned but skin on

½ tsp (2 mL) salt

Canola oil, for frying

MASALA:

2 tbsp (30 mL) canola oil

1 onion, minced

1 clove garlic, grated

1 tbsp (15 mL) grated fresh ginger

¼ tsp (1 mL) cayenne pepper (approx)

½ tsp (2 mL) turmeric

2 tbsp (30 mL) water

1½ tbsp (25 mL) tomato paste

1 tsp (5 mL) salt

1 cup (250 mL) water

1 tsp (5 mL) garam masala

½ tsp (2 mL) ground roasted fennel seeds *

¼ tsp (1 mL) cinnamon

⅛ tsp (0.5 mL) ground cloves

¼ tsp (1 mL) freshly ground pepper

½ cup (125 mL) chopped coriander leaves

Cut the fish into small serving portions and sprinkle with salt. Heat about 1 inch (2.5 cm) oil in a heavy skillet. Fry fish, skin side down, turning with tongs, until browned. Remove to a paper towel and refrigerate if not using immediately.

MASALA: About 30 minutes before serving, heat the oil in a large skillet or heavy saucepan; fry the onion until browned. Stir in the garlic, ginger, cayenne and turmeric; cook for a few seconds. Add the water, tomato paste and salt. Stir in enough additional water

to make a thin sauce. Sprinkle with the garam masala, ground fennel seeds, cinnamon, cloves and pepper. Add the reserved fish pieces and simmer until the fish is thoroughly reheated. Sprinkle with the chopped coriander; stir gently and serve.

*To roast the fennel seeds, lightly brown them in a dry skillet or in a 350°F (180°C) oven until toasted. Remove from heat and let stand for 2 to 3 minutes before pulverizing finely in a coffee grinder. Store the powder in a small, tightly covered glass jar.

Kashmiri Mint Chutney

This is a brilliantly easy condiment to make. It can be made ahead and refrigerated for up to three days.

YIELD: About 1½ cups (375 mL)

1 cup (250 mL) packed mint leaves

½ cup (125 mL) packed coriander leaves

4 green cayenne peppers or 2 jalapeño peppers

1½ tsp (7 mL) salt

1 cooking onion, chopped coarsely

Juice of ½ lemon

2 tsp (10 mL) grated orange rind

6 walnut halves

¼ cup (60 mL) plain yogurt

In a food processor, combine the mint, coriander, cayenne peppers (including seeds), salt, onion, lemon juice, orange rind, walnuts and yogurt; process until finely chopped. Use immediately or refrigerate for up to 3 days.

Planked Okanagan Trout with Seasoned Butter

This recipe is from Trudy Heiss, who co-founded Gray Monk Cellars with her husband, George, near Kelowna, B.C. Gray Monk is the last of the original "estate" wineries in the valley. The Heisses, two of the most well-loved and well-known growers in British Columbia, pioneered many European varietals, including rare Ehrenfelser, Auxerrois, Müller Thurgau, Rotberger and Siegerrebe, along with more common varieties like Cabernet Franc and Chardonnay. Their first vintage, in 1980, was of their namesake grape, Pinot Gris, which when translated means "grey monk." Their wine library holds 700 cases, including some of George's early, unlabelled experiments.

Trudy serves the trout with Spiced Summer Berry Sauce (page 255) and Barbecue-Roasted Baby Potatoes (page 181). Virtually all the ingredients she uses are local. And the wine? It *must* be a Gray Monk Pinot Gris.

The two apple, maple or cedar planks should be between ⅝ to 1 inch (2 to 2.5 cm) thick and measure roughly 10 inches (25 cm) long. Soak them overnight before preparing the fish.

YIELD: 4 servings

2 shallots, finely minced
1 tsp (5 mL) freshly coarse-ground pepper
1 tbsp (15 mL) lemon juice
3 tbsp (45 mL) unsalted butter, at room temperature
½ tsp (2 mL) salt
2 trout, about 1½ lb (750 g) each

A female rainbow trout at the University of Guelph's Alma Aquaculture Station is one of hundreds of breeding fish used to stock the waters in fish farms across Ontario.

In a small bowl, combine shallots, pepper, lemon juice, butter and salt.
Wash trout and pat dry inside and out. Stuff belly cavity with butter mixture.
Preheat barbecue on high. Place soaked planks directly on the grill and heat for 3 to 5 minutes or until they begin to crackle. Place fish on hot planks; close lid and grill for about 15 minutes or until flesh is opaque and flakes easily.
With large spatula, remove fish from planks and serve immediately with Spiced Summer Berry Sauce and Barbecue-Roasted Baby Potatoes.

Ali's Amazing Halibut

My best friends' son, Vince Morris, met Ali Kendall when she was cooking and he was tree-planting near Lake Revelstoke, B.C. Being the camp cook means being the undisputed reigning monarch of whatever remote location the crew finds themselves in. Vince, a young man who had spent as much time chowing down at my kitchen table as he did playing hockey and fishing with my sons, immediately realized on which side his bread was buttered. Ali not only understands hard work (she truly has inherited the gene), but she also understands flavour. Vince and Ali were married in the summer of 2006.

This recipe speaks to Ali's Dutch love of butter and fresh coastal ingredients. The story of her family (the Brinkmans) is similar to that of many recent Dutch immigrants to Canada.

"Oma and Opa, my grandparents, came over from Holland in 1950. My Oma was pregnant with my mom at the time, baby number five of 10! They started out living with a farmer and then moved around Ontario before settling in Bowmanville. My uncle and his family still live in the family house there. My grandparents moved to the Kootenays about 15 years ago, then my Opa passed away about three years ago, and my Oma moved back to Ontario [Whitby] because she missed her old friends. Half of my mom's siblings, who are Dutch Christian Reformed, stayed in Ontario and the other half (the 'tree-planting types') live here in B.C. I have about 30 or so blond-haired, Dutch-looking cousins. Oma is still alive and is totally great!"

This is Ali's recipe—simple and utterly perfect. The shallots brown just a bit in the oven, and the butter helps to keep the fish moist. Serve with a great B.C. Pinot Blanc or even a Chardonnay, or with fresh water from a mountain glacier.

YIELD: 4 servings

> 2 lb (1 kg) fresh boneless halibut
> 3 shallots
> ¼ cup (60 mL) butter
> Salt and freshly ground pepper
> ½ lemon

In a skillet, sauté shallots in 1 tbsp (15 mL) of the butter. Sprinkle with salt and pepper. Place the halibut in a lightly buttered or parchment-lined baking dish. Spread with the shallots and top with the remaining butter. Squeeze the lemon over the fish and season with more salt and pepper.

Bake, uncovered, in a preheated 375°F (190°C) oven for 20 to 25 minutes or until the fish begins to flake.

Grilled Pacific Halibut with Indian Spiced Yogurt

Vancouver food writer and yoga teacher Eve Johnson took me on my first tour of Vancouver's East Indian food stores. This dish showcases one of her favourite ways of combining Indian flavours with fresh Pacific seafood. She marinates the fish in spiced yogurt, making enough to pass as a pungent sauce.

YIELD: 4 servings

1 cup (250 mL) plain non-fat yogurt
1½ tbsp (25 mL) grated fresh ginger
4 cloves garlic, minced
2 tsp (10 mL) ground coriander
2 tsp (10 mL) ground dry-roasted cumin
1 tsp (5 mL) ground turmeric
1 tsp (5 mL) salt
Juice of 1 lime
4 halibut steaks (each 5 to 6 oz/150 to 175 g), about 1 inch (2.5 cm) thick
Canola oil
Salt and freshly ground pepper

In a bowl, whisk together the yogurt, ginger, garlic, coriander, cumin, turmeric, salt and lime. Reserve half and refrigerate. Add the fish to the remaining spiced yogurt, turning to coat evenly. Cover and refrigerate for at least 4 hours or overnight, stirring and turning fish occasionally.

Heat the barbecue to medium-high and brush the grill with canola oil. Remove the fish from the marinade, scraping off excess; discard marinade. Sprinkle the fish with salt and pepper. Place on oiled grill; grill fish until just opaque in centre, about 6 minutes per side. Transfer to plates and serve with the reserved spiced yogurt.

Fishing boat in Johnstone Strait, north coastal B.C.

Salt and Chili Pickerel

This recipe was inspired by one of Vancouver food writer Stephen Wong's, which is for preparing local Dungeness crab. Using freshwater fish fillets like pickerel or whitefish allows all the flavour of the sauce to soak into the sweet flesh.

YIELD: 4 servings

1 lb (500 g) fresh pickerel or whitefish fillets, cut into serving-size pieces
   with skin on
2 tbsp (30 mL) fish sauce
2 tbsp (30 mL) sake or dry sherry
1 tbsp (15 mL) minced or grated fresh ginger
1 tsp (5 mL) salt
½ tsp (2 mL) freshly ground pepper
½ cup (125 mL) cornstarch
1 cup (250 mL) canola oil, for frying
3 cloves garlic, finely chopped
2 large shallots, minced
2 jalapeño peppers, seeded and thinly sliced
½ cup (125 mL) finely chopped fresh coriander or green onions
Several lime wedges
Coarse sea salt

In a large bowl, toss together the fish pieces, fish sauce, sake and ginger. Let stand for 10 to 20 minutes. Remove the fish from the marinade and pat lightly with paper towels.

Combine the salt, pepper and cornstarch in a resealable plastic bag. Add the fish and shake until evenly coated.

In a medium saucepan or large wok, heat the oil over medium-high heat until very hot (about 350°F/180°C). Shallow-fry the fish until the coating is golden, 1 to 2 minutes per side. Remove with slotted spoon, drain well and place in baking dish lined with paper towels; keep warm.

Meanwhile, transfer about 1 tbsp (15 mL) of the oil to a separate wok and heat over medium-high heat for 30 seconds. Add the garlic, shallots and jalapeño peppers; stir-fry until fragrant, about 30 seconds. Place the fish on a heated platter; top with garlic mixture. Sprinkle with coriander or green onions. Serve immediately with lime wedges to squeeze over top and sea salt to sprinkle on top.

Greek Fish Soup with Hazelnut Garlic Mayonnaise

This recipe originally came from George Koyionis, a Greek Cypriot fish vendor at Toronto's St. Lawrence Market. In the late '80s his reputation for providing customers with some of the finest seafood in the city was firmly entrenched. I was introduced to him by Helen Kates, the undisputed doyenne of Arowhon Pines in Ontario's Algonquin Park. The kitchen there was, and still is, one of the best in the province.

Soup

YIELD: 6 to 8 servings

8 cups (2 L) chicken or fish stock
2 lb (1 kg) fresh fish, such as rock cod, flounder or sole
2 tbsp (30 mL) butter
3 celery stalks, diced
1 large onion, diced
2 cloves garlic, minced
2 tsp (10 mL) dried oregano
3 potatoes, peeled and diced
Salt and freshly ground pepper
2 eggs, beaten
Juice of 2 lemons

In a saucepan, bring the stock to a boil. Add the fish; cover and simmer until tender. With a slotted spoon, transfer the fish to a separate bowl; let cool and remove any bones. Reserve the stock and fish separately.

In another saucepan, melt the butter over medium heat; sauté the celery, onion and garlic until translucent. Add the oregano and potatoes, seasoning lightly with salt and pepper. Add the reserved fish stock and return to a boil; reduce heat and simmer until the vegetables are softened.

In a separate small bowl, whisk together the eggs and lemon juice.

Just before serving add the reserved fish to the stock and reheat completely. Whisk in the egg mixture and heat but do not boil. Taste and adjust seasoning with salt and pepper. Ladle into heated soup bowls. Top each serving with Hazelnut Garlic Mayonnaise.

Hazelnut Garlic Mayonnaise

YIELD: Makes 1½ cups (375 mL)

½ cup (125 mL) skinned roasted hazelnuts

1 egg

2 to 3 large cloves garlic

½ tsp (2 mL) salt

1½ tbsp (25 mL) lemon juice

1½ tbsp (25 mL) cider or wine vinegar

¾ cup (175 mL) canola oil

In a blender or food processor, pulverize the nuts. Set aside.

Add the egg and garlic to the blender or food processor, along with the salt, lemon juice and vinegar. Process until smooth. With machine still running, add the oil in a thin stream to create a thick mayonnaise. Stir in the nuts and transfer to a serving bowl; cover and refrigerate until using. Can be refrigerated for up to 2 days.

On Grand Manan Island, a girl sells the day's catch.

Peppery Portuguese Fish Stew (Caldeirada)

This dish is almost a direct transposition of the Portuguese national fish stew that Margaret Timmins' (a.k.a. Margarida Ferreira) mother, Maria, made in her Mississauga, Ontario, home and later her Cambridge, Ontario, home for years after her family immigrated in the 1950s. Rather than ocean fish, which once arrived daily in Maria's island kitchen on São Miguel, she substituted pickerel and a bit of extra salt. Last year, this identical recipe, which is really more of a method than a set of hard and fast rules, was cooked for me by Margaret's niece, Rosa Maria Mauricio, on the north coast of that same island near the village where Margaret's mother was born.

The goal is to make a flavourful bed for the fish, which is added toward the end of the cooking and steamed to spicy perfection. Like any classic homestyle recipe, this one lends itself to many variations. Don't be afraid to modify it. If you don't have ripe tomatoes, add ½ cup (125 mL) tomato sauce or crushed tomatoes. If banana peppers aren't available, add a sweet red pepper and ramp up the amount of pimento sauce. It's wonderful served with crusty fresh bread and a good salad.

Yield: 6 to 8 servings

2 large cooking onions, sliced
3 or 4 ripe tomatoes, sliced
3 or 4 banana peppers, seeded and diced
6 cups (1.5 L) sliced peeled potatoes
3 large cloves garlic, crushed
¼ cup (60 mL) minced fresh parsley
¼ cup (60 mL) minced fresh mint
⅓ cup (75 mL) olive oil
¼ cup (60 mL) pimento sauce*
1 tbsp (15 mL) coarse salt
1½ tsp (7 mL) ground white pepper
2 or 3 large bay leaves
1 cup (250 mL) water
2 lb (1 kg) whole fish fillets, such as pickerel or
    whitefish

In a large heavy pot or Dutch oven, layer the onions, tomatoes, peppers, potatoes and garlic. Sprinkle each layer with some of the parsley, mint, olive oil, pimento sauce, salt and white pepper, retaining a bit of each for the fish. Embed the bay leaves at random. Add water, cover and cook over medium heat or until the potatoes are nearly tender, 15 to 20 minutes. Top with the fish and reserved seasonings. Cover and continue to steam until the fish begins to flake, about 10 minutes, adding additional water if necessary to prevent burning. Ladle into warmed soup bowls.

*Available at Portuguese grocery stores.

Traditional Dutch Mess with Scrunchions

My Haligonian friend, author Marie Nightingale, traced the roots of this dish to Lunenburg, Nova Scotia. The "Dutch" in the title refers to the German settlers of that coast, men and women who were lured there to work. According to Marie, this dish was originally called "house bankin," but I've seen it in other kitchens across Atlantic Canada merely called by the name of whatever dried fish happens to be around. For Flossie MacDonald of Souris, Prince Edward Island, it's "hake and potatoes," but nothing goes better with either version than her own Green Tomato Pickle (Flossie's Chow, page 280).

Be it cod or hake or whatever, the salt fish is soaked in several changes of water, shredded and then boiled with the potatoes. Marie encourages her readers to top it with onions, cream and rendered salt pork, called scrunchions. She also suggests that leftovers be mashed and made into fish cakes by just shaping them into patties, rolling them in dry bread crumbs and frying them in a mixture of "butter for flavour, and canola oil so they won't burn."

This is basic food, created with ingredients that could be found in most Atlantic Canadian cupboards. Like so many quasi-peasant meals, it's really, really good.

YIELD: 5 to 6 servings

1 lb (500 g) salt cod
4 large potatoes
1 cup (250 mL) diced salt pork or thick-cut bacon
1 large onion, diced
1 cup (250 mL) whipping cream (35%)
Freshly ground pepper

Place the cod in a medium bowl and cover with cold water. Let soak for 4 hours; drain and cover with more cold water. Let stand for 2 more hours. Tear (rather than cut) the cod into strips. Cover with cold water and soak for 4 to 6 hours. If the fish is very salty (hard and dry), change the water several times. Drain the water into a large saucepan and add the potatoes to it. Cover and bring to a boil.

Meanwhile, with your fingers, shred the fish into small pieces and set aside.

When the potatoes are partially cooked, add the shredded fish, cover and return to a boil. Reduce heat and simmer until the potatoes are tender and the fish flakes easily.

As the fish and potatoes are cooking, fry the salt pork in a heavy skillet over medium heat until all the fat has been rendered. Drain and set the crisp bits aside to drain on a paper towel. Discard fat.

Add the diced onion to the hot pan and cook, stirring, until tender and beginning to brown. Stir in the cream and heat until steaming.

To serve, drain the fish and potatoes and turn out onto a heated platter. Pour the onion cream over top. Season with a generous grinding of pepper and sprinkle the reserved crisp pork scrunchions over top.

NUTRIENTS IN OYSTERS

Oysters are filter feeders, siphoning up to 25 gallons of water a day through their system, so the flavour of their meat is a function of the trace minerals (especially salt) in the water. They're prized for being an excellent source of vitamins A, B1 (thiamin), B2 (riboflavin), B3 (niacin), C (ascorbic acid) and D (calciferol). Four or five medium oysters supply the recommended daily allowance of iron, copper, iodine, magnesium, calcium, manganese and phosphorus. They also contain high levels of zinc, a sexual performance enhancer. This is one of the reasons oysters are claimed to be an aphrodisiac.

PACIFIC OYSTERS

Fifty thousand gallons of the world's finest Pacific oysters are harvested annually in the Tofino-Clayoquot region, and residents of the Pacific Rim need help in knocking them back. Every November, shellfish freaks, seafood geeks, bona fide connoisseurs and some of North America's savviest chefs make the pilgrimage to Tofino to gobble, gorge and munch as many of the briny critters as humanly possible. With over 25 growers in the region and ideal conditions for cultivating the Pacific oyster, Tofino attracts top culinary talent to work wonders with the area's bumper crop. During November, a.k.a. Oyster Month, local chefs profess their love for this versatile shellfish, preparing oysters in as many ways as you can eat them. How does a miso- and mayo-slathered oyster with pancetta sound? Or perhaps a fried oyster tostada with avocado purée? If that doesn't rock your boat, try a hemp seed oyster concoction. What could be more B.C. than that? This celebration of oysters really takes hold during the annual Clayoquot Oyster Festival weekend in mid-November.

John Bil's Oyster Mignonette

This simple recipe is from the Canadian Champion Oyster Shucker himself!

YIELD: 1 cup (250 mL), or enough for about 2 dozen oysters

½ cup (125 mL) red wine
½ cup (125 mL) apple cider vinegar
2 tbsp (30 mL) minced shallots
1 tsp (5 mL) cracked black pepper

Combine the red wine, cider vinegar, shallots and pepper. Let stand at room temperature for 1 hour to allow the shallots to marinate. Use a small spoon to drizzle on top of fresh oysters. Refrigerate leftover sauce for up to 1 week.

Tonging for Johnny Flynn's extraordinary Colville Bay oysters, Souris, P.E.I.

West Coast Clam Chowder

When I first sailed through Discovery Passage near Campbell River, B.C., with the Canadian Coast Guard, the rain seemed to fly sideways. There, in the late 1980s, Wendy Abram was a lightkeeper on Quadra Island. Digging clams was part of her life. This chowder, adapted from her original recipe, is the sort of soup that wards off the foggy winter dampness. It's great with Portuguese Cornbread (page 42). If you don't have clams, almost any other fish or shellfish would work. It's particularly good with cooked prawns.

YIELD: 6 to 8 servings

¼ cup (60 mL) butter
1 large onion, finely chopped
1 cup (250 mL) diced celery
4 cups (1 L) diced peeled potatoes
¼ cup (60 mL) minced fresh parsley
½ tsp (2 mL) salt
½ tsp (2 mL) freshly ground pepper
4 cups (1 L) chicken stock
5 or 6 strips bacon, coarsely chopped
¼ cup (60 mL) cornstarch
3 cups (750 mL) milk
2 cups (500 mL) chopped cooked clams

Melt the butter in a large soup kettle over medium heat. Add the onion and celery; cook and stir until transparent, 7 to 10 minutes. Add the potatoes, parsley, salt and pepper; stir to combine. Pour in the stock; cover and bring to a boil. Reduce heat and simmer until the potatoes are tender.

Meanwhile, fry the bacon until crisp. Drain on paper towels and add to the soup kettle.

Mix the cornstarch with a little of the milk, stirring until smooth. Pour into the simmering stock; cook until slightly thickened. Add the remaining milk and cooked clams. Gently reheat for 5 to 10 minutes or until steaming. Taste and adjust seasonings if necessary.

"Socks" of mussels, Murray River, P.E.I.

Prawns Peri-Peri

South African cooking relies heavily on the barbecue, or *braai*. Like Canada, South Africa has tons of great shellfish. This is chef Michael Allemeier's recipe, which features British Columbia's spectacular prawns, cooked the way he and his family had done in their home in Johannesburg and on the coast near Durban, where they escaped the summer's heat. Serve with warm crusty bread. (For more of Michael's story, see page 115.)

YIELD: 4 to 6 servings

> 2 peri-peri peppers or red jalapeño peppers
> 1 tbsp (15 mL) minced garlic
> ¼ cup (60 mL) fresh lemon juice
> 1 tbsp (15 mL) paprika
> 1 tsp (5 mL) salt
> ⅔ cup (150 mL) corn oil
> 2 lb (1 kg) fresh prawns (16 to 20 count), peeled and deveined
> ¼ cup (60 mL) chopped fresh parsley

Remove the stem from the peppers. Place in a food processor along with the garlic, lemon juice, paprika and salt. Process to make a paste. Pour in the oil slowly and continue to process until it becomes a smooth emulsion.

Place the prawns in a glass bowl and toss with the marinade. Cover and let the prawns absorb the marinade for 30 minutes at room temperature or for up to 4 hours in the refrigerator. Remove prawns from the marinade and grill over hot coals.

To serve, strew the prawns with fresh parsley.

IS IT A SHRIMP OR A PRAWN?

There's a fair bit of confusion between these two terms, each of which applies to the most delicious of ocean foods. The names often are used interchangeably, as I use them here. A passage in *Sea Life of the Pacific Northwest* (McGraw-Hill Ryerson, 1976) is a great illustration of the linguistic uncertainty:

> The Pacific Prawn (*Pandalus platyceros*) is the largest of the commercial shrimps growing to 22.5 cm (9"). Like other shrimps, it functions first as a male, changing sex during its third and forth years.

When my so Mark fishes for prawns he sets the traps (you can buy them at good old Canadian Tire) with bait cans full of fish scraps, cat food or fish farm pellets, which dissolve fastest. He drops them into the very deep water—"over 250 feet"—of Discovery Passage or around Quadra Island. In two to three hours, depending on the bait, he'll return to haul in the harvest.

The tails of the Spot Prawn are utterly delicious, but often smaller Side-striped Shrimp, one of some 80 species of shrimps in the Northwest, are also part of his catch.

On the east coast of Canada, sweet Cold-water Shrimp, often thought of as salad shrimp when they're tossed with a little mayonnaise, are landed by the ton in a large commercial fishery off the coast of Newfoundland.

Fried Rice Noodles with Chinese Sausage and Prawns (Char Kuay Teow)

Linda Chin is a delightful, community-focused hotel manager in Vancouver. When we met, we instantly started talking about her particular food customs. Her family emigrated from Malaysia to Vancouver in the 1970s, and today they all live on the Lower Mainland. "Aunty Betty is the oldest of the three sisters, Aunty Lucy is the middle sister, and my mom is the youngest," she explained.

The recipes that Linda provided, largely from memory, are among the most elegant and easy in this book. The flavours are complex and well balanced. Today, in Canada's multi-ethnic urban areas, the ingredients are also quite accessible.

Linda's mother, Rosemary, shared this extraordinary dish with me. Linda advises that it's best cooked in small batches so as not to break the noodles too much. Rosemary suggests using strips of chicken breast rather than prawns, if you like. Fresh rice noodles are available at most Asian grocery stores. Dried radish was a new and delicious flavour to me, so when I made the dish I added quite a lot more than the amount Rosemary requires.

You'll note that there is no liquid added, and at first I thought it was a mistake. In fact, the heat of the stir-frying releases the water from the bean sprouts, cooking the noodles perfectly.

YIELD: 4 servings

Moss covers the pilings at Alert Bay.

2 tbsp (30 mL) canola oil

4 cloves garlic, chopped

4 tsp (20 mL) minced dried radish

4 Chinese sausages, sliced diagonally

½ lb (250 g) raw prawns, peeled and deveined

4 eggs

Salt and freshly ground white pepper

1 lb (500 g) fresh flat rice noodles (or Hor Fun noodles)

2 cups (500 mL) bean sprouts

1 bunch (about 10) green onions, cut into 1½-inch (4 cm) strips

1 tbsp (15 mL) oyster sauce or fish sauce

1 tbsp (15 mL) dark soy sauce

1 tbsp (15 mL) light soy sauce

Chinese chili sauce (optional)

Heat wok over medium-high heat and add the oil, swirling to coat pan. Add garlic and radish, cooking until golden. Stir in the sliced sausages and prawns; sauté for a couple of minutes.

Break the eggs into the wok and scramble, seasoning to taste with salt and pepper.

Add the noodles, separating them before frying. Add the bean sprouts, green onions, oyster sauce, dark and light soy sauces, and chili sauce (if using). Stir-fry until lightly browned. Serve immediately.

Shelling Lobster

In its brochure entitled "No More Shell Games," Ocean Choice International, a Newfoundland-based company, outlines how it has developed an innovative shelling procedure for lobster that leaves the flesh whole and the shell intact. In its Souris, P.E.I., plant, the hyper-baric shelling process humanely dispatches the crustaceans and loosens 100 percent of the sweet meat. The results are perfectly formed whole lobsters or lobster claws and tails with no shell. They are then flash frozen and vacuum packed under the label HyperFresh. At the time of writing, they are mainly sold to the food service industry.

Steaming Lobster

The late author Ron Nickerson's method of steaming lobsters works well and is quicker because steam is infinitely more effective than boiling water when cooking lobsters. He recommended using clean seawater, but if you don't have access to any, add 1 tbsp (15 mL) coarse salt to each 4 cups (1 L) water used. For even cooking, the lobsters should be about the same size. Here's his method for cooking lobsters that are about 1½ lb (750 g).

In a very large pot over high heat, bring 1 inch (2.5 cm) seawater or salted water to a rapid boil. Remove bands from lobsters' claws and add lobster to the pot. Cover quickly and return water to a rapid boil. Adjust heat so steam is still escaping from under the lid. Cook for 18 to 20 minutes. Plunge cooked lobsters into a sink of ice water for 30 seconds. "This prevents the meat from sticking to the shell and makes meat removal easier," wrote Nickerson.

Cape Island Lobster (Sweet-and-Sour Lobster)

Ron Nickerson was born and grew up in Liverpool, Nova Scotia. His family was active in the East Coast fishery, and he was deeply involved in the industry until his death in 2005. His other passion was recipe collecting and cooking. His massive self-published cookbook, *Favourites Then and Now,* is a testament to the foods of the region and his huge circle of culinary friends. This Maritime treasury took 40 years to complete and is in its fourth printing.

Barb Nickerson recalls that she'd never tasted lobster done in this fashion till Ron's mother made it for her in Shelburne, Nova Scotia. If you choose to use frozen lobster, make sure that it's "knuckles and claws." Barb's favourite brand comes from Shediac, New Brunswick.

Barb's late husband wrote:

This presentation is unquestionably my favourite way to have lobsters. I think I can speak on behalf of several generations of family members (including the in-laws). . . . I think it originated in New England/Western Nova Scotia. My first recollection of this dish came from my maternal grandmother's side of the family. Here again, you can see the influence of the lack of fat in the coastal diet and the flavourings of vinegar and molasses (not to mention the abundance and early unmarketable situation for this crustacean).

Yield: 4 to 6 servings

⅓ lb (150 g) salt pork
2 lb (1 kg) cooked lobster meat
Boiling water
½ tsp (2 mL) freshly ground pepper
7 tbsp (105 mL) white vinegar
3 tbsp (45 mL) molasses
2 tbsp (30 mL) all-purpose flour
⅓ cup (75 mL) water
Mashed cooked potatoes

Cut the pork into ¼-inch (5 mm) cubes. In a heavy skillet over medium heat, cook the pork until all the fat has been rendered, 15 to 20 minutes. Remove the crisp bits (scrunchions) and drain on paper towels. Set aside.

Cut the lobster meat into bite-sized pieces, removing cartilage from the claws. Add to the skillet. Fry the lobster in the rendered pork fat until the fat has been absorbed, being careful not to overcook. This step will take about 2 minutes.

Almost cover the lobster mixture with boiling water (¾ to 1 cup/175 to 250 mL); add the pepper and stir. Add the vinegar and molasses. Taste to make sure that neither the vinegar nor the molasses overwhelms the flavour; adjust accordingly.

Stir or shake together the flour and water, stirring into the lobster mixture to create a colourful sauce. Taste again, adding more molasses or vinegar to create a balance of sweet and sour. Simmer on low for 7 to 10 minutes or until thickened. Remove from heat and let stand for 2 to 3 hours to allow the flavours to develop. Reheat and serve over mashed potatoes.

Left: At the end of the season, the traps are stacked high on the dock at North Lake, P.E.I. Middle and right: On Johnny Flynn's boat, the Owen Mor, *a lobster is measured with callipers to determine whether it is to be kept or thrown back into the sea.*

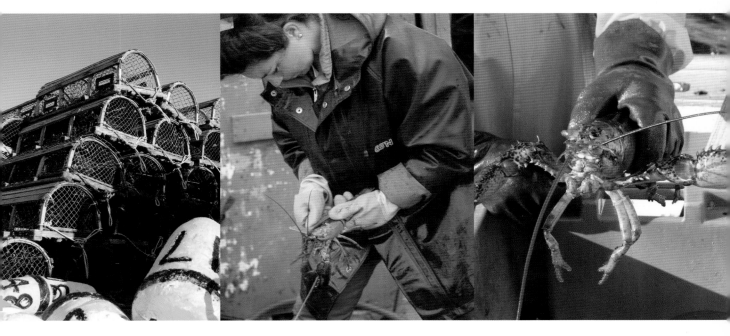

Lobster Fishing in P.E.I.

I was running late. A salmon-coloured slit backlit the dawning Prince Edward Island day. Dots of light, like so many bobbing stars, marked the boats already hauling in the lobster traps for the final day of fishing. North Lake was washed with dawn by the time I drove by the fish plant and across the harbour bridge. Traps were already heaped high as the boats emptied their gear and charged out to sea to pull more from the depths. I was waiting for Johnny Flynn—*the* Johnny Flynn of Colville Bay Oysters, and lobster fisherman in his "spare time." His boat, the *Owen Mor,* was named after an old Irish monarch, but it was also a statement, like *Undaunted,* another boat from another harbour I'd been aboard years before. Lobster fishing may be an occupation, but it's also a deeply personal tradition that, like farming, courses through the blood of countless Islanders.

Cool and salty, the air smelled good. Conversations could be overheard—hearty greetings, talk of parties to be thrown after the heavy work was finished. The harbour was a scene of crashing activity. Season 2007 had been a good one—not great, but the quality of the catch was very high. Ninety-seven boats had sailed out of North Lake that season, each licensed for 300 traps. "The man who invented hydraulics is sittin' at the right hand of God," Flynn observed wryly when we were underway. "They used to pull 'em in by hand. There were smaller traps and stronger men!"

The north shore of P.E.I. has never been dragged, so its bottom is an ideal habitat for lobsters. Fishing begins offshore, where the waters are about 120 feet deep, then moves inward, with the lobsters, on their spawning run. No females with roe are kept, and undersized and oversized lobsters are quickly tossed back. The market-sized ones—big and often beautifully tinged with red—are most often destined for the U.S., and the "canners" stay closer to home. Both sizes are quickly banded and put into a cool bin.

Flynn has seen island life change dramatically. He grew up on a family farm. "It's gone. I was the end of the ground fishery," he says. In 1989, he bought his first lobster boat. It wasn't till 1993 that he began experimenting with oysters. He bought another boat in 2003. "I used to have the smallest boat. Now I just have the oldest," he quips.

Loaded high, we headed through the 40-foot slit at the harbour's mouth. Working quickly—there was only one more run to do—the men heaved the traps on shore. The party would soon begin, and the stories, like the rum, would flow.

Meat & Poultry

A Barred Rock hen treads carefully on the first snow of winter.

$\mathcal{I}$t's odd how early childhood tastes influence the rest of one's life. I have to admit that I still love the darkened, drier ends of a beef roast that my mom overcooked beyond description; to her, meat that looked even remotely raw was considered downright dangerous. The juices must have caramelized, and the seasoning had already stuck to the exposed ends, so they were crusty and salty and good. Most Canadians, unlike many of our ancestors in their less bountiful homelands, have such remembrances about the importance of meat on the table. It is often these main dishes like the Basque Boeuf Bourguignon or the Acadian Meat Pies or the Braised Beef Stew with Dried Lemons that effectively nail a particular culture onto the map of modern Canada.

The New World provided an extraordinary larder, particularly for those European peasants used to a monochromatic diet of grains, pulses and potatoes. The Aboriginals who were originally in the St. Lawrence Valley had fled, so when the families of early French, and later English, settlers arrived, they had little competition for the game that they found there. In *A Taste of History,* Yvon Desloges and Marc Lafrance write eloquently about how the settlers were amazed "at the sight of the abundant large game in the colony." There were myriad animals, many of which had never been seen, let alone consumed, by a European. The settlers began to think in different ways. Early Quebeckers, with the unfamiliar, even odd, animal kingdom of New France, were able to create their own assessment of what they perceived to be delicious. Desloges and Lafrance observe:

> The taste of moose was compared with that of beef, bear to pork, porcupine to suckling pig and beaver to mutton, while marmot was said to be 'better than hare,' and the taste of deer . . . surpasses that of all types of venison. Everyone spoke of the excellence of the snow geese, Canada geese, partridges, teals and other wild ducks, and of course, passenger pigeons.

Much of the meat savoured during this era of the mid- to late 18th century was wild. "Caribou and ptarmigan meant a feast, since they came down the St. Lawrence Valley only in very cold weather." Each winter, snow bunting were eaten "so plump and so delicate that connoisseurs called them *ortolans.*" Even the strangest ingredients struck the fancy of the French, including beaver tail, bear paw, moose muffle and bison tongue.

Quebeckers ate well—and still do, for that matter—likely better than the peasants in France who were their contemporaries. "All we are missing is the wine and the eau de vie," wrote Simon Denys in 1651. At about the same time, Baron de La Hontan observed wryly, "The peasants here are extremely well off, and I would wish such good cooking upon all our dilapidated nobility in France."

From as early as 1676, urbanites had the option of buying their meat at the market in Quebec City. There, the *habitants,* the rural farmers who were tenants on the *seigneuries,* sold their wares. Cattle around the city had been imported from France, but because of the hard winters they were smaller in stature than their French ancestors. Nonetheless they flourished. Beef became the main dietary protein for the poor and was, according to Desloges and Lafrance, "as little as a quarter of the price of pork at the market." In 1806, one observer listed "seven types of meat, eight of poultry or game, thirteen of fish. . . ."

The English brought their own meat culture. In the early part of the 19th century, say Desloges and Lafrance, "grilled meat, steak, chops and croquettes, pies, especially mutton, oysters and soups . . . appeared on most taverns' à la carte menus, imitating the English chop houses which specialized in grilled meats and soups."

During the dynamic and turbulent times prior to Confederation, French *voyageurs* and English traders paddled into the heartland of the continent, where they encountered a land rich in history and, unlike the St. Lawrence River Valley, already populated by three of Canada's 16 language groups: the Siouan, Algonquin and Athapaskan. All had well-entrenched meat cultures. For thousands of years, they had hunted and collectively slaughtered the buffalo that thundered across the open plains. But with active settlement, the picture changed dramatically.

By 1885, when the Canadian Pacific Railway was completed, eastern markets were accessible. The railway became the conduit to the expanding packing houses in the east. By 1901, there were over three million cattle in western Canada. Meat on the Prairies came to mean beef. Far more than mere sustenance, it was a way of life. Cattle defined power over the land, domination of

THE WORLD'S LONGEST BARBECUE

In 2003, the Canadian cattle industry was ravaged by the closure of the American border over the fear of mad cow disease. Communities were devastated. It was that summer that I began what has become an annual challenge to Canadians: "Head to your grills, cook local food and tell me your menus!" They did, and since then we've recorded thousands of great barbecues from coast to coast.

The World's Longest Barbecue (www.flavoursofcanada.ca) is always held at 6 p.m. on the first Saturday in August. We've had virtual entries from around the globe. My goal is to create a national food day for Canada. We need one and it really *is* time!

The Berkshire Hog

It is said that the Berkshire hog was discovered in the 1600s by Oliver Cromwell's army in the English shire of Berks. The veterans of that troop carried the news to the outside world of the wonderful hogs of that region; they were larger than any other swine of that time and produced hams and bacon of rare quality and flavour. The Berkshire hog became an early favourite with the upper class of English farmers. For years, the royal family kept a large Berkshire herd at Windsor Castle. In fact, a famous Berkshire of a century ago was named Windsor Castle, having been raised within sight of the towers of the royal residence. This boar was imported to Canada in 1841, creating a stir in the rural press. From news accounts, it appears he must have weighed around 1,000 pounds at maturity.

one of the largest ranges on earth, a space that is well over six times the size of modern France. The cowboy was the new crown prince. Cattle, so similar to buffalo in their need of large open pasture, ranged and multiplied.

Settlers across all of early Canada also loved pork—it was the cornerstone of many early meals, and was of huge importance in their cooking since it was the most versatile of all meats. Fat was slowly heated and the lard rendered out of it for use in pastries or simply for frying. Pork was salted and stored in barrels so chunks could be fished out to flavour the pots of baked beans or simply fried into scrunchions to top the salt fish and potatoes. A pig was used in its entirety, from the head for head cheese to the roasted tail.

Pigs came on shore in 1518 with the Portuguese Baron de Leury as he made the first recorded European attempt at settlement, and in 1606, pigs were part of Champlain's agricultural inventory (the cattle died en route). Journal entries in Churchill, Manitoba, dating from 1777, record the slaughter of hogs that had been brought from the Orkney Islands. On the Red River, the Selkirk settlers had pigs in 1822, and in 1835 the Yorkshire breed arrived from England. In fact, there was little mention of the various breeds of hogs, but we do know the Berkshire pig was likely one of the earliest. A heritage breed that seemed to fall from culinary favour, it is seeing a substantial revival. Particularly in Nova Scotia and Manitoba, it is becoming the kobe beef of the pork world because of its marbled flesh. Landrace, Duroc, Hampshire and Tamworth, as well as Lacombe, a breed established in Alberta in the 1940s, are all raised across Canada.

Today, pork is still an incredibly popular meat. The reason is likely twofold. Modern pork has less and less visible fat—it really is a lean choice. And because so many of our immigrant communities come from cultures that relish pork, we are seeing more flavourful recipes, from the ginger-spiced Japanese dumplings known as Gyoza (page 127) to fiery South African Sosaties (page 124).

Sheep and lamb played a historic role for providing wool and "mutton." Many early Canadians, my own ancestors included, didn't enjoy mutton as much as beef or pork. The earliest record of sheep in what is now Canada was a description written in 1583 about an expedition led by Sir Humphrey Gylberte [sic].

The soyle along the coast is not deepe of earth, bringing forth abundantly peason, small yet good food for cattel. Roses, passing sweet, like unto our muske roses in form, raspases, a berry called harts, good and holesome to eat. The grasse and herbe doth fat sheepe in very short space, proved by

English merchants which have carried sheepe thither for fresh victual, and had them raised exceedingly fat in lesse than three weeks.
(*Sir Humphrey Gylberte and His Enterprise of Colonization in America*, ed. John C. Slafter, Boston, 1903, Wilson & Son Publishers.)

Today lamb is a very important component of the Canadian diet, partly because the home kitchens of many newer Canadians require lamb—from the well-spiced curries of India to the perfumed tagines of Morocco. The lamb of today is absolutely delicious, with none of the boiled-wool overtones that infused early mutton stews.

Chickens originated in Asia as the Red Jungle Fowl of Indonesia and spread throughout Europe. Canada's early chickens would have been the Old World varieties with which the settlers were familiar, but the breeds were not considered worth noting. They were simply judged on how handsome they were and whether they performed well.

According to retired professor Don Crober, of the Nova Scotia Agricultural College near Truro, poultry is truly global in nature. "The fundamental difference is between the purebred and the commercial industry. The latter is in the hands of a few companies. The industry is hardly farming any longer." Turkeys originated in Mexico, he explains, but were taken to Europe and really domesticated in England before they were returned to the New World. Pheasants may have originated in Russia, and it seems that ducks came from Asia. He is opinionated on the subject of flavour. When I asked which breed, if any, tasted better, he said, "Chicken flavour has to do with their age and what they have been fed. Period! The older they are, the more flavour." He's right—there *is* nothing like a plump yellow-skinned bird purchased at a local farmers market and then simmered gently to make Classic Chicken and Dumplings (page 139).

Few chefs write a menu quite like Mike Smith, known to Food Network Canada viewers as "Chef at Home." In 2006 he hosted a chefs' retreat, and all weekend long chefs cooked, ate and partied communally.

Beef with Barley Soup

This recipe has evolved with generations of soup makers who've allowed themselves the freedom to adjust the ingredients as necessity required. Fresh beans, shelled peas, chopped tomatoes, parsley and even celery root were added. It became a very creative and ultimately delicious exercise in frugality. In today's kitchens, either homemade or purchased stock can be used, but it's my belief that every cook should make beef stock at least once in his or her career.

YIELD: 4 generous servings

> 4 to 6 cups (1 to 1.5 L) beef stock (page 105)
> 1 large onion, minced
> ½ cup (125 mL) pearl or pot barley
> 1½ cups (375 mL) cubed, uncooked beef
> 2 or 3 carrots, peeled and diced
> 1 or 2 potatoes, peeled and diced
> 1 or 2 celery stalks, diced
> ½ tsp (2 mL) crushed dried rosemary
> Salt and freshly ground pepper

In a heavy soup pot, combine stock, onion, barley and beef cubes. Cover and bring to a boil; reduce heat and simmer for 1½ hours or until beef is tender and barley is swollen.

About 30 minutes before serving, add carrots, potatoes, celery and rosemary. Season with salt and pepper to taste.

Barley heads at Elora research station.

Paul's Homemade Beef Stock

There's no secret to making stock other than patience, and in my case having a son, Paul, who dictated the how-tos over the phone on a particularly cold winter's day. Since then, I've used this same recipe for venison bones, and the results were simply superb. If there is a "trick," it's the long reduction of the stock at the end of the cooking process. Try to obtain bones that still have a lot of marrow in them.

YIELD: **6 to 8 cups (1.5 to 2 L) stock**

8 to 10 lb (3.5 to 4.5 kg) beef bones
1 head garlic
2 onions, quartered
2 or 3 carrots, cut into chunks
1 or 2 celery stalks, coarsely chopped
2 leeks, cleaned and coarsely chopped
2 to 3 tbsp (30 to 45 mL) canola oil
2 or 3 bay leaves
1 or 2 sprigs fresh thyme or 2 tsp (10 mL) dried
2 tsp (10 mL) whole peppercorns
½ cup (125 mL) chopped fresh parsley
1 bottle (750 mL) dry red wine
1 cup (250 mL) canned tomatoes
Salt

Spread the bones in a shallow roasting pan. Break apart the garlic and scatter over the bones along with the onions, carrots, celery and leeks. Drizzle with oil. Roast slowly in a 375°F (190°C) oven for 2 to 3 hours, stirring occasionally, or until the bones are very dark but not burned.

Transfer to a large stockpot. Add enough water to cover the bones. Stir in the bay leaves, thyme and peppercorns; cover and bring to a boil. Reduce heat and simmer for 3 to 4 hours, skimming occasionally. Remove from heat and let cool slightly; when cool enough to handle, strain the stock. Refrigerate to allow the fat to rise to the surface. Remove fat and return to the heat. Stir in the parsley, wine and tomatoes. Simmer, uncovered, until reduced to one-third the original volume. Season with salt to taste. Let cool, then transfer to storage containers and freeze for up to 6 months.

Oakley the energetic puppy peeks from beneath the barn door. He was named by most of Marion Whale's 10 grandkids, who were spending a P.D. day at the farm. Out of four suggested names, "Oakley" won.

Scotch Broth

A quintessential comfort food, this recipe came out of a conversation I had with an elderly neighbour whose roots were Scottish. Millie Hartley was an independent, hardy woman. She built much of her own house and gardened until well into her late 80s.

Look for dried soup vegetables in the bulk section of supermarkets selling dried beans and peas.

YIELD: 6 to 8 servings

2 lb (1 kg) lean lamb shanks
8 cups (2 L) cold water
2 onions, minced
⅔ cup (150 mL) dried soup vegetables
1½ tsp (7 mL) salt
½ tsp (2 mL) freshly ground pepper
2 or 3 diced carrots
2 cups (500 mL) shredded cabbage
1½ cups (375 mL) diced turnip

In a large soup kettle, combine the shanks and cold water; cover and bring to a boil. Add onions, dried vegetables, salt and pepper. Reduce heat and simmer gently for 1½ to 2 hours, skimming occasionally, or until meat is very tender.

With a slotted spoon, transfer the meat to a bowl. Let cool; when cool enough to handle, remove meat from bones and return to soup kettle. Refrigerate the soup for several hours. Remove the solidified fat. Add the carrots, cabbage and turnip. Heat until simmering. Simmer for 30 to 40 minutes or until vegetables are tender. Serve piping hot.

Spicy Saskatchewan Braised Beef

This dish, which was developed by Joan Heath of Radisson, Saskatchewan, to take into the field as part of a hot lunch for her husband, Corey Loessin, makes incredibly flavourful gravy.

YIELD: 8 to 10 servings

> 4 lb (2 kg) cross rib or boneless blade pot roast
> 4 cloves garlic, minced
> 2 tbsp (30 mL) Montreal steak spice
> 3 tbsp (45 mL) canola oil
> 2 onions, sliced
> 2½ cups (625 mL) beef stock
> ⅓ cup (75 mL) all-purpose flour
> ½ cup (125 mL) water
> ¼ cup (60 mL) minced fresh parsley

Pat the roast dry. In a large shallow dish, combine the garlic and steak spice; rub all over the roast. In a large Dutch oven, heat 2 tbsp (30 mL) of the oil over medium-high heat; brown the roast all over, turning with a wooden spoon, for about 8 minutes. Transfer to a plate; set aside.

Drain off any fat in the pan. Reduce heat to medium and add the remaining oil. Sauté the onions until golden, stirring often to loosen browned bits, about 4 minutes.

Transfer onions to a 24-cup (6 L) slow cooker. Top with the browned roast. Add the beef stock to the Dutch oven; bring to a boil, stirring and scraping up the brown bits. Pour over the roast. Cover and cook on low until fork-tender, about 7 hours.

Remove the roast; cover and keep warm. Skim the fat from the pan juices. Whisk the flour with the water, then whisk into the slow cooker. Cover and cook on high until thickened, about 15 minutes. Sprinkle with parsley. Serve the gravy with the roast.

Basque Boeuf Bourguignon

Basque chef Roger Dufau's full-flavoured version of the classic wine-soaked braised beef is absolutely unique—you'll never see it in another cookbook. The technique he uses to ramp up the flavour is to "burn" the wine. At home, one really needs a good gas cooktop or a high-powered side burner on an outdoor gas grill. And you *must* be careful! The flames from the burning wine leap higher than when one flames brandy. You can cool this stew and refrigerate it for up to 2 days.

YIELD: 6 to 8 servings

1½ lb (750 g) lean stewing beef (preferably meat from beef shanks)

1 or 2 carrots, peeled and diced

1 celery stalk, diced

3 cloves garlic, crushed

1 large onion, diced

1 tsp (5 mL) dried thyme

½ tsp (2 mL) freshly ground pepper

1 bottle (750 mL) dry red wine

Cut the stewing beef into serving-size chunks and place in a glass or stainless steel bowl. Add the carrots, celery, garlic, onion, thyme and pepper. Pour half of the wine over top, reserving the remainder for the stew. Stir the mixture well; cover and refrigerate for at least 48 hours or preferably for 3 days.

¼ cup (60 mL) chopped fresh parsley

2 cloves garlic

⅓ cup (75 mL) canola oil

½ cup (125 mL) all-purpose flour

1 tbsp (15 mL) dried tarragon

1½ cups (375 mL) canned diced tomatoes

1 cup (250 mL) beef stock

1 to 1½ tsp (5 to 7 mL) salt

½ tsp (2 mL) cayenne pepper

2 oz (60 g) bittersweet chocolate, finely chopped

¼ lb (125 g) lean bacon, chopped

1 to 1½ lb (500 to 750 g) cremini or portobello mushrooms

Chop the parsley and garlic together until fine; set aside. Remove the meat from the marinade, reserving the marinade. Heat the oil in a large heavy pan (cast iron is perfect) over medium-high heat. Dredge the meat in the flour, shaking off the excess. Sear it in batches until dark brown, transferring each batch to a plate. When it is all richly coloured, return the meat and any juices to the same pan and stir in half of the parsley mixture. Cook briefly and pour in the reserved marinade and vegetables, tarragon, tomatoes, beef stock, salt, cayenne and chocolate.

On a gas stove (skip this step if you have an electric stove), in a separate pot with a sturdy handle, heat the reserved wine over high heat, holding the handle of the pan with a kitchen towel or oven mitt in order to quickly remove it from the stove if needed. Swirl the wine until it begins to boil. It will catch fire on its own if the heat is high enough. Remove it from the stove if the flames are too high for your kitchen. This step could be done outdoors on the side burner of a barbecue.

As soon as the flames die down, pour the wine into the stew. Stir well and bring the stew to a boil, uncovered. Reduce heat and simmer gently for 2 to 2½ hours or until meat is tender. Add water, as needed, if the stew becomes too thick.

About 30 minutes before the stew is finished, sauté the bacon in a skillet until beginning to brown. Drain any excess fat from pan and add mushrooms along with the remaining parsley mixture; cook until the mixture begins to brown. Stir the mushroom mixture into the stew, and serve.

IRANIANS IN CANADA
From the land once known as Persia,
Iranian Canadians have come to Canada
relatively recently, beginning in 1964.
Locating mostly in Toronto (24,800),
Iranians have settled mainly in urban
areas, where many have become
successful business people.

Braised Beef Stew with Dried Lemons (Gormeh-Sabzi)

Gormeh-Sabzi is a great stove-top stew and can be made in a tagine. Although dried beans would have been used originally, canned are a time-saving substitute, and in the busy household of Iranians Farouk and Abi Dadashi, such shortcuts are essential.

Farouk and Abi arrived in Toronto from the violence of Iran in 1988 with $57. Abi is an extraordinary artist, having come from generations of painters in Iran. He's even done restoration work at the Musée du Louvre. They found a motel where Abi could paint and that they could afford on Kingston Road, a distance from the city centre. Every day, Abi would trudge downtown to visit galleries and sell his work. It's a marvellous success story, for today they own two flourishing galleries on Yonge Street, and Abi's works hang in collections around the world.

Farouk is an excellent home cook. She makes traditional foods, and because so many families come to Canada from the Middle East, there are a good number of Persian grocery stores in the Greater Toronto Area where she can purchase the traditional ingredients. The beans must never be allowed to break down and become soft, so Farouk adds them with the dried lemon at the end of the cooking. Fresh lemon juice is an excellent substitute for the traditional dried lemons.

YIELD: 4 servings

3 tbsp (45 mL) canola oil

1 onion, thinly sliced

1 lb (500 g) lean beef, cut into 1-inch (2.5 cm) cubes

1½ tsp (7 mL) salt

½ tsp (2 mL) freshly ground pepper

1 tbsp (15 mL) dried fenugreek

½ tsp (2 mL) curry powder

2 to 2½ cups (500 to 625 mL) water

1 leek, well washed and finely chopped

1 cup (250 mL) finely chopped green onions

2 cups (500 mL) minced fresh parsley

2 cups (500 mL) chopped spinach

Juice of 1 large lemon (or 2 dried lemons, pierced with a skewer)

1 can (19 oz/540 mL) kidney or romano beans, drained and rinsed

In a Dutch oven or large heavy saucepan, heat 2 tbsp (30 mL) of the oil over medium heat; sauté the onion until tender. Add the beef cubes and sprinkle with 1 tsp (5 mL) salt and the pepper; cook until beginning to brown. Add the fenugreek and curry powder, cooking for 1 to 2 minutes longer. Add 2 cups (500 mL) water; cover and bring to a boil. Simmer for 35 to 40 minutes or until meat is nearly tender.

Meanwhile heat the remaining oil in a skillet or wok over medium-high heat. Add the leek, green onions, parsley and spinach; sprinkle with remaining salt. Stir-fry until the vegetables are wilted and bright green. Stir into the meat mixture, adding more water if needed.

Stir the lemon juice into the simmering meat. Add the beans. Cover and continue to stew for 10 to 15 minutes or until the meat is fully cooked.

The Wilmers, Ann and her late husband, Ned, were often seen gathering their salad greens in the garden of the inn their son David still operates at Bay Fortune on the eastern shore of Prince Edward Island.

Frederique's Fabulous Garlic Steak

My friend Frederique Philip came to Canada from France in 1978 and moved to Vancouver Island the following year. As the co-owner of Sooke Harbour House, one of the finest inns on earth, she has very little time to cook for herself. Her dinners are simple and fast and full of flavour. She showed me this amazing recipe when she visited Elora one autumn. The amounts can be varied to suit your personal taste and how many servings you need. Grilled medium-rare with fresh garlic from the Guelph Farmers Market, it was the best steak I've ever eaten. We drank the finest Niagara red wine we could afford, and I served the steak with barbecue-roasted Bijou Rouge potatoes, a variety that will be in general distribution soon. Watch for them—they taste as though they've already been buttered. For extra zip, serve this steak with Sarah's Chimichurri Sauce (page 114).

YIELD: 1 serving

For each serving:
1 filet or strip loin, 4 to 6 oz (125 to 175 g)
Salt
1 or 2 cloves garlic
1 tsp (5 mL) butter, slightly softened

Lightly salt the steak and grill it to the desired doneness. Meanwhile, crush a clove or 2 of garlic onto the dinner plate; top with the butter. When the steak is done, simply lay it on top. Grind a bit of pepper over top.

Sarah's Chimichurri Sauce

After a trip to Buenos Aires, where red meat is a huge part of the day-to-day diet, Sarah Mitchell developed this recipe to serve with the wild venison and the Highland beef that her sister raises on her ranch in northern British Columbia. "Make it as spicy or mild as you wish by adding a variety of fresh chilies," says Sarah. "The only prerequisite is a tremendous amount of garlic. The best garlic is local; imported bulbs lose their pungency with travel. For additional heat, leave the seeds in the jalapeño." Being a bit of a culinary nationalist, she substituted cider vinegar but says a great red wine vinegar can also be used.

This sauce is absolutely perfect with a grilled steak or filet. Actually, I rather like heaping it onto crusty bread or using it to jazz up simple barbecued chicken. One word of caution about the garlic content: if you're having guests, everyone must eat this dish!

YIELD: 4 to 6 servings

> 8 to 10 large cloves garlic, crushed
> 1 jalapeño pepper, seeded and coarsely chopped
> 1 sweet red pepper, seeded and coarsely chopped
> 2 or 3 green onions, coarsely chopped
> ⅓ cup (75 mL) minced fresh coriander
> ½ cup (125 mL) apple cider vinegar
> 2 tbsp (30 mL) olive or canola oil
> ½ tsp (2 mL) salt

In a food processor, combine the garlic, jalapeño pepper, red pepper and onions. Pulse off and on to chop finely, scraping down the sides once or twice. Transfer to a mixing bowl; stir in the coriander, cider vinegar, oil and salt. Serve at room temperature. Refrigerate any leftovers, well covered!

South African–Style Sausage with Spicy Tomato Sauce (Boerewors and Tomato Bredie)

Michael Allemeier is one of Canada's most talented chefs. He's now well and duly ensconced at Mission Hill Winery in B.C.'s Okanagan Valley. But no matter where he hangs his chef's toque, his South African roots are strong. His recipes reflect that heritage but, in true Allemeier fashion, the ingredients reflect his passion for Canada.

"Speck is smoked pork belly fat—and it's delicious!" says Michael. "A good substitute for speck—although any German butcher will carry it—is fatty bacon."

Michael's original recipe—three times this amount—calls for the sausage mixture to be stuffed into casings. However, few cooks have access to the equipment, so this recipe has been adapted to make eight large sausage patties or 16 small sausage-shaped rolls. In South Africa, the casings are not twisted; instead, the one-metre-long sections are rolled into a coil. They're then grilled over charcoal on a traditional braai, or barbecue, and served with a peppery tomato sauce called Bredie and a soft, buttered cornmeal roll.

Boerewors Sausage

YIELD: 8 large patties or 16 small sausage-shaped rolls

1 lb (500 g) lean ground beef
1 lb (500 g) lean ground pork
6 oz (175 g) speck
6 oz (175 g) pork belly fat
½ tsp (2 mL) salt
1 tsp (5 mL) freshly ground pepper
1½ tbsp (25 mL) roasted coriander seeds, finely ground
¼ tsp (1 mL) freshly grated nutmeg
¼ tsp (1 mL) ground cloves
¼ tsp (1 mL) ground allspice
2 cloves garlic, minced
1½ tbsp (25 mL) Worcestershire sauce
1½ tbsp (25 mL) white vinegar

Coarsely grind the meats. Mix with all ingredients except the vinegar. Let stand for one hour, then add the vinegar. Form into patties, either round or sausage shaped. Or stuff into casings. Cook over low-burning coals on your barbecue or roast on a baking sheet in a 400°F (200°C) oven until juices run clear.

Serve as is, or on crusty rolls, with warm Tomato Bredie as a condiment.

Tomato Bredie

While the sausage meat is standing, make the Tomato Bredie. If the peppers are very hot, remove the seeds.

YIELD: About 6 cups (1.5 L)

1 large onion, diced
2 fresh hot peppers, chopped
3 tbsp (45 mL) corn oil
12 ripe tomatoes, chopped
2 tbsp (30 mL) granulated sugar
Salt and freshly ground pepper

In a skillet, sauté the onions and peppers in the oil until tender and fragrant. Add the tomatoes and sugar. Simmer, covered, for 30 minutes.

Season with salt and pepper to taste. Keep warm.

Acadian Meat Pies

When I stayed at Hôtel Paulin in Caraquet, New Brunswick, my second-floor room overlooked the clothesline filled with white linens and, just beyond, the Bay of Chaleur. Whitecaps randomly rolled in. The ocean is different here. If there is a word to describe it, it's "practical." Flat, expansive, panoramic—a plateau of steel-blue water with painted villages solidly built on the shore of the shallow bay and centred on a particular fishery. In this case, it's clams—delicious ones—oysters and lobster.

In the Acadian region of New Brunswick many excellent authentic recipes are still being used. This one comes from Gerard Paulin. Gerard's roots run deep—the boutique hotel has borne the family name for over a century. He knows and loves the cuisine of his ancestors. In the hotel, which he runs with his wife, Karen Mersereau, and young son, Jules, he serves some of the finest renditions of his culture's food that can be found.

These meat pies can be made with moose or wild rabbit, *la lièvre,* which can be purchased at the local grocery store in Acadian New Brunswick. This recipe makes enough filling for 12 3-inch double-crust meat pies. Lard pastry is essential—you will need the entire package of Tenderflake, and the recipe is printed on the inside of the box.

YIELD: 2 deep-dish meat pies

4 lb (2 kg) total mix of pork, chicken and beef, cubed
1 celery stalk
1 large Spanish onion, finely chopped
3 cups (750 mL) chicken or beef stock
3 tbsp (45 mL) butter
2 large cloves garlic, minced
1 tbsp (15 mL) minced fresh ginger
1 tbsp (15 mL) salted herbs*
1 tbsp (15 mL) summer savory
1 tsp (5 mL) dried thyme
⅛ tsp (0.5 mL) ground cloves
⅛ tsp (0.5 mL) ground allspice
Salt and freshly ground pepper
¼ cup (60 mL) all-purpose flour
Lard pastry for 12 3-inch (7.5 cm) double-crust pies

*Available in grocery stores and markets throughout Quebec and Acadian Atlantic Canada. I picked up my last jar in Montreal's Jean-Talon Market. For more about salted herbs, see page 298.

Place the meat, any reserved bones, celery stalk and onion in a large saucepan. Add the stock, reserving ½ cup (125 mL). Bring to a boil; cover, reduce heat and simmer until the meat is tender, about 1½ hours, skimming occasionally. Remove celery and bones; discard.

Melt the butter in a large skillet; cook the garlic and ginger until softened. Add the cooked meat, stock, salted herbs, summer savory, thyme, cloves and allspice. Season with salt and pepper to taste. Stir the flour with the reserved stock until smooth and add to the meat, stirring to thicken slightly. Remove from heat and let cool.

Fill the pastry shells with the filling and cover with the top crusts, pinching the edges together well. Place on a baking sheet. Bake in a preheated 425°F (220°C) oven for 15 minutes. Reduce heat to 350°F (180°C) and bake for 10 to 15 minutes or until golden. If not serving immediately, let cool and wrap.

Carleton County Mincemeat

In November 2006, I received a telephone call from my friend Archie McLean, who was very excited. His son-in-law had just bagged a 400-kilogram moose near their home in Carleton County, New Brunswick. This heavily forested area of the province is near the Saint John River, and wild game abounds.

Janet and Keith Wright live in the same neck o' the woods, but this recipe was first shared with me in Vancouver by their daughter, Jill Killen, while she was working in media relations in one of that city's poshest hotels. Food memories are powerful, and Jill became nostalgic talking about hers, particularly when she recalled her mother's Christmas mincemeat. Keith hunts for venison, and this recipe uses the leanest cuts.

The recipe calls for homemade jam since it has the most concentrated flavour. If none is available, purchase jam that has a lot of fruit. You can substitute good lean ground beef for the venison, and I've used ground bison, which is also quite lean, from a ranch near Earlton, Ontario. The original recipe calls for suet, but since it's not as widely available as it once was, I've suggested butter.

As a filling for pies or tarts, use the mincemeat as is or with the addition of one or two finely chopped apples or pears. Allow about 3 cups (750 mL) mincemeat per 9-inch (23 cm) pie.

YIELD: 16 to 18 cups (4 to 4.5 L)

2 lb (1 kg) lean venison
5 lb (2.3 kg) sour apples (like Cortland), peeled, cored and coarsely
    chopped
½ lb (250 g) butter
3 lb (1.5 kg) seedless raisins
Rind and juice of 2 oranges
Rind and juice of 1 large lemon
1 cup (250 mL) packed brown sugar
1 cup (250 mL) granulated sugar
½ cup (125 mL) molasses
½ cup (125 mL) apple cider vinegar
½ cup (125 mL) homemade strawberry jam
1 tbsp (15 mL) salt
1 whole nutmeg, grated
1½ tbsp (25 mL) cinnamon
1½ tsp (7 mL) ground cloves
Apple cider

Place the venison in a roasting pan and pour in ½ cup (125 mL) water. Cover and roast in a preheated 350°F (180°C) oven for 1½ to 2 hours or until well done, stirring every 15 to 20 minutes. Remove from pan and let cool for 30 minutes. Using a food grinder or a food processor, grind the meat until it's like coarse crumbs.

Meanwhile, in a heavy pot, combine the apples and 2 cups (500 mL) water; cook until soft, 20 to 25 minutes, stirring frequently and adding more water as needed to prevent sticking. Stir in the meat, butter, raisins, orange rind and juice, lemon rind and juice, brown sugar, granulated sugar, molasses, cider vinegar, jam, salt, nutmeg, cinnamon, cloves and 1 cup (250 mL) apple cider. Bring to a gentle boil and simmer, covered, for 2½ to 3 hours or until thickened and brown. Add more apple cider as needed to prevent the mincemeat from drying out. Stir frequently to keep it from sticking.

Ladle into sterilized jars; store in the refrigerator. Or let cool and freeze in plastic containers.

Normally the Farmers Feed Cities sign is posted where the public can be reminded of the connection between urban and rural, but here, on Deborah and Bruce Whale's Clovermead Farm north of Alma, Ontario, Deb has nailed it to a small shed, where it can be seen by everyone who works on the farm. It's her way of reminding her family, their employees and anyone else who visits, that farmers themselves have an enormous responsibility to provide good food for the consuming public.

Where the Buffalo Roamed

The buffalo, also known as the bison, was king, the *provider*. It had defined spiritual status among the Aboriginals, who depended upon the great beast for survival. To encourage the passage of large herds, Aboriginals built huge rock configurations called medicine wheels on hilltops, and placed buffalo skulls overlooking certain valleys. The skull, placed at the base of a tall pole in the sun-dance lodge, located the animal at the junction between the Great Spirit and the humans below.

The buffalo hunt was communal and, until the Spanish brought horses to the Americas in the 1700s, was done on foot. It was a complex and cooperative affair, with band members concealing themselves along constructed boulder-line runways that gradually narrowed toward a high cliff. The women and children hid behind the first widely spaced rocks, frightening the animals, and as the pathway narrowed, men took over until, at the base of the cliff, other men slaughtered the animals that plummeted over the precipice. Both Head-Smashed-In-Buffalo-Jump, a UNESCO World Heritage Site in Alberta, and Wanuskewin Heritage Park in Saskatchewan are located at buffalo jumps.

In her paper "The Development of the Prairie Palate: The Red-Meat Eaters," published in the book *Northern Bounty: A Celebration of Canadian Cuisine* (Random House Canada, 1995), Edmonton food journalist Judy Schultz describes the importance of bison in early prairie life. As a virtual "one-stop shop," the animals, about 900 kilograms each, provided warm, furry clothing and robes, and plentiful meat along with the essential by-products of sinew and bone. Some parts, like the fatty hump and the fat from around the teats and the heart, were particularly relished, while others had spiritual significance. The blood was drunk warm to ensure bravery, and "the tongue was given to the medicine men to ensure a safe hunt."

Temiskaming Bison and Cheddar Meat Pie (Tourtière du Témiscaming au bison et au cheddar)

Debbie Demers of Earlton, Ontario, uses local ingredients to make this fabulous rendition of meat pie: great cheddar cheese from Thornloe; local bison from Biz Meats in Earlton; and pungent garlic scapes preserved in oil by Ghislain Trudel of Val d'Or, Quebec; Ghislain calls them "flowers." I love this dish with a hearty northern beer.

YIELD: 6 servings

1½ lb (750 g) ground bison meat
1 onion, chopped
2 tbsp (30 mL) garlic scapes, either fresh or preserved in oil
   (or 1 tbsp/15 mL minced garlic)
1 celery stalk (including leaves), chopped
1 cup (250 mL) beef stock
2 tbsp (30 mL) cornstarch
½ to 1 tsp (2 to 5 mL) freshly ground pepper
1 tsp (5 mL) Worcestershire sauce
1 tsp (5 mL) hot sauce
Chili powder
1½ cups (375 mL) shredded old cheddar, preferably Thornloe
10-inch (25 cm) unbaked deep double-crust pie shell

In a heavy skillet over medium heat, brown the bison thoroughly. Add the onion, garlic and celery. Cook over low to medium heat until vegetables are tender. Combine the beef stock and cornstarch; stir into the bison mixture. Add the pepper, Worcestershire and hot sauces, and chili powder to taste. Taste and adjust seasonings. Add the cheese and stir until melted. Let cool for 10 minutes before pouring into the unbaked pie shell. Cover with the remaining pastry; crimp edges and cut small slits in the top crust to let steam escape.

Bake in a preheated 350°F (180°C) oven for 40 to 45 minutes or until golden brown. Let stand for about 15 minutes to cool before serving.

Wine-Braised Veal Shanks (Osso Buco)

Perfect in its simplicity, osso buco is true Italian country cooking. I love it with buttermilk-mashed potatoes. The essential flavouring is called gremolata, a mixture that always has lemon, garlic and parsley in it. Some cooks add anchovies, too. It's quickly minced with a mezzaluna, a two-handled rounded knife that's becoming more widely available in Canada.

YIELD: 6 servings

6 veal shanks (about 3 lb/1.5 kg)
All-purpose flour, for dredging
2 tbsp (30 mL) canola oil
3 cups (750 mL) dry white wine
1½ tsp (7 mL) salt
1 tbsp (15 mL) tomato paste

GREMOLATA:
1 lemon
½ cup (125 mL) chopped fresh parsley
2 or 3 cloves garlic

Dredge the veal shanks in flour, shaking off any excess. Heat the oil in a large heavy skillet over medium-high heat. In batches, brown the veal thoroughly on both sides. Add wine to almost cover the meat. Sprinkle with salt; cover and bring to a boil. Reduce heat to low and simmer for 50 to 60 minutes or until the veal is tender. Stir in the tomato paste and add more wine if the mixture is too dry. Cover and cook gently for 30 to 45 minutes longer.

GREMOLATA: Remove the rind from the lemon with a vegetable peeler. Using a mezzaluna or sharp knife or in a food processor, mince the peel very finely with the parsley and garlic. About 15 minutes before serving, sprinkle the gremolata over the veal. Cover and heat thoroughly.

Transfer the shanks and the sauce that has formed to a wide serving bowl. Serve with warm crusty bread onto which diners can spread the marrow.

Pork Medallions with
Cru du Clocher Cheese and Sun-Dried Tomatoes
(Médaillons de porc au Cru du Clocher et tomates séchées)

Before Hélène Lessard and Christian Barrette opened Le Fromage au Village in Lorrainville, Quebec, there hadn't been an artisanal cheesemaker in the Temiskaming area since 1972. When they bought their farm, they started by making cheese curds but soon graduated to cheddar. A fire destroyed their operation, and they turned to other dairy farms in the region for help in meeting their milk needs. Today they use only locally produced milk from herds of Holsteins, which in the summer feed on clover and alfalfa, and in the winter on dried grasses rather than silage.

The cheese, particularly the Cru du Clocher, their flagship raw milk cheddar, is extraordinary, well aged and crumbly. This is Hélène's recipe.

YIELD: 4 servings

1 lb (500 g) pork tenderloin
1 tbsp (15 mL) canola oil
4 oz (125 g) Cru du Clocher or other sharp cheddar
  cheese, thinly sliced
6 to 8 dried tomato halves, cut into slivers
Salt and freshly ground pepper

SAUCE:
1 tbsp (15 mL) butter
1 shallot, minced
1 cup (250 mL) white wine
⅔ cup (150 mL) whipping cream (35%)

Slice the pork into 12 medallions, each ¾ to 1 inch (1 to 2.5 cm) thick. In a heavy skillet, heat the oil over medium-high heat and sear each medallion for about 1 minute per side. Place pork in an ovenproof pan; top with the cheese and tomatoes. Sprinkle lightly with salt and pepper. Bake in a preheated 350°F (180°C) oven for 8 to 10 minutes or until cheese is melting. Remove pork medallions and set aside; keep warm.

SAUCE: Add the butter and minced shallot to the pan; cook, stirring, over medium heat until shallot is soft and just beginning to brown. Add the wine, stirring to deglaze the pan; cook, uncovered, until reduced to half the original volume. Whisk in the cream, cooking until slightly thickened. Season with salt and pepper to taste.

Arrange the medallions on heated serving plates and spoon the sauce over top.

Spicy Skewered Pork (Sosaties) with Tomato and Red Onion Salad

This is one of chef Michael Allemeier's South African classics. "As a whole, many elements of the food of South Africa can be spicy—it's a hot country," he says. "The chili's recommended in this recipe but is optional. However, the curry and apricot are the lynchpins. They are much better cooked over the charcoal-fired braai."

This recipe can be made in the winter if you want to dig out the barbecue to do it, but it's best in late summer when tomatoes are at their finest. In case you wonder about the amount of hot pepper, fear not—the flavour of the grill and of the meat comes through loud and clear.

YIELD: 8 servings

MARINADE:
¼ cup (60 mL) corn oil
1 small onion, diced
¾ cup (175 mL) curry powder
4 cups (1 L) white vinegar
½ cup (125 mL) granulated sugar
¼ cup (60 mL) chili flakes
1 cup (250 mL) apricot jam

SALAD:
1 egg
1 tsp (5 mL) dry mustard
⅓ cup (75 mL) white wine vinegar
3 tbsp (45 mL) olive oil
Salt and freshly ground pepper
4 large vine-ripened tomatoes
1 small red onion, thinly sliced

3 lb (1.5 kg) lean pork, cubed
1 large green pepper, seeded and cubed
3 red onions, cubed
20 button mushrooms

Heat the oil in a large saucepan over medium heat; sauté the onions until wilted and beginning to brown, 1 to 2 minutes. Add the curry powder; cook, stirring, for 10 to 15 seconds. Stir in the vinegar, sugar, chili flakes and apricot jam. Reduce heat and simmer for 1 to 2 minutes. Remove from heat and let stand for 10 minutes before transferring to a food processor or blender. Purée and let cool.

SALAD: Meanwhile, in a bowl, whisk together the egg and mustard. Slowly whisk in the vinegar and then the oil. Season to taste with salt and pepper. Cut the tomatoes into wedges and add the onions. Pour the dressing over the tomatoes; taste and adjust seasonings. Cover and refrigerate until needed.

Soak 10 to 12 wooden skewers in hot water for 1 hour. Thread the meat, pepper, onions and mushrooms onto the skewers and layer them in a large roasting pan. Pour the marinade over them. Cover and marinate for 4 hours. Drain and place skewers on the grill over medium coals; cook until meat is starting to brown and vegetables are tender-crisp. Serve with the tomato salad.

Tomatoes, peppers, ground cherries, parsnips—great local, and often heritage, vegetables are always part of the annual Feast of Fields celebration, be it near Toronto as it was in this picture, in Vancouver or on Vancouver Island.

Jamaican Jerk Pork

Emigrating from Jamaica to Canada in 1963, Laurice de Gale quickly realized that people loved the flavours she brought with her Caribbean traditions. She showed off her expertise by preparing this brilliantly seasoned jerk pork recipe on stage at the 2000 Royal Agricultural Winter Fair as a representative of the Women's Culinary Network, an organization that connects Canadian women in all facets of the food industry.

Laurice uses scotch bonnet peppers but cautions that they should be handled very carefully and recommends wearing rubber gloves.

YIELD: 6 to 8 servings

4 scotch bonnet peppers, seeds removed and discarded, minced
2 large cloves garlic, minced
8 green onions, white and light green parts, chopped
1 large onion, diced
1 tbsp (15 mL) thyme leaves
1 tbsp (15 mL) brown sugar
1 tbsp (15 mL) whole allspice
2 tsp (10 mL) salt
1 tsp (5 mL) ground cloves
½ tsp (2 mL) whole black peppercorns
¼ cup (60 mL) dark soy sauce
¼ cup (60 mL) cider or red wine vinegar
4 lb (2 kg) boneless pork shoulder roast

JERK SEASONING: Place the peppers, garlic, green onions, onion, thyme, brown sugar, allspice, salt, cloves and peppercorns into the work bowl of a food processor. Add the soy sauce and vinegar. Grind till the mixture becomes a paste, about 2 to 3 minutes. Set aside.

Wash and dry the pork. With a sharp knife, slash every ¾ inch (2 cm). Place in a large bowl and coat evenly with the Jerk Seasoning. Cover and refrigerate overnight, turning occasionally.

Remove pork from marinade and transfer to a large roasting pan. Reserve marinade for basting. Cover and roast at 350°F (180°C) for 2 hours. Remove cover and continue to roast and baste for an additional hour, or until the meat is tender.

Keep warm till serving.

Ginger-Spiced Pork Dumplings (Gyoza) with Chili Dipping Sauce

This is the first dish that my son Mark and his Kyoto-born wife, Kaori, made for me as a couple before they were married. These dumplings use lean pork and are a simple, quick and impressive appetizer. I've also used ground chicken and turkey. The round dumpling wrappers are available in Asian food markets and are sometimes labelled for use in making "Shanghai dumplings."

Adjust the amount of chili oil in the dip to your own taste. The real trick, as in all Japanese cooking, is in the patient chopping of the ingredients that go into the filling. The other "essential" is a good non-stick skillet or a well-seasoned cast-iron skillet. If you wish, use a food processor to chop the filling ingredients finely.

YIELD: 30 to 40 dumplings

½ lb (250 g) lean ground pork
3 large dried shiitake mushrooms, soaked and minced
1 cup (250 mL) minced garlic chives or green onions
2 cloves garlic, minced
2 tbsp (30 mL) minced fresh ginger
1½ cups (375 mL) finely shredded green cabbage
1 tsp (5 mL) sesame oil
1 tbsp (15 mL) light soy sauce
½ tsp (2 mL) cayenne pepper (optional)
30 to 40 dumpling wrappers
Canola oil, for frying

DIPPING SAUCE:
3 tbsp (45 mL) rice wine vinegar
1 tbsp (15 mL) light soy sauce
Chili oil

DUMPLINGS: Combine the pork, mushrooms, chives, garlic and ginger. Blanch cabbage in boiling water 30 seconds. Drain and squeeze out excess liquid. Add to pork mixture. Stir in the sesame oil, soy and cayenne (if using). Place a wrapper in the palm of your hand and moisten one edge. Mound with about 2 tsp (10 mL) of the filling. Fold over and pinch edges tightly to seal. Crimp edges attractively, if desired.

Heat a non-stick skillet over medium-high heat. Moisten the pan with a little oil. Add about half the gyoza in a single tightly packed layer. You will be cooking only one side so there is no need to leave room for flipping. Add ¼ cup (60 mL) water and cover. Cook and steam, adding a little extra water if needed, for 10 minutes. At the end of the cooking time, the pan should be dry and the dumplings will have started to brown. Check for doneness by slicing through a gyoza. The filling should not be pink.

Repeat with the remaining dumplings. Keep warm until serving.

DIPPING SAUCE: Stir together the vinegar, soy and chili oil. Pass with the gyoza.

While there were three stages of Danish immigration to Canada (1860–1914; 1919–1930; 1945–1970s), it appears that the first Dane to set foot in Canada was an explorer, Jens Monk, who had been sent to find the Northwest Passage in 1619. He landed on the shores of Hudson Bay. Since 1945, about 42,000 Danes have come to Canada. According to the 1991 census, B.C. has the largest population. Alberta is second, and Ontario third.

Danish Meat Patties (Frikadeller)

When Tulle and Peter Knudstrup were children, their parents owned The Highway Inn (Lindelse Kro) at Langeland on an archipelago in Denmark. As an adult, Peter regularly made this quick supper dish for his wife, Nancy, and their growing family. It's traditionally served with pickled beets, a cucumber salad (see accompanying recipe), boiled potatoes and his sister Tulle's red cabbage or Ródkål (page 251).

There are many versions of this dish, but Peter's is lightened considerably by the addition of a can of soda water. More traditionally, beer would have been used. The meat must be very finely ground.

YIELD: 4 servings

> ½ lb (250 g) each ground pork and veal (or 1 lb/500 g lean ground beef)
> 1 onion, chopped
> ⅓ cup (75 mL) all-purpose flour
> 1¼ cups (300 mL) soda water (1 can, 10 oz/300 mL)
> 1 egg, well beaten
> 1 tsp (5 mL) salt
> ½ tsp (2 mL) freshly ground pepper
> 2 tbsp (30 mL) canola oil
> 2 tbsp (30 mL) butter

Thoroughly mix together the meat and onion using either a meat grinder or by pulsing in a food processor for a few seconds.

Transfer the meat to a large mixing bowl; using a wooden spoon, beat it well to lighten it. Add the flour and beat again thoroughly. Gradually whip in the soda water until mixture is light and fluffy. Mix in the egg, salt and pepper. Cover and refrigerate for at least 1 hour or until firm enough to handle.

With moistened hands, shape the meat mixture into oblong patties about 4 inches (10 cm) long or into small patties, whichever you prefer.

Heat oil and butter in a large heavy skillet over medium heat. Cook the patties slowly, 6 to 8 minutes per side or until well browned. Drain briefly on paper towels before serving piping hot.

Cucumber Salad (Agurkesalat)

According to her granddaughter Alessandra, Tulle Knudsen was the queen of open-faced sandwiches, on which she'd pile this cucumber salad with some pâté or Danish meatballs. "I still have such a vivid memory of my grandmother—*Mormor* in Danish—and great aunt, Moster Gurli, preparing the Danish smorgasbord at Sunset Villa near Guelph, Ontario, every Sunday," says Alessandra. "My sister and I would come down and watch as the two of them worked quickly and meticulously to arrange all the sandwiches, which were a work of art. The aromas are very distinct as well. I recently went to a Danish butcher and as soon as I walked in, I was taken back to my grandmother's kitchen just by the smell! Mormor's hands never seemed to stop, whether they were cooking or knitting or wrapping around me to give me a hug, they were always in motion."

In her notes, Tulle suggests that, if you add a few spices to the vinegar mixture, it can be used for pickled beets as well. She also cautions that if you pour the vinegar mixture over the cucumber while it is still hot, it will turn the cucumber grey.

YIELD: 6 to 8 servings

1 cup (250 mL) white vinegar
½ cup (125 mL) granulated sugar
½ tsp (2 mL) freshly ground pepper
2 English cucumbers
1 tbsp (15 mL) salt

Combine the vinegar, sugar and pepper in a pot; bring to a boil. Set aside to cool. When completely cold, pour over the cucumber and let marinate for a few hours or overnight in the refrigerator.

Slice the cucumber finely, preferably using a mandoline. Place the cucumber in a bowl and cover with salt. Stir the cucumber and let stand for 10 minutes. Rinse and squeeze dry with your hands.

A DANISH RECIPE FOR LIFE

Alessandra and Jean-Francis Quaglia own two of Vancouver's top restaurants, Provence Mediterranean Grill and Provence Marinaside. They met and fell in love in Europe, where Jean-Francis's mother was a Michelin-star chef. In Europe, Alessandra, who grew up in a tightly knit Danish family in Toronto, was homesick for her grandmother Tulle's traditional cooking, so she often called across the Atlantic to extract her recipes, particularly her red cabbage (Ródkål) and her cucumber salad (Agurkesalat). This is a tiny part of Tulle's culinary story.

Tulle Knudstrup came to Canada in 1956 with her husband, Bruno Knudsen. Her first job was at Little Denmark in Toronto. Nothing other than memories remains of that restaurant now. She was an exceptional homestyle cook, and when the opportunity arose to run Sunset Villa, a Danish retirement community south of Guelph, Ontario, she and her husband headed to the country. It was here that Tulle put pen to paper in order to share her culinary traditions.

Her handwritten binder begins with an ingredient list and is followed by the method: "Dear Everybody, Some Meat, Some Fish, Some Green, Some Fruit, Some Time, Some Patience, Some Planning, Some Luck, Some Imagination, Some Understanding and Lots of Love. Mix all the ingredients and some will come out of it. You can have a little on the table and you can have a lot, it is not important, as long as you are all together to enjoy the Time you are lucky to have together."

Latvians in Canada

The first wave of Latvian immigrants arrived in the Prairies before the 1920s. It's difficult to determine the exact dates of their arrival and the number of Latvians because they were lumped together with Russian immigrants. Latvia was an oppressed, war-ravaged country. It wasn't until 1921 that they were registered as a distinct group. Before the post–Second World War influx, most resided in the Prairies, whereas after the war, most settled in Ontario.

Latvian Bacon and Onion–Stuffed Rolls (Piradzini)

A celebration in the scattered Latvian communities of Canada often includes these bacon-filled buns. They are fabulous with a salad for a quick lunch or, if you make them smaller, they're great cocktail appetizers.

This recipe was one that the late Tanya Barsevski shared with me years ago while she still lived in the farming community of Mount Forest, Ontario, and cooked at the local high school, a time when secondary schools had real kitchens.

Yield: 16 rolls

Dough:

- 1 potato, peeled and diced
- 1 cup (250 mL) water
- 1 tsp (5 mL) salt
- 1 tbsp (15 mL) granulated sugar
- 2 tbsp (30 mL) butter
- 1½ to 2 cups (375 to 500 mL) all-purpose flour
- 2 tsp (10 mL) instant yeast

Filling:

- ¼ lb (125 g) lean side bacon, finely diced
- 2 small onions, finely minced
- 1 green onion, minced
- ½ cup (125 mL) finely diced ham
- ½ tsp (2 mL) freshly ground pepper

Egg Wash:

- 1 egg yolk
- ¼ cup (60 mL) milk

In a saucepan, combine the potato, water and salt; cover and bring to a boil. Reduce heat and simmer for 15 to 20 minutes or until tender. Drain, reserving liquid, and mash thoroughly. Stir in the sugar, butter and reserved water. Let cool until lukewarm.

Beat in ½ cup (125 mL) of the flour. Add the yeast, beating vigorously until well combined, 1 to 2 minutes. Add enough of the remaining flour to make a stiff dough. Turn out onto a floured surface and knead, adding more flour as needed to keep from sticking, until smooth and elastic, 4 to 5 minutes. Place in a well-oiled bowl; cover with a damp towel and let rise until doubled, 1 to 1¼ hours.

FILLING: Meanwhile, in a heavy saucepan, cook the bacon, onions, green onion, diced ham and pepper until onion is softened and bacon begins to crisp. Let cool completely.

When the dough has doubled, punch down and divide into 16 pieces. Roll each piece to flatten slightly. Place a spoonful of the bacon mixture in the centre of each piece of dough. With floured fingertips, pinch edges together to make crescent. Place about 2 inches (5 cm) apart on a parchment-lined baking sheet. Slash tops with a sharp knife. Cover loosely with a towel; let rise until doubled, 50 to 60 minutes.

Whisk together the egg yolk and milk. Brush over the crescents. Bake in a preheated 375°F (190°C) oven for 15 to 20 minutes or until very well browned.

A plate of freshly baked Piradzini in my home kitchen.

Arabs in Canada

When Arabic-speaking immigrants first arrived in Canada, they were simply classified as Syrians and Turks. The label Syrian was applied not only to those from Syria but also to immigrants from Lebanon, Jordan and Palestine. Immigration began in 1882; by 1992, well over 200,000 had arrived, the vast majority after 1962.

Iranian or Persian Cooking

Iranian or Persian food is ancient, and although it is not static, it can be quite defined. It uses ingredients that are very familiar in Canada: wheat, lentils, chickpeas, fresh fruit and dairy products, particularly yogurt. But Iran is also a dry, hot land, and many of its people were nomadic, so what sprang up was a reliance on foods that were dried; that not only preserved them in the desert heat, but also made them infinitely lighter to carry. These include dried sour cherries and sour plums and lemons, the sweetest dates, and tiny red berries called *zarashk*, which are cooked briefly and used with saffron, sliced pistachios and almonds to top rice. Even yogurt was dried and reconstituted when needed.

Persian food is about balance, and great use is made of the sour spectrum. Pomegranate paste, tiny pickled green grapes and ground lemon are only part of the puckering palate. A skilled cook counters their flavours with a sprinkling of sugar or a drizzle of honey or, here in Canada, a good pouring of maple syrup.

Asian-Spiced Lamb Kebabs with Garlic Cucumber Dressing (Tzatziki)

This is serious cross-cultural cuisine—the aromatic spices of the Orient cooled with the traditional cucumber and garlic mixture found all over the Middle East. It's reminiscent of the cooling raita that blends so beautifully with the spiced dishes of India and of those that create a wave of flavour from Africa across the subcontinent.

English cucumbers are a recent introduction to the Canadian marketplace. They were first researched by Dr. Arthur Loughton at the University of Guelph's Vineland Research Station.

To grate garlic, I use a kitchen rasp, one of the neatest tools in my drawer. If lamb is not available, use chunks of veal or even chicken.

YIELD: 4 to 6 servings

2 lb (1 kg) lean lamb shoulder
1 small onion, minced
2 or 3 cloves garlic, grated
1 tbsp (15 mL) grated fresh ginger
1½ tbsp (25 mL) garam masala
¼ cup (60 mL) soy sauce
¼ cup (60 mL) canola oil
¼ cup (60 mL) Canadian brandy

GARLIC CUCUMBER DRESSING (TZATZIKI):
2 cups (500 mL) plain yogurt
½ English cucumber, grated
2 cloves garlic, grated or finely minced
3 tbsp (45 mL) olive oil
1 tsp (5 mL) sea salt

Cut the lamb into 1-inch (2.5 cm) cubes and place in a medium bowl. Add the onion, garlic, ginger, garam masala, soy sauce, oil and brandy; toss together. Cover and refrigerate for 10 to 12 hours, turning the meat several times.

DRESSING: Line a sieve or colander with cheesecloth and set in the sink. Spoon the yogurt into the sieve and let drain for 1 to 2 hours or until quite thick. Transfer to a small bowl and stir in the cucumber and garlic. Cover with plastic wrap and refrigerate until thoroughly chilled.

When ready to grill, remove the meat from the marinade and thread onto soaked wooden skewers. Grill the kebabs over high heat on a gas barbecue or over hot coals, turning with tongs often, until richly browned but still pink inside. Dribble the olive oil over the dressing; sprinkle with the salt and serve with the kebabs.

Lamb and Prune Tagine
(Agneau aux pruneaux)

Sanaa El Asfi is a graceful lady. Even her entrance into the Ville Marie par-
ish basement hall was striking the day a group of us were there to judge the
regional dishes of northern Quebec. In a long camel-coloured robe, which
had been her wedding dress in her native Morocco, she bore a steaming
tagine of local lamb from the rolling farmland near Lake Timiskaming, seasoned with the spices of her homeland. At her side were her beaming husband and son. The dish was spectacular.

A tagine is a deep, glazed clay dish with a domed top that has a vent in it to
allow the excess steam to escape. It must be seasoned before use by placing it
over low heat, adding 1 cup (250 mL) milk, covering it and heating it for 20 to
30 minutes. The milk should only simmer but not boil dry. Let the tagine cool
before disposing of the milk, washing the pot and drying it.

YIELD: 6 servings

1¼ to 1½ lb (625 to 750 g) lean lamb or beef
3 tbsp (45 mL) canola or olive oil
2 onions, thinly sliced
4 cloves garlic, minced
1 tsp (5 mL) cinnamon
1 tsp (5 mL) salt
1 tsp (5 mL) ground ginger
½ tsp (2 mL) freshly ground pepper
½ tsp (2 mL) turmeric
½ tsp (2 mL) saffron
2 tsp (10 mL) grated fresh ginger
2 tbsp (30 mL) minced fresh parsley
2 tbsp (30 mL) minced fresh coriander
1 cup (250 mL) pitted whole prunes
8 to 10 small potatoes, halved
2 or 3 potatoes, scrubbed and quartered

GARNISH:
½ cup (125 mL) whole blanched almonds
1 tbsp (15 mL) sesame seeds
Icing sugar, for dusting

*The Foire Gourmande is held annually on
the third weekend in August. It's one of
the neatest culinary fairs I've been to over
the years, with tastes and talent from all
over the Abitibi–New Liskeard region.*

Cut the meat into ½- to ¾-inch (1 to 1.5 cm) cubes. Set aside.

Place the tagine base over medium heat. Add the oil and sauté the onion and
garlic until tender, covering with the lid for part of the cooking time.

Add the cinnamon, salt, ground ginger, pepper, turmeric, saffron, fresh ginger,
parsley, coriander and prunes. Stir in the meat and arrange the potatoes
around the perimeter of the pot. Add the water, cover and bring to a boil.
Reduce heat and simmer, covered, for 1½ to 2 hours or until the meat is
tender, adding water as needed.

GARNISH: Meanwhile, in a shallow dry skillet over medium heat, brown the
almonds. Just before they are fully golden, toss in the sesame seeds and
continue to dry-roast for 1 to 2 minutes. Remove from heat and set aside.

To serve, top the dish with the almond and sesame seed garnish. Dust with a
little icing sugar.

*Le Domaine des Ducs, near Ville-Marie,
Quebec, is so far north that few believed
the vines would grow, much less flourish.*

Quick and Easy Pan-Roasted Chicken

Stephen Wong of Vancouver swears by this easy recipe. As with Mark Mitchell's Grilled Salmon (page 56), these are free-form instructions, guidelines for a quick chicken dinner. Although Stephen has provided a few ideas, use your own imagination, too. "This is more of a general method for a quick chicken dinner than a specific recipe," he says.

Any number of dry or wet rubs can be used to season the chicken. Just use what you have on hand. Here are some suggestions:

- seasoning salt with minced garlic mixed with a dollop of butter
- Cajun spice mix
- rind and juice of a lemon with a splash of olive oil and chopped rosemary leaves
- minced fresh ginger and green onions with spiced salt
- minced lemongrass with lime juice, sweet chili sauce and soy sauce
- curry powder or garam masala with onion salt and a dollop of yogurt

YIELD: 3 to 4 servings

1 chicken (about 3 lb/1.5 kg)
Spice rub or other seasoning mixture
1 small onion, finely chopped
1 large carrot, finely chopped
1 celery stalk, chopped
2 cups (500 mL) chicken or vegetable stock or water
2 tsp (10 mL) cornstarch
1 tbsp (15 mL) water
2 tbsp (30 mL) half-and-half cream (10%) (optional)
2 tsp (10 mL) Dijon mustard (optional)

BUTTERFLY THE CHICKEN: Using a sharp knife, make a cut on the back of the chicken along one side of the backbone from shoulder to tail (cutting through the rib cage). Open up the chicken, skin side up; using the heel of your hand, press down on the chicken to flatten it. Sprinkle a spice or seasoning mixture of your choice on both sides of the chicken and rub all over.

Campbell River, B.C.'s Pier Street Farmers Market is held in a spectacular location by the water and near the Marine Heritage Centre.

Toss chopped vegetables into a large cast-iron skillet or shallow but heavy casserole dish. Add ½ cup (125 mL) stock or water. Place chicken over vegetables and bake in a preheated 450°F (220°C) oven, basting once or twice with pan juices, for 50 to 60 minutes or until juices run clear when the chicken is pierced. If using a meat thermometer, the internal temperature should be 185°F (85°C) at the thickest part of the meat. During roasting, if the skin is browning too quickly, cover with a loose tent of foil.

When chicken is cooked and deeply browned all over, transfer it to a platter and cover loosely with foil. Add remaining stock or water to the vegetables in the skillet and bring to a boil on the stovetop; cook for 3 minutes to reduce volume slightly, scraping up the brown bits with a wooden spatula. Strain the sauce into a small saucepan and discard the vegetables. Bring the sauce to a boil; add the cornstarch slurry and stir until the sauce thickens. (To "sweeten" the sauce, you can add a splash of half-and-half cream, if desired; to spice it up a little, try a spoonful of Dijon mustard, if desired.)

Carve and serve chicken with sauce.

Classic Chicken and Dumplings

The only chicken to use for this recipe is a larger, meaty broiler that you'll likely have to buy at a specialty butcher or a farmers market. Young birds won't work. If it's free range, all the better. The fat that rises to the top of the broth can be discarded, or it can be used to fry potatoes until golden brown and utterly delicious.

YIELD: 6 to 8 servings

1 large broiler chicken (5 lb/2.3 kg)
2 tsp (10 mL) salt
2 cups (500 mL) diced celery, including leaves
2 onions, diced
1½ cups (375 mL) diced carrots
1 cup (250 mL) diced turnip
1 small tomato, diced
½ tsp (2 mL) freshly ground pepper
½ tsp (2 mL) dried thyme
2 bay leaves
¼ cup (60 mL) minced fresh parsley
1 cup (250 mL) fresh or thawed frozen peas

DUMPLINGS:
1 cup (250 mL) all-purpose flour
1 tbsp (15 mL) baking powder
½ tsp (2 mL) salt
¼ cup (60 mL) chilled butter
½ cup (125 mL) milk

In a large soup kettle, barely cover the chicken with cold water. Add salt and bring to a boil. Cover, reduce heat and simmer for 2 to 3 hours or until the meat is very tender, skimming occasionally and adding more water as needed. Remove the chicken from the stock; let cool, then remove the meat from the bones. Discard bones and refrigerate meat.

Skim the fat from the stock or, if necessary, refrigerate it to allow the fat to solidify. Return the stock to medium-high heat and add the celery, onions, carrots, turnip and tomato. Season with pepper, thyme, bay leaves and parsley. Reduce heat, cover and simmer until the vegetables are tender. Taste and adjust the seasonings as needed. Remove the bay leaves. Stir in the peas and reserved chicken meat.

DUMPLINGS: In a small bowl, sift together the flour, baking powder and salt. Cut in the butter until it resembles fine crumbs. Add the milk all at once and stir quickly to blend. Drop the batter by spoonfuls onto simmering liquid. Cover tightly and cook over medium heat for 7 minutes without peeking. The dumplings will more than double in size. Ladle into warmed serving bowls.

There's nothing that Deb Whale likes better than to talk farming. With her husband, Bruce, she lives it every day of the year at Clovermead Farm, near Alma, Ontario, where they milk 180 dairy cows. She's as comfortable holding her cousin Marion's Barred Rock laying hen as she is chairing meetings and rattling agricultural cages across the nation. At this writing she is the vice-chair of the Ontario Farm Products Marketing Commission, an umbrella agency that oversees all the province's marketing boards. She sits on the Board of the Poultry Research Centre, an Alberta-based organization, and is part of the Ontario Livestock and Poultry Council.

Grain

Chef and baking guru James MacGuire brought artisan bread to Montreal. From there, his reputation (and sourdoughs) spread to great kitchens across Canada.

Wheat is the symbol of civilization. For the ancients, grain, with its corollary, wine, made the eater human. I remember my first communion—I suppose as only a "food person" might. At 12, I was older than most communicants and already had a healthy appetite. The bread that I'd anticipated as having some sort of extra, even magical, flavour turned out to be a cube of sliced white bread and nothing like the delicious loaves my mother baked and which, still warm from the oven, I slathered with butter. It was even further removed—light years away—from the bread I was to taste decades later in Montreal, baked by James MacGuire, the expat New Yorker who almost single-handedly brought good bread to the restaurants of Canada.

When I first tasted James MacGuire's bread at Le Passe Partout, a bakery-restaurant that has become one of Montreal's legends since it closed in 2004, it *was* almost a religious epiphany. Having been raised on the often home-baked breads of central Ontario, when we depended upon commercial yeasts and bleached flours and plenty of butter, I finally understood why bread is called the "staff of life." Ours was delicious, but his was splendid!

Late in the winter of 2003, I headed to Montreal. I hoped to understand the *why* and, more important, the *how* of bread. I wanted to learn, to experience, to absorb, to smell the intimacies of bread.

I got a particularly early wake-up call in order to crawl out of the cosy bed long before the freezing-cold crack of dawn. The winter had been very hard and deep, so I trudged, boots crunching on the snow-covered sidewalks, to the bakery to work, or, more accurately, observe those who worked there. My glasses steamed over when I opened the door—now *that* was aromatherapy. My God, I needed a coffee.

The bakery was piled high with sacks of flour—OCIA-certified organic flour from Humboldt, Saskatchewan, deep in the heart of the Canadian Prairies. I could envision the grain fields and the 360-degree Saskatchewan horizon. I could feel the sun. Or was it the fiery oven that was hovering at 240°C?

The day began with the *levain*. This dough had been tucked away to rise all night long. It was the first to be baked on the floors of the massive ovens. The smells became intoxicating. *Pain de campagne* was next, then the loaves filled with walnuts and sometimes laced with raisins. With a little razor, James slit another batch of unbaked loaves to give them some growing space, and the ovens were loaded again. Misted with water to develop the crust, the next batch of *boules* puffed and rose and baked until they developed a thin layer of crust, which prevented them from expanding further. The misting ended, and they turned deep golden brown, a few shades darker than the colour of ripe wheat. The brioche seemed to wait almost impatiently, so light and airy it actually quivered when washed with egg. It needed the oven soon.

As the dawn showered pink across the high snowbanks in Montreal's Notre-Dame-de-Grâce region, the bakery windows filled with loaves and buttery croissants and *pains au chocolat* and the perfect, feathery brioche artfully arranged in wicker baskets.

Later in the day, during a drive back from the city's bustling Atwater Market, where we'd headed to buy some cheese, for which Quebec is now internationally renowned, James launched into what he called his "bread speech." According to him, there are two pillars of great bread: unbleached flour to give the loaves a creamy colour and nutty, wheaty flavour, and long, cool fermentation to develop the "architecture" and still more flavour. Finally, he was insistent that "millers of grain must know how to bake."

The story of Canadian wheat is mythic in its proportions. Not only was it the foundation of the economies of vast regions within our country, it remains Canada's largest agricultural export.

Wheat was first grown in Canada during the short Newfoundland summers in the mid-1500s. Then Marc Lescarbot, the diarist of Samuel de Champlain, recorded that in July 1606, M. de Poutrincourt sowed the first wheat in Nova Scotia at Port Royal.

As traders and *voyageurs* dove deeper into the continent, agriculture became an absolute necessity to support the chain of outposts. Virtually every settlement log listed wheat, often first. Along the St. Lawrence River, most villages had a communal bread oven. Without wheat, survival was questionable.

By 1829, the grain had reached British Columbia, not only from the east but also from the west with the spread of cultivars brought to California by settlers who journeyed north by ship rather than overland. The first documented planting on Vancouver Island was in 1825.

The story of Canada's first identified wheat cultivar, Red Fife, has taken on a mystique. Myths abound of how the famous grain was "discovered." In 1842, two young Ontario settlers, Jane and David Fife from near Peterborough,

RED FIFE WHEAT

For wheat pioneer Sharon Rempel, the Red Fife Wheat Project has been an exercise in tenacity. In spite of countless roadblocks and challenges—even growing out the seed in a quantity large enough to distribute was no easy task—Red Fife is once again starting to flourish in small growing communities across the nation. It has great flavour but, most important, it provides another level of biodiversity and an opportunity for an identity-preserved flour, something that has not happened to date. At the time of writing, a number of tons have been harvested and are ready for milling.

asked a friend in Scotland to send them some seed. Jane was the daughter of a farmer and seed man, so she understood the selection process. The friend went to the docks in Glasgow to collect samples of wheat and sent them to the Fifes. They planted them but only one stem was productive, branching out with three sturdy heads. They propagated it and it flourished. Over the ensuing years, this cultivar was grown throughout Canada and parts of the United States, and was simply called Fife.

We now know that this particular grain was a variety called Halychanka, a Galacian spring wheat from Danzig, Poland, but during those early years, other growers tinkered with it and attached new names: Bernard Fife, MacKendry Fife, McKissing Fife, and so on. In the 1870s, with the marketing of a revolutionary new milling machine that used steel rollers rather than millstones, it became possible to mill spring wheat as effectively for bread baking as it was for the long-used winter varieties. A market was quickly established for spring wheat, and the Fife varieties took centre stage.

Eventually named Red Fife, it became the most important spring wheat in Canada, and for more than 60 years, it served as a crop, as breeding stock and as a rather creative incentive for settlers. Red Fife seed was given away free to potential immigrants by both the Canadian government and the CPR in hopes of attracting them to the heartland. Canada's reputation for high-quality wheat was founded on Red Fife, particularly when it was grown in Manitoba, where it fetched a higher price than that grown in the Dakotas.

That province's first wheat shipment to the United Kingdom was probably in 1878—somewhat ironically to Glasgow—and in 1879, another shipment went to Liverpool. In 1880, Manitoba's reputation for producing the highest-quality wheat was so well established that the entire surplus was purchased by American buyers at a price higher than that of Dakota wheat; the explanation given was that this particular grain was "rich in gluten." It was recognized as the finest milling wheat on earth. Seeing an opportunity, in 1881 the Ogilvie company built the first country elevator in Manitoba, at Gretna.

This was the old-fashioned background from which the modern story of wheat exploded. In 1892, Dr. William Saunders, the first director of Canada's experimental farm system, encouraged dozens of crossings of various wheat varieties in the hope of finding one that ripened earlier than Red Fife. His two sons, A.P. "Percy" and Charles, did a great deal of work. By 1901, 58 new grains had been identified, but one stood out—a cross of Red Fife with Hard Red Calcutta. It was made by Percy Saunders in 1892, when he was working in Agassiz, British Columbia. With a handful of other cultivars, he sent it to his brother, Charles, at the Central Experimental Farm, where all the seeds were grown out. Charles had such a poorly equipped lab that he

From the dome car of The Canadian, VIA Rail's transcontinental service, travellers pass by Prairie elevators such as this one, near Edmonton.

had to chew the various grains to determine the gluten strength and, hence, their bread baking attributes. He figured that his brother's cross was excellent, but it took until 1906, when he finally had some decent equipment, to confirm that finding. Ten kilograms of the seed was sent to Agassiz in 1907, and in 1908 the grain was shipped to Brandon's Experimental Farm. In 1909, it was sent to the Prairies for general trials and was embraced by the farming community. Named Marquis, it quickly became the most revolutionary grain ever to hit North America. While Red Fife is currently being lauded and honoured, it is Marquis that is Canada's premier wheat. By 1920, Marquis constituted 90 percent of the 6.9 million hectares of hard, red spring wheat that were seeded on the Canadian Prairies. Maturing earlier and standing strong in the field, Marquis could be grown in areas that had previously been far too cold or inhospitable for wheat production. The annual increase of 25 million bushels in production between the years 1915 and 1918 was because of Marquis. It made superb flour and was *the* milling standard until the 1970s, when it was replaced by Winnipeg-bred Neepawa.

It was likely Marquis that filled the flour bags of young George Weston. As an apprenticing baker, he purchased a Toronto bread route from his boss in 1882 for the lordly sum of $200. By 1884, he had started The New Model Bakery at the corner of Phoebe and Soho Streets. There, in 1898, he and his wife, Emma, had a son, Garfield. While George expanded his operation to 30 delivery wagons, which sold to 500 stores across the city, young Garfield was growing up with "the smell of bread in his nose." Upon the death of his entrepreneurial father in 1924, Garfield took the reins and, on the already solid foundation, began to build an empire. When the chance came to buy 30 bakeries in Great Britain, he shrewdly saw it as an opportunity, well laced with nationalistic pride, to "merchandise Canadian wheat."

The other wheat variety of great note is durum, the grain that, when milled into semolina, makes the finest pasta on earth and the unleavened flatbreads and couscous of the Middle East.

Durum is a relatively new player, originally grown in Canada in the early 1900s for animal feed or to add strength to blends of bread flour. When it was recognized as a superb ingredient for pasta, the market expanded. By the 1930s, several hundred thousand tons were exported. The war temporarily interrupted trade, but as new cultivars came on stream, production increased. Today it travels the world and, sometimes, back again in the form of Italian pasta.

Oats were brought to Canada by an Englishman in 1578; he wrote home bragging that he'd planted them in what is now Newfoundland. He tossed the seeds about, then sailed off into the sunrise. Later, in 1622 at Ferryland,

OATS IN CANADA

Oat breeding began at the Central Experimental Farm in Ottawa in 1906, under the watchful eye of "aggie" pioneer Charles Saunders. The first variety he released was called Legacy, and it's still being sold in Canada.

FOR HORSES *AND* PEOPLE

Duane Falk, the University of Guelph's barley and wheat expert, likes to recount how English scholar Samuel Johnson (1709 to 1784) described oats as a grain which, in England, is generally given to horses but in Scotland supports the people. In response, Johnson's Scottish colleague James Boswell suggested that this is why England breeds such fine horses and Scotland such fine men.

Lord Baltimore's early settlement outside of present-day St. John's, the leader of that troop, Captain Wynne, detailed the staples of the two-acre garden as "Barley, Oates, Pease and Beanes."

Although oats are dearly loved for breakfast cereal and cookies, nowhere are they such a culinary pillar as on Cape Breton Island, Nova Scotia. Cape Bretoners even make oats into suet-laced sausages, a serious specialty known as marag pudding (the plural is maragan). They're delicious. Not well known outside of the island, maragan are time-consuming to make, but as the old saying goes, "Many hands make light work." Their production is a community activity, and they're used as a fundraiser for a number of church groups across the island, including the United Church Women in Whycocomagh.

Another Cape Breton Scots tradition is fuarag, a very old dish based on cream whipped so stiff it almost becomes butter, finely ground uncooked oats and maple sugar. Mint leaves might be used for decoration. According to Cape Bretoners Janice Beaton, who is in the cheese business in Calgary, and historian Alex St. Clair, it is supposed to be eaten communally and often had small trinkets buried in it. If you found a thimble, you'd have to sew on your own buttons; a ring meant you'd soon be married. *Stapag* was raw oatmeal steeped in water, the best thirst quencher for men in the hot summer fields at haying time.

One has to wonder whether those old Scots knew something we didn't because, in fact, oats have real health benefits! The bran is rich in dietary fibre that sponges up blood cholesterol.

While research into new oat varieties was carried on side by side with other grains across the country, it wasn't until 1970 that four plant explorers, two from Ottawa and two from Winnipeg (home of the Grain Research Lab) really made headlines. They did for oats what Gary Johnston had done for Yukon Gold potatoes. Whereas Johnston went to Peru and brought back one spectacular spud from the cradle of potato civilization, this team headed to the Mediterranean, where oats had been originally domesticated, and brought back 15,000 samples. In less than a decade, 10 new oat hybrids were released. Because of their adaptability to cold climates, premium oat varieties are being studied in New Liskeard, a very new growing region in Ontario that boasts 165,000 acres of agricultural land and potential for another three million acres up Highway 11 in Earlton.

Barley is another plant that hailed from the Mediterranean and was first planted in Canada in 1578 by that same anonymous English fisherman in an attempt to supplement the meagre diet of the men who were working off the coast of Newfoundland; it had nothing to do with the great beer for which Canada is now justifiably well known. Its association with beer came about when the prolific plant breeder Charles Zavitz, who ironically was a tee-totaller, obtained the superior-yielding Mandscheuri barley line from Russia in 1889. He evaluated seed from the 33 best lines of the strain and selected one, OAC 21, which went on to revolutionize the brewing industry in Canada. Released in 1910 and named because it was number 21 in a group of some 10,000 plants, it soon became the dominant barley in the province, constituting 98 percent of the barley acreage in Ontario in the 1920s, and eventually monopolized acreages on the Prairies and in Scandinavia and South America. OAC 21 showed such exceptional malting qualities that it became the preferred variety for beer making in Canada for more than 50 years. In fact, most new barley varieties trace their ancestry back to OAC 21. The modern malting industry owes its existence to this amazing plant.

While, in my opinion, great beer is close to being a food group, barley is infinitely more than its essential base. For me, it replaces rice. I use it in a very passable, if not superior, version of risotto. Aside from culturally specific foods like sushi or congee or paella, where good rice is essential, there is little need for it in a Canadian kitchen. Heresy perhaps to the purists, but I figure that the use of alternative grains gives us infinitely more direct ownership of our food supply. Some call this import replacement; I call it common sense.

Canada was founded on substantial dishes with ingredients that could be grown and cooked in our local kitchens. Grain of all sorts played a central role, not only to the survival of the early settlers but in the development of our national food culture. Is there anything more quintessentially Canadian than Beef with Barley Soup (page 104) or butter tarts (page 222) or the foods of this chapter, many with names from afar but rooted in our land? Karen Baxter's Brazilian family, the Gerlingers, taught her how to make spätzle (page 160), those soft, floating noodles they in turn had brought with them from Germany. Alex Sgroi's extraordinary pasta (page 158) may have been invented somewhere else, but every single ingredient is our own, including the exceptional semolina. Italian pasta makers cut their basic recipe with flour of lesser quality before they ship it back to us. My Prussian ancestors, whose names I never knew, taught my great-grandmother how to make what Grandpa called German Buns (page 169). The Portuguese adopted corn from the New World, blended it with wheat from the Old and created their signature cornbread (page 42). The Irish made soda bread in the Old World. It was easy, fast and cheap. Then they brought it with them (page 155). Indeed, if one could draw a map of the earth using the journey of grain, Canada, with its millions of acres of cropland, would be at its core.

I met Lise Brunn in 1987 when she was keeping the light station at the tip of Langara Island, the most northerly of the Queen Charlottes. Resilient and hard-working, she baked extraordinary bread and harvested the wild shoreline, some 120 feet below the lighthouse, for mussels that she'd preserve in oil.

Nana's (Utterly Fabulous) Multi-Grain Rolls

When Joan Heath of Radisson, Saskatchewan, shared this great recipe, she explained its title: "My mom (a.k.a. Nana to our children, Audra and Aidan) bakes the best rolls and bread I have ever had; they're so light and fluffy. I had no interest in cooking or baking as a teenager and, in fact, left home having never cooked a meal. But I did spend hours watching her method and something must have stuck. I always thought her secret was the triple rise—and *never* using anything but traditional yeast. She usually makes white, sometimes whole wheat, not more than about 50 percent whole wheat, whereas I like grainy, seedy bread, so this recipe is my adaptation of her original. On a whim, I decided to make a batch and enter it into the local fair. I phoned Mom and she just recounted what she did, not really a recipe as the flour and water always vary based on the day. I still have the recipe scrawled in a Western Producer notepad. Beginner's luck—I won some prizes."

YIELD: 12 buns

¼ cup (60 mL) canola oil

¼ cup (60 mL) + ½ tsp (2 mL) granulated sugar

2 tsp (10 mL) salt

1 cup (250 mL) boiling water

1 cup (250 mL) tepid water

3 cups (750 mL) whole wheat flour

2 cups (500 mL) multi-grain flour

¼ cup (60 mL) warm water

1 tbsp (15 mL) active dry yeast

¼ cup (60 mL) Red River cereal

⅓ cup (75 mL) sunflower seeds

¼ cup (60 mL) cornmeal

In a bowl, combine the canola oil, ¼ cup (60 mL) sugar, salt and boiling water. Mix until sugar has dissolved. Add tepid water, 1 cup (250 mL) whole wheat flour and 1 cup (250 mL) multi-grain flour. Stir until it forms a thick, souplike texture. In a separate bowl, stir together remaining sugar, warm water and active yeast; let stand and puff for 10 minutes. Add yeast mixture to flour; combine thoroughly.

In another bowl, stir together 1 cup (250 mL) whole wheat flour, 1 cup (250 mL) multi-grain flour, Red River cereal, sunflower seeds and cornmeal. Add to yeast mixture, mixing until it forms a sticky ball. Add remaining 1 cup (250 mL) whole wheat flour. Knead on a lightly floured surface for approximately 10 minutes or until a smooth, elastic dough forms. Let rest for 5 minutes. Brush or rub the top of the dough with oil and place in an oiled bowl. Cover with a tea towel and let rise until doubled in size, about 2 hours, depending upon the temperature of the kitchen.

Punch down and let rise a second time until doubled in size, about 1 hour. Punch down and, with a sharp knife, divide into 12 equal pieces. Shape into mounds resembling large hamburger buns. Place on a parchment-lined baking sheet. Let rise for another 40 to 50 minutes or until doubled.

Bake in a preheated 375°F (190°C) oven for 35 to 45 minutes or until well browned.

On the acreage near the Wellington County Museum, between Elora and Fergus, Ontario, sheaves are stacked into stooks in a demonstration of heritage grain harvesting.

THE RYE CROP

In 1622, Captain Edward Wynne, who helped Lord Baltimore open up the settlement of Ferryland in Newfoundland, wrote glowingly, "At the Bristow Plantation, there is as goodly Rye now growing as can be in any part of England."

Rye has never been a huge crop in Canada, which is somewhat surprising because it is very cold hardy. One variety developed at the Central Research Station in Ottawa was named Polar. It's generally used as feed, but some finds its way into the specialty market to make Canada's fabulous rye whisky.

Tuula's Christmas Limpa Bread (Finnish Rye Bread with Raisins)

Both the Finnish community and its food culture thrive in Sointula, a small village on Malcolm Island in north coastal British Columbia. Tuula Lewis is at the heart of many of its activities. Her limpa, a delicious molasses-laced rye bread, is part of the tradition. Served on the Christmas table, it's simply sliced and buttered or used for great open-face sandwiches, with good ham and dill pickles.

YIELD: 2 loaves

BATTER:
   2 cups (500 mL) warm water
   2 tsp (10 mL) salt
   1 tbsp (15 mL) active dry yeast
   1½ cups (375 mL) rye flour

DOUGH:
   1 cup (250 mL) raisins
   ⅓ cup (75 mL) warm water
   1 tsp (5 mL) granulated sugar
   2 tsp (10 mL) active dry yeast
   ½ cup (125 mL) molasses
   2 tbsp (30 mL) melted butter
   1 tbsp (15 mL) whole aniseed
   1 tbsp (15 mL) cocoa powder (optional)
   4½ cups (1.125 L) all-purpose flour

BATTER: In a large bowl, stir together the water, salt and yeast. Beat in the rye flour; cover and let stand in a warm place for 1½ hours or until very bubbly.

DOUGH: Cover the raisins with boiling water; set aside to plump for 10 minutes. Drain well, discarding soaking liquid. In a small bowl, combine ⅓ cup (75 mL) warm water with the sugar and yeast. Let puff for 5 minutes. Add the raisins to the rye flour batter. Beat in the molasses, melted butter, aniseed, cocoa (if using) and yeast mixture.

Add flour, a cupful at a time, until the dough becomes very thick. Turn out onto a floured surface and knead in any remaining flour. Continue to knead for 5 to 6 minutes or until very smooth and elastic.

Transfer to a well-oiled bowl; cover and let rise in a warm place until doubled in bulk, about 1½ hours. Punch down, divide in half and shape into 2 round or oblong loaves.

Place on parchment-lined baking sheets. Cover and let rise a second time in a cool kitchen until almost doubled, about 1½ hours.

Bake in a preheated 375°F (190°C) oven until well browned, 35 to 40 minutes. The bottom of the loaves should sound hollow when tapped. Let cool on a wire rack.

If one wants grapes to really flourish on an island in north coastal British Columbia, it's best to build a greenhouse, as fishing guide and gardener Jim McDowell does near Sointula.

Tuula's Pulla
(Finnish Coffee Bread)

Tuula often provides many loaves of this delicious sweet bread for the local museum in Sointula. When I visited there, before I was even allowed into the collection of Malcolm Island memorabilia, I had to have a thick slice of this fabulous cardamom bread, spread with butter and wild blackberry jam. A cup of tea was also de rigueur. Like most good Scandinavian bakers, Tuula grinds her cardamom in a coffee grinder just before using it; however, an old-fashioned mortar and pestle will also do the trick.

YIELD: 4 braids

YEAST PUFF:
>   ¼ cup (60 mL) warm water
>   1 tsp (5 mL) granulated sugar
>   1 pkg (1 tbsp/15 mL) active dry yeast

DOUGH:
>   1 cup (250 mL) granulated sugar
>   2 cups (500 mL) very hot water
>   ½ cup (125 mL) table cream (18%), warmed
>   2 eggs, well beaten
>   1 tbsp (15 mL) ground black cardamom
>   2 tsp (10 mL) salt
>   ½ cup (125 mL) melted butter, slightly cooled
>   6 to 7 cups (1.5 to 1.75 L) all-purpose flour

In a small bowl, stir together the water and 1 tsp (5 mL) sugar until sugar is dissolved; sprinkle with the yeast. Let puff for 5 to 7 minutes.

Meanwhile, in a large bowl, dissolve the 1 cup (250 mL) sugar in the very hot water. Whisk in the cream, beaten eggs, cardamom and salt. Add the yeast mixture, stirring to combine. Add the melted butter, combining thoroughly.

Add the flour, a cupful at a time, beating well after each addition to ensure it is well blended. When the dough is dense and stiff, turn out onto a well-floured board and knead in any remaining flour. Knead for 5 to 7 minutes or until the dough is smooth and elastic. If the kitchen is warm, simply cover the dough with a kitchen towel and let rise until doubled. Otherwise, transfer it to a well-oiled bowl, cover and let rise in a warm place for 1½ to 2 hours or until doubled.

Punch down and divide into 4 equal pieces. Roll each piece into a flat rectangle, about 10 inches (25 cm) long. Make 2 lengthwise cuts to within 1 inch (2.5 cm) of the end of each rectangle. Braid the dough, pinching the loose ends tightly. Place on a parchment-lined baking sheet. Let rise a second time for 50 to 60 minutes.

Bake in a preheated 350°F (180°C) oven for 25 to 30 minutes or till golden brown.

A wall mural in Sointula, Malcolm Island, B.C. The Finnish community attempted to create a utopia for themselves here in the very early 1900s. Their food culture is still strong!

Portuguese Sweet Bread

Yeast breads reflect the superb baking talent of the Portuguese. Served at Easter time, these loaves are studded with raisins and walnuts. They could be braided and iced. The original recipe, the one that's the foundation of this adaptation, came from a lightkeeper on the B.C. coast, the late Fil McMurray, who said that it's essential that the loaves be cooled before being sliced. I tasted similar loaves, both with and without the raisins and nuts, in Ontario's Portuguese community and in the Azores.

YIELD: 4 loaves

> 2 tbsp (30 mL) yeast
> ½ cup (125 mL) warm water
> 1 cup (250 mL) milk
> ½ cup (125 mL) butter
> 2 tsp (10 mL) salt
> 6 eggs
> 1½ cups (375 mL) granulated sugar
> 7 to 8 cups (1.75 to 2 L) all-purpose flour
> 1½ cups (375 mL) raisins
> 1½ cups (375 mL) walnuts
> Melted butter

In a large bowl, sprinkle the yeast over the warm water and set aside. Warm the milk, butter and salt in a small saucepan just until the butter is melted. Let cool to lukewarm.

Whisk together the eggs and sugar until light coloured. Add the milk mixture to the eggs and combine with the yeast. Gradually beat in 3 cups (750 mL) of the flour. Mix in raisins and nuts. Continue to add flour, a cupful at time, mixing well after each addition.

Turn out dough onto a floured surface and knead until smooth, 5 to 7 minutes, adding more flour as necessary. Gather into a ball and transfer to a well-oiled mixing bowl, turning dough to oil the top. Cover with a damp towel and let rise until doubled, about 1½ hours. Punch down and let rest for 10 minutes. Cut into 4 equal pieces, shaping each into a smooth ball. Flatten into 4 rounds and place on well-oiled or parchment-lined baking sheets. Cover again and let rise until doubled.

Bake in a preheated 350°F (180°C) oven for 30 minutes or until well browned. Brush with a little extra melted butter while hot. Let cool before slicing.

Holly's Whole Wheat Buttermilk Soda Bread

This quickest of breads has its roots in Ireland, where it's known as wheaten soda bread, but this particularly great recipe was developed by Holly Rowland, a Victoria-based food writer, when she lived in Halifax. Serve thick, warm slices of it with butter.

YIELD: 2 loaves

2 cups (500 mL) whole wheat flour
2 cups (500 mL) unbleached all-purpose flour
1 tbsp (15 mL) baking powder
1 tsp (5 mL) baking soda
½ tsp (2 mL) salt
2 tbsp (30 mL) packed brown sugar
¼ cup (60 mL) chilled butter
1 egg, beaten
1¾ cups (425 mL) buttermilk

Measure the whole wheat flour into a large mixing bowl. Sift the all-purpose flour, baking powder, baking soda, salt and brown sugar into the bowl. Cut in the butter until it looks like fine crumbs. Whisk together the egg and buttermilk; add to the dry ingredients, stirring until just combined and no dry spots remain.

Turn out onto a floured surface and knead 8 to 10 times. Cut in 2 equal pieces and shape each into a round loaf. Place on parchment-lined baking sheet, slashing tops with a sharp knife.

Bake in a preheated 400°F (200°C) oven for 35 to 40 minutes or until hollow-sounding when tapped on the bottom.

Evolution of Yeast

Our Canadian "bread culture" also includes yeast. We first used wild yeasts to create the sourdoughs that prospectors carried with them. Old Canadian cookbooks contained recipes for yeast that used hops, which were widely grown in early Canada, flour and potatoes. Commercial yeast made life much easier for housewives, who bought flour in 100-pound sacks (about 45 kilograms) and would use eight to 10 such bags over the winter. The empty bags were then made into everything from underwear to dish towels.

Tanya's Latvian-Style Bagels

The late Tanya Barsevski was a lovely lady who cooked at our high school in Mount Forest, a farming community in central Ontario. She was a renowned baker. When we were talking about these bagels years ago, she told me that you know you have enough flour in the dough when it puffs back at you.

While the original instructions were to poach them in batches, I've found that it's best to have two or even three pans of the sweetened water simmering. The bagels rise quickly after they've been shaped, and if not handled quickly, they'll deflate before baking. Nonetheless, homemade bagels are a treat. Every true bagel fan should bake them at least once in a lifetime.

Yield: 24 to 30 bagels

2 cups (500 mL) warm water
1 tbsp (15 mL) granulated sugar
2 tbsp (30 mL) active dry yeast
4 eggs, beaten
½ cup (125 mL) canola oil
1 tsp (5 mL) salt
6 to 6½ cups (1.5 to 1.625 L) all-purpose flour

Poaching Liquid:
16 cups (4 L) water
⅔ cup (150 mL) granulated sugar

Glaze:
1 egg yolk
¼ cup (60 mL) milk
Poppy or sesame seeds

In a large bowl, combine 1 cup (250 mL) of the warm water with the sugar. Sprinkle in the yeast and let stand for 8 to 10 minutes or until frothy. Beat in the remaining water, eggs, oil and salt. Beat in the flour, a cupful at a time, working the final cupfuls in by hand to make a soft sticky dough. Turn out onto a floured board; knead for 5 minutes or until smooth and elastic. Cover and let rise until doubled, about 1½ hours.

Punch down and divide into 24 to 30 pieces. Roll each piece into a 6-inch (15 cm) cylinder; form into a circle, twisting and pinching ends together. Place on parchment-lined baking sheet. Cover and let rise for 8 to 10 minutes or until puffy. The bagels should not be allowed to double in size at this stage as you would for other breads.

POACHING LIQUID: In 2 or 3 large saucepans, combine water and sugar. Bring to a boil over medium-high heat. Add bagels, 3 or 4 at a time, turning with chopsticks or the handle of a long wooden spoon. Cook for 3 minutes. Remove with slotted spoon and return to the parchment-lined baking sheets.

GLAZE: Whisk together the egg yolk and milk; brush onto bagels. Sprinkle generously with poppy or sesame seeds. Bake in a preheated 450°F (220°C) oven until golden brown, 20 to 25 minutes.

An old-fashioned harvest near the Wellington County Museum.

Alex's Perfect Pasta

Over the years, I've tasted a lot of pasta. But it was the tissue-thin lasagna in Bologna that made me realize how feeble my own attempts had been. About five years ago, a Swiss chef, Alex Sgroi, landed in the Fergus/Elora region of Ontario. He'd grown up in a canton (province) of southern Switzerland that routinely had been traded back and forth with Italy. His mother taught him to make pasta before he even began attending elementary school. He went on to attend the famous Swiss hotel school in Lausanne and came to Canada to work for the Four Seasons in its earliest days. Although he moved between Canada and Europe frequently while his wife, Barbara, was deeply involved with the fashion beat, they settled permanently in Canada in 1978 so their children could go to school here and because it was basically "a safer country." In all his restaurants, from his upscale ventures in Toronto to their country place near Shelburne, Ontario, and finally Elora, he made his mother's pasta. Alex spent a day with me in my kitchen, teaching and coaching me through this recipe. It forms the foundation of many pasta dishes, and I would encourage you to begin with the simplest—a perfect linguine—then branch out into the tad more complex ravioli.

There are several important steps. First of all, ignore any recipe that tells you that good pasta can be made with all-purpose flour. *No!* You must have durum semolina, a rough-textured product found in the Italian section of most large grocery stores. The brand that is most widely available is Unico. The finest pasta on earth is made from Canadian Prairie durum wheat. Second, buy a good pasta roller. There are electric models, which are fine, but a less expensive hand-operated one is what Alex uses now that he no longer has a restaurant. The third must-have is a good pasta cutting wheel. When you're making ravioli, it's essential. Alex's well-worn implement makes a zigzag cut as it seals the pasta.

Once you're comfortable with making the thin eggy ribbons of linguine, try your hand at his Roasted Winter Squash Ravioli with Sage Browned-Butter Sauce (see page 32) or, more simply, roll the pasta into the thinnest sheets to make your own lasagna or linguine.

You can use the finished pasta immediately or pile it loosely into a plastic bag. Or, in the case of ravioli or lasagna, you can layer it between parchment in an airtight freezer container and freeze it for up to a month. It can also be refrigerated, uncooked, for several days.

The bag of durum semolina that we used was labelled 750 g (1.65 lb). Its contents measured 4½ cups (1.125 L). For that amount, Alex used seven eggs.

7 eggs
2 tsp (10 mL) salt
4½ cups (1.125 L) durum semolina
All-purpose flour

Break the eggs into a large bowl. Whisk vigorously to combine. Add salt. Pour in the semolina, a cupful at a time, whisking to combine until it becomes too stiff to mix. Work in the remaining semolina by hand. Turn out onto a well-floured surface; knead dough for 3 to 5 minutes, working it well to make a compact dough. Cover and wrap with a damp towel. Let stand at room temperature for 1 hour.

Divide the dough into 4 or 5 pieces. While you work with one of the pieces, keep the remaining pieces covered with the damp cloth.

Pat or roll out the dough with a rolling pin to about ½-inch (1 cm) thickness, flouring it lightly on both sides. Dust the roller of the pasta machine with flour. Beginning with the highest number (the higher the number, the thicker the pasta will be), pass the dough through the roller. If it tears, fold it over and do it again. Reduce the number and repeat until you reach number 1. Roll carefully and remove from the machine. Use to make ravioli (page 32) or simply cut it into linguine, dust lightly with a little additional flour and set aside until the rest of the pasta has been rolled. (With a generous dusting of flour, this pasta can be frozen after rolling and cutting. The uncooked pasta will keep for at least 2 days if refrigerated.)

When cooking pasta, the ratio of water to pasta is 7:1. Bring the water to a boil and then add the salt (½ tsp/2 mL salt per 4 cups/1 L water). This will prevent a scum from forming on the water. Drop in the pasta and boil for 2 to 3 minutes. Drain and serve.

Fresh Basil Pesto

Another recent addition to the repertoire of Canada's home cooks is pesto.

To be totally true to our roots, you can use raw or roasted hazelnuts from British Columbia rather than pine nuts, or, if you can find them, heart nuts from Ontario. I've used blanched almonds and pecans on occasion. This is one of the few recipes that really does require the use of olive oil. Make it when basil is in season, toward the end of August in much of southern Canada. Pesto freezes beautifully.

To serve it, simply toss the pesto with hot pasta—this amount will serve four—and generously grate in a hard aged cheese. In Canada, we make excellent Parmesan-style cheeses, but even an aged Gouda or hard sheep's milk cheese would be a fabulous alternative.

YIELD: 1 cup (250 mL), enough for 4 servings

3 cloves garlic
2 cups (500 mL) packed basil leaves
⅓ cup (75 mL) nuts
1 tsp (5 mL) salt
½ tsp (2 mL) freshly ground pepper
¾ cup (175 mL) olive oil

In a blender or food processor, finely chop the garlic, basil, nuts, salt and pepper. With the machine still running, pour in the oil and purée the mixture. Use immediately or freeze for up to 6 months. To refrigerate, transfer to a small bowl and cover with a thin layer of olive oil to prevent darkening; refrigerate for up to 4 days.

Karen's Spätzle

This is an example of a quintessential well-travelled recipe. Spätzle, small nuggets of egg-laced pasta, is a German tradition, either dropped as a thin batter into boiling water, as Karen Gerlinger-Baxter does, or, more authentically, quickly scraped off a board with a very sharp knife into boiling water, as distiller Roswitha Rosswog does in her home kitchen near Baie Verte in New Brunswick.

The route of Karen's recipe is fascinating. Her grandfather emigrated from Nuremberg in southern Germany to Brazil in the 1940s, raising money to help the Jews escape. He eventually married one of his charges, a lovely German Jewess who became Karen's grandmother. In Brazil, they kept this Swabian specialty in their culinary repertoire and would serve it with a stroganoff-style beef. Karen came north to complete a graduate degree and has now permanently settled in Canada, where she, too, makes this fast but often ignored noodle. It is *perfect* with the rich, fragrant stew her husband, David, a skilled hunter and Air Canada pilot, cooks all winter long using Wellington County's amazing wild venison that "pastures" at night on local corn and soy fields—to some farmers' dismay.

The batter must be well beaten, and when it's ready, it will fall from the spoon in loose sheets. A spätzle press is essential; they are now widely available in cookware stores. Spätzle is best made just before serving. It can be served as is with a good stew or reheated by tossing with a little melted butter and a few fresh herbs. I love it!

YIELD: 4 servings

1 cup (250 mL) all-purpose flour

2 eggs

½ tsp (2 mL) grated lemon rind

½ tsp (2 mL) salt

2 tsp (10 mL) melted butter

½ cup (125 mL) cold water

Salted water

1 tbsp (15 mL) canola oil

Measure the flour into a bowl and make a well in the centre of it. Break in the eggs and add the lemon, salt and butter. Stir to combine. Add the water and beat by hand for 3 to 4 minutes or until you can easily see the batter becoming stretchy. It must sheet off the spoon. Let it rest while you bring a large pot of boiling salted water to a boil over high heat. When the water is boiling, add oil and place the spätzle press over top. Working in batches, add the batter to the press, and with gentle back and forth movements, allow the batter to drip into the boiling water; it will bob to the top and float when it's done. With a slotted spoon, transfer the cooked spätzle to a buttered or oiled serving bowl. Keep warm in the oven while boiling the remaining batter.

At Kings Landing Historical Settlement, a marvellous historic village on the Saint John River in central New Brunswick, daily life means milling the harvest and operating the farm in the most traditional manner.

Vij's Pearl Barley Pilaf

Vij's restaurant in Vancouver is legendary. It is owned and lovingly operated by the husband and wife team of Meeru Dhalwala and Vikram Vij.

They've established a no-reservation policy—a democratic way of dining which means that all would-be customers line up for a table. As one of them, I can attest that it is absolutely worth the wait, even on the dampest coastal evening. Mark Bittman waited . . . and called Vij's "easily among the finest Indian restaurants in the world" (*New York Times*, 2003).

But it was a meal at Vij's years before the Bittman review that was a turning point in my personal understanding of the concept of Canadian cuisine. After a particularly fine and beautifully spice-laden feast, my friend Les Anthony asked me what region of India I'd guess the meal represented. I answered that I'd never been to India, so I couldn't possibly say. He told me that he had travelled throughout India, and hadn't ever tasted food like it. It was an "A-ha!" moment for me. So this is it! Canadian ingredients + the spices/flavourings/techniques of one's homeland = Canadian cuisine. Every time I return to Vij's, I am further enamored with Meeru and Vikram's dedication to the food of the coast. I always come away inspired and satiated.

This all-Canadian dish was adapted from one in Vij's award-winning book, *Vij's Elegant & Inspired Indian Cuisine* (Douglas & McIntyre, 2006). In it, Meeru wrote:

> Sometimes it's just nice to eat something other than rice and bread with Indian food. This pilaf can be served in place of a rice pilaf with any dish and many actually prefer it, as the barley can take more spices than rice. Unlike rice pilafs, though, we don't think the pearl barley tastes good with raita or yogurt.

Serve it with a good curry, or simply as a side dish with an old-fashioned roast chicken dinner.

YIELD: 6 servings

Is there anything more beautiful than the sky being reflected on the water as it is here off the south end of Sointula Island?

¾ cup (175 mL) pearl barley

3 cups (750 mL) water

2 tsp (10 mL) canola oil

1 tsp (5 mL) salt

Masala:

¼ cup (60 mL) canola oil

1½ cups (375 mL) (1 large) chopped onion

2 tbsp (30 mL) finely chopped garlic

1½ tbsp (20 mL) finely chopped ginger

1 tbsp (15 mL) finely chopped jalapeño pepper

⅓ cup (75 mL) chopped fresh coriander

Rinse barley in cold water. Combine water, oil and salt in a medium pot and heat on high heat. When water reaches a vigorous boil, add barley. Reduce the heat to low, cover and simmer for 25 minutes. Stir barley, replace lid and turn off the heat. Allow to sit for 5 to 10 minutes.

Meanwhile, make the masala.

In a separate frying pan, heat the oil on medium-high for one minute. Add the onions and sauté until golden, about 5 to 8 minutes. Add the garlic and sauté for another 3 to 4 minutes. Stir in the ginger and jalapeño pepper, cooking for 2 or 3 minutes. Add the cooked barley to the masala and just before serving stir in the coriander. Serve immediately.

To reheat, add ½ cup (125 mL) water to the barley pilaf and heat it on medium heat. As soon as you see steam, reduce the heat to low, cover and simmer for 5 minutes.

On a late summer day, then Campbell River city councillor Morgan Ostler (on right) poses proudly with Pier Street Farmers Market manager, Inge Kettler. It's a great market, where fishermen on their way to cast their lines from the pier mingle with regular market-goers and tourists who have journeyed to see the famous boat BCP 45 (see page 66), the famous ship from Canada's old five-dollar bills.

Buckwheat-Buttermilk Crêpes

Buckwheat, or "sarrazin," was one of the first grains settlers planted when they came to Canada. In Quebec, buckwheat grew where many grains wouldn't have survived. To serve these crêpes, fill with apples poached in maple syrup or simply enjoy them as one would on the streets of Paris—with a handful of shredded cheese liberally seasoned with freshly ground pepper.

YIELD: About 16 crêpes

⅔ cup (150 mL) all-purpose flour
⅓ cup (75 mL) buckwheat flour
1¾ cups (425 mL) buttermilk
2 eggs
2 tbsp (30 mL) canola oil

In a food processor, blender or bowl, combine all-purpose and buckwheat flours. Add buttermilk, eggs and oil. Process or vigorously whisk until blended. Let stand for 30 minutes before using.

Heat a lightly oiled crêpe pan or skillet over medium heat. In batches, pour in about ¼ cup (60 mL) batter per crêpe. Swirl and tilt pan to spread batter evenly. Cook for 1 to 2 minutes or until bottom is golden and edges begin to lift. Flip and cook for 10 to 15 seconds, until lightly browned. As they are cooked, keep warm under a kitchen towel.

Buckwheat ready to mill.

Joan Heath's Prairie Grain Cookies

This is another recipe from the Saskatchewan farm kitchen of Joan Heath. It's packed with flavour and travels so well that she frequently uses it as part of the lunches she prepares for her husband, Corey, as he works their thousands of acres of wheat, lentils, canola and beans.

YIELD: 2 dozen cookies

1 cup (250 mL) whole wheat flour

1 tsp (5 mL) baking soda

½ tsp (2 mL) salt

2 cups (500 mL) rolled oats

¼ cup (60 mL) Red River cereal

¾ cup (175 mL) canola-based margarine

1½ cups (375 mL) packed brown sugar

2 eggs

1 tsp (5 mL) vanilla extract

¾ cup (175 mL) raisins

½ cup (125 mL) sunflower seeds

In a bowl, combine the whole wheat flour, baking soda, salt, rolled oats and Red River cereal; set aside. In another bowl, cream together the margarine, brown sugar, eggs and vanilla. Add flour mixture, raisins and sunflower seeds to creamed mixture. Mix well. Refrigerate dough for about 1 hour.

Drop by the tablespoonful onto non-stick or parchment-lined cookie sheet; shape and flatten slightly. Bake in a preheated 350°F (180°C) oven for 12 to 15 minutes or until golden brown.

NUTRITIONAL BENEFIT OF OATS

It took 37 studies over 30 years, some of which were done at the University of Guelph as early as the 1980s, before the U.S. FDA made its first food-specific health claim, in January 1997, in support of the consumption of oats. Now we see that oats can be a good medicine, and in the U.S., this claim can be used on packaging: "may reduce the risk of heart disease." B-Glucan is the active agent; it lowers LDL, or the "bad" cholesterol. To obtain the health benefits of oats and lower the LDL, we must consume 3 grams of oat-soluble fibre daily. This translates into 1½ cups (375 mL) cooked oatmeal or 1 cup (250 mL) cooked oat bran or two oat bran muffins.

Glencoe Mills Oatcakes

Deep in the rolling hills near Glencoe Mills, Cape Breton, Elizabeth "Mrs. Angus" Beaton bakes utterly amazing oatcakes. They are so good that she packs them with great care and ships them to Calgary, where her daughter Janice, entrepreneur extraordinaire, shares them with lucky customers in her two upscale cheese shops, called Janice Beaton Fine Cheeses.

These oatcakes are made with ingredients that might be a bit challenging to find. Gone are the days of the gristmills that populated the Atlantic region. These are made with two kinds of oats: one a grainy type that Elizabeth buys from Speerville Mills; and a coarser one that she buys on her infrequent trips to Halifax, then freezes until she bakes another batch.

Scottish oats are steel-cut shards of the oat grain, smaller, sharper and coarser than rolled oats. Speerville Mills oats are freshly processed so the nuttiness of the grain comes through beautifully when baked.

When Elizabeth has finished, she cuts the oatcakes evenly with the rim of an empty corned beef tin (corned beef is one of her husband's favourite foods), bakes them and ships them. Laced with a mom's love, these are the finest biscuits I've ever had with cheese.

The Speerville Mill is located outside of Woodstock, New Brunswick, and its products can be found all over Atlantic Canada.

YIELD: 3 to 4 dozen

2 cups (500 mL) Scottish oatmeal
1 cup (250 mL) rolled oats
2 cups (500 mL) unbleached all-purpose flour
1 tsp (5 mL) salt
⅓ cup (75 mL) granulated sugar
1¼ cups (300 mL) cold butter
1 tsp (5 mL) baking soda
⅓ cup (75 mL) boiling water

Stir together the oatmeal, oats, flour, salt and sugar. Cut in the butter and then, using your hands, rub it into the flour mixture until crumbly. Dissolve the baking soda in the boiling water; stir into the oat mixture, combining with a fork until all the liquid is incorporated. Gently gather up the dough and transfer to a lightly floured surface. Roll out to ¼-inch (5 mm) thickness and cut into desired shapes. Transfer to parchment-lined baking sheet and bake in a preheated 425° to 450°F (210° to 220°C) oven until golden, 10 to 12 minutes. Let cool on the pans or slide parchment carefully onto counter.

All-Butter Oatmeal Cookies

These old-fashioned cookies are crisp and utterly delicious. They've been a favourite in my family for so long that I've committed the recipe to memory. My mother's addition of grated orange rind is a good one, and she comments that, rather than raisins, finely chopped dates would be great. They are!

YIELD: About 2 dozen, depending on the size

> ½ cup (125 mL) packed brown sugar
> ½ cup (125 mL) granulated sugar
> 1 cup (250 mL) melted unsalted butter
> 1 egg
> 1½ cups (375 mL) all-purpose flour
> 1 tsp (5 mL) salt
> 1 tsp (5 mL) baking powder
> 1 tsp (5 mL) baking soda
> 1½ cups (375 mL) rolled oats
> 1 cup (250 mL) raisins
> ½ cup (125 mL) chopped walnuts or heart nuts
> Grated rind of 1 orange

In a large mixing bowl, combine the brown and granulated sugars. Beat in the melted butter and egg until well blended and light in colour.

Sift the flour, salt, baking powder and baking soda into the creamed mixture. Blend well with a wooden spoon. Add the rolled oats, raisins, nuts and orange rind.

Place small spoonfuls of the dough onto parchment-lined cookie sheets. Press down with the tines of a fork dipped in milk. Bake in a preheated 350°F (180°C) oven for 10 to 12 minutes or until golden. Let cool before storing in an airtight container for up to 1 week.

German Buns

When she was about 16, Annie Augusta Wilhemina Frederika (Klug) Ovens immigrated from Prussia to Canada aboard a ship that ran out of every scrap of food save hard tack, or sea biscuits. She was my great-grandmother. This is her recipe. I found it pencilled into my grandmother's cookbook of family favourites.

YIELD: 1 dozen

2 cups (500 mL) all-purpose flour
½ tsp (2 mL) salt
⅓ cup (75 mL) granulated sugar
1½ tsp (7 mL) baking powder
1 tsp (5 mL) baking soda
½ cup (125 mL) butter
1 egg
⅔ cup (150 mL) buttermilk

FILLING:

1 egg
¾ cup (175 mL) packed brown sugar
1 tsp (5 mL) cinnamon
2 tbsp (30 mL) melted butter
½ cup (125 mL) all-purpose flour
½ cup (125 mL) raisins
Maple syrup (optional)

Grain stook at a heritage farming plot near the Wellington County Museum.

In a medium bowl, sift or stir together the flour, salt, sugar, baking powder and baking soda. Cut in the butter finely. Whisk together the egg and buttermilk; add to the dry mixture and stir lightly to combine. Turn out onto floured surface, kneading 5 or 6 times. The dough will be very soft. Roll or pat out into an 8- x 12-inch (20 x 30 cm) rectangle.

FILLING: Combine the egg, brown sugar, cinnamon, melted butter and flour. Spread evenly over the dough and sprinkle with the raisins. Roll the dough into a cylinder. Cut into 1-inch (2.5 cm) pieces. Place on a parchment-lined or well-oiled baking sheet. Brush with maple syrup (if using) and bake in a preheated 375°F (190°C) oven for 20 to 25 minutes or until deep golden.

Nutmeg-Scented Walnut, Farina and Phyllo Pastry (Bougatsa)

This Greek dish uses wheat in two forms—in the pastry and as farina—and is my favourite phyllo dessert. Like the Baklava on page 272, this also comes from the Stroutzas family of Toronto. Farina is known commercially as Cream of Wheat or wheat hearts.

Alex and Patricia Stroutzas left their small grocery store in Greece and came to Canada in 1968, when, as Alex puts it, "being adventurous was in style." Like so many new Canadians, they started with very little, but through extraordinarily hard work have built a flourishing cheese business. When they immigrated, their daughter, Effie, was 16 months old. Today she is deeply involved in their family's business, which has grown from a stall at Toronto's St. Lawrence Market to seven retail locations across the Greater Toronto Area.

YIELD: 6 to 8 servings

1¼ cups (300 mL) homogenized milk

¼ cup (60 mL) farina

½ cup (125 mL) granulated sugar

2 eggs

½ tsp (2 mL) freshly grated nutmeg

1½ tsp (7 mL) vanilla extract

5 or 6 sheets phyllo pastry

⅓ cup (75 mL) melted butter

¼ cup (60 mL) ground walnuts

1 tbsp (15 mL) icing or superfine sugar

In a heavy saucepan, heat the milk until it begins to steam. Stir in the farina and ⅓ cup (75 mL) of the sugar, stirring until it bubbles and thickens, watching it carefully to prevent scorching. Beat eggs in a separate bowl and whisk in the boiling mixture. Return to the saucepan, stirring and cooking thoroughly over low heat for about 1 minute. Stir in the nutmeg and vanilla; set aside.

Unwrap the phyllo and cut the large sheets in half. Butter an 8-inch square (20 cm) glass baking dish. Place half a sheet in the bottom and brush with melted butter; top with another half sheet and brush with butter. Stir together the walnuts and remaining granulated sugar; spread half on the phyllo. Repeat layering and buttering pastry 2 more times. Pour in the custard mixture, spreading it evenly over the bottom phyllo layer. Top with the remaining phyllo, buttering each sheet and spreading the second-last one with the remaining walnut mixture. Brush top with butter and bake in preheated 350°F (180°C) oven for 25 to 30 minutes or until golden. Let cool for 30 minutes before dusting with either icing or superfine sugar. Cut into squares.

Classic Lemon Jelly Roll

This is such an easy dessert. Fill it with Lemon Butter or simply spread it with a high-quality jam, preferably homemade. Spoon the tangy Lemon Butter into small tartlets for a sweets tray. It's an essential for afternoon tea.

Yield: 8 to 10 servings

3 eggs, separated
¾ cup (175 mL) granulated sugar
3 tbsp (45 mL) water
1 cup (250 mL) all-purpose flour
1 tbsp (15 mL) baking powder
Icing sugar
Lemon Butter (recipe follows)

Line a rimmed baking sheet with parchment.

In a large bowl, beat the egg whites until soft peaks form; gradually beat in ¼ cup (60 mL) of the sugar and continue beating until the peaks are stiff. Set aside.

In a separate bowl, whip the egg yolks for 1 to 2 minutes or until lighter in colour. Gradually add the remaining sugar, beating for 2 to 3 minutes and adding the water during the last minute. Sift the flour and baking powder over the yolk mixture; gently fold in the egg whites.

Spread evenly in the prepared pan and bake in a preheated 400°F (200°C) oven for 12 to 15 minutes or until golden. Immediately invert onto a kitchen towel well dusted with icing sugar. Peel off the parchment and gently roll up the cake lengthwise in the towel. Let cool.

Unroll carefully, spread with Lemon Butter and re-roll without the towel.

Lemon Butter

Yield: 3 cups (750 mL)

4 lemons
2 cups (500 mL) granulated sugar
½ cup (125 mL) butter
6 eggs

Grate the rind of 2 of the lemons before juicing all 4. Whisk together the rind, juice, sugar, butter and eggs in the top of a double boiler. Place over boiling water and cook until it is the consistency of honey. Pour into a jar, cover with lid and let cool for 10 to 15 minutes before refrigerating.

FLAMING THE PUDDING

Warm the whisky by placing the bottle in a saucepan of hot water. Place over low heat and warm for 3 to 4 minutes. Pour a little over the pudding and light with a match.

Lillian Phillips' Christmas Plum Pudding with Traditional Buttered-Brandy Sauce

During the 65 years of her marriage, Lillian Phillips made this pudding for her family and friends. In our home, receiving her gift, delivered with affection in its cream-coloured bowl, was as much a part of our holiday traditions as our Christmas tree. Made in October or early November, the pudding was allowed to ripen until Christmas. This recipe makes three—one for the cook and two to give away.

Long before she passed away, Lillian explained to me that when reheating the pudding, "the longer you steam it the darker and better it will be."

Her daughter, also named Lillian, has taken over the stove and continues the tradition. "When pudding was made, Mum had everyone in the family come and stir the batter and make a wish before she put it into the bowls," says Lillian. "Years ago, I think puddings were made on 'Stir-Up Sunday.' They were covered with well-buttered waxed paper and a cloth before being tied twice. A stick was placed though the loop and the pudding was set over the copper pot and steamed over an open fire."

In the original, suet was used, but because it is no longer easy to find, I've substituted butter and was able to cut the fat by more than half. The pudding is lighter in colour and in texture than the original. If you wish to be true to the British roots, however, the amount of suet called for in the original recipe was 2 cups (500 mL).

The Buttered-Brandy Sauce is another essential. I was fortunate enough to have some Johnny Ziegler Aged Fruit Brandy from New Brunswick's Rosswog Distillery in my cupboard—I'd picked it up on a culinary foraging trip in the summer of 2006. Added to the steaming sauce, the fragrance alone was intoxicating. This year I'll be using the great aged brandy from Niagara's Kittling Ridge.

YIELD: Three 2-cup (500 mL) puddings, each 6 to 8 servings

1 cup (250 mL) all-purpose flour

1 tsp (5 mL) baking soda

1 tsp (5 mL) salt

1½ tsp (7 mL) cinnamon

1½ tsp (7 mL) mace

1½ tsp (7 mL) freshly grated nutmeg

1 tsp (5 mL) ground allspice

1½ cups (375 mL) sultana raisins

2 cups (500 mL) currants

2 cups (500 mL) mixed candied fruit

1½ cups (375 mL) fine dry bread crumbs

⅔ cup (150 mL) butter, softened

1 cup (250 mL) packed brown sugar

3 eggs

¼ cup (60 mL) orange juice

⅓ cup (75 mL) molasses

⅔ cup (150 mL) beer

Whisky

In a large bowl, sift together the flour, baking soda, salt, cinnamon, mace, nutmeg and allspice. Stir in the raisins, currants and candied fruit, tossing well to coat thoroughly. Add the bread crumbs, stirring well.

In a separate bowl, cream the butter and brown sugar until light. Beat in the eggs, one at a time. Add the orange juice, molasses and beer. Add the dry ingredients, stirring until completely combined.

Divide the batter among three well-buttered 2-cup (500 mL) pudding basins. Completely cover the surface of each pudding with a round of parchment paper. Using a large square of foil, cover the top of each bowl tightly, crimping the foil tightly to form a rim around the outer ridged edge of the bowl.

Place the bowls in a large roasting pan with a rack or on metal jar rings to keep them from direct contact with the heat. Pour in enough hot water to come one-third of the way up the side of the bowls. Cover tightly and bring to a boil over medium heat. Reduce heat and let the puddings steam for 3 hours, replenishing water when necessary. Remove from the steamer and let bowls cool before refrigerating, well wrapped, for 2 to 3 weeks or even several months.

To serve, re-steam the pudding for 1 to 1½ hours or until completely warmed through. Unwrap, remove parchment paper, loosen edges, and invert onto large, warmed serving dish. Flame with warmed whisky. Serve with Traditional Buttered-Brandy Sauce.

Traditional Buttered-Brandy Sauce

This is the sauce that Lillian Philips served for decades with Christmas pudding. Custard powder is generally sold under the brand name of Bird's, and is also an essential ingredient in that other delicious Canadian invention, Nanaimo bars.

YIELD: 2¾ cups (675 mL)

1¼ cups (300 mL) packed brown sugar

¼ cup (60 mL) custard powder

1½ cups (375 mL) water

¼ cup (60 mL) butter

1 tsp (5 mL) brandy flavouring

½ cup (125 mL) brandy

In a small heavy saucepan, stir together the brown sugar and custard powder. Whisk in the water and cook over medium heat until bubbling and thickened. Stir in the butter until melted. Add the brandy flavouring. Just before serving, stir in the brandy.

Potatoes

You'll find Raymond Loo at the Charlottetown Market most Saturdays throughout the summer selling his superb Island Sunset and Island Sunrise potatoes.

*T*anned and smiling, Raymond Loo mans his family's stall at the Charlottetown Farmers Market. He talks rapid-fire, in staccato syllables. His mind seems to race. This is a man with a mission—to select, propagate and share a great-tasting, disease-resistant potato. He was inspired by his late father, Gerrit, who believed it was possible for a farmer to understand a crop enough to improve it, and that it should be possible to grow potatoes with few pesticides and less fertilizer. For years, Gerrit let potatoes go to seed and then watched them grow. "Dad lived in the potato patch all summer, named them everything he could think of," says Loo. "One was Apple Twig because of the apple twig he'd marked its location with; another Splash because it had purple and white stains on the skin—it's lovely for home fries. People didn't really understand what he was doing. Then he became an organic farmer on top of everything else. "Dad didn't like weeding," Raymond recalls with a broad grin. "He just wasn't interested in the mundane stuff, especially after an accident he had in the 1970s. His kids did the work. There are still daffodils and tulips all over the place under the pear trees."

Raymond still lives on Springwillow Farm, where "Dad planted everything. We have gooseberries, currants, even some things we don't know what they are. If anyone had told me 25 years ago that I'd be a broccoli, cauliflower and potato farmer, I'd have shot myself. But here I am," he comments wryly, "and now I realize why."

Raymond Loo's mission is to produce a brand of potato that is recognized as being solely from P.E.I., and when he does it, it will likely be with two of the potatoes his dad created. Island Sunset is a very light feeder, and Island Sunrise is so resistant to blight that it doesn't need to be sprayed. Island Sunset may be one of the newest, brightest stars of the spud world, a delicious, buttery-fleshed potato with a skin that keeps its pinkish hue when cooked. It would be spectacular in a potato salad.

Potatoes have a long history in Canada but, particularly in the early days, were not held in high regard. Even Samuel de Champlain did not note them, but that was more likely a class issue. They were considered the food of the poorest in France, fit only for pigs, in spite of the fact that they are very nutritious. This misconception was encouraged by the government itself because potatoes were not taxed. By growing them, the poor could avoid the tithes that were levied on wheat and other products.

Potatoes likely reached our shores with the Acadians, but it was the Irish who brought their almost genetic love of them to Canada. Few other countries have the potato so ingrained into their culture as Ireland. The potato arrived on that island in the late 1600s, where it became a main staple, a fallback crop if wheat failed. Because of its enormous agronomic success, Ireland's population grew from 2 million to around 4.4 million by 1790. All a family of six needed to survive was a single acre of good potatoes every year.

The potato that most of the three million poor of Ireland relied upon was one known as Lumper. When a fungus appeared in 1845, it hit that particular variety the hardest. The crop failed, and because the Lumper provided up to two and sometimes three meals every day, starvation set in. It was during that time that Canada received thousands of Irish immigrants. They settled everywhere from Newfoundland to Ontario, bringing with them the staple dishes they still cherish, like champ, potatoes mashed with butter and green onions, and colcannon, a buttery, meatless version of Stamppot (page 196), the Dutch dish featuring kale, potatoes and sausage, but colcannon uses cabbage rather than kale.

Canadians adore potatoes. Whether whipped into fluffy cream-laced mounds or fried to golden perfection at our myriad chip wagons, in Ontario alone we mow down 72.67 kilograms per person annually. In a province of roughly 12 million people, that totals 87,204,000 kilograms every year. Across the nation, we eat them, we export them, we love them. But a spud's not just a spud, according to those who work with these seemingly wily tubers.

"Potatoes are smart!" says Rickey Yada, currently both a professor of food sciences at the University of Guelph and holder of a prestigious Canada Research Chair. "As soon as you start drilling down on one thing, they'll change the path and try to subvert you and try to trick you into looking at something else."

Getting inside a potato, at least metaphorically, requires analysis, a bit like a botanical chess game. Weather, bugs, regulations, soil, genetics—they all play a role. Breeding the next earthy star, the next Yukon Gold, requires patience and creativity on the part of the breeder. And the potato has to taste terrific! This is why Vanessa Currie, the energetic potato point person at the university, connects with her spud network across the continent to assemble as many different varieties as she can. (In 2006, there were 95 varieties and in 2007 well over 100, including fresh, processing, specialty and standards.)

NEW BRUNSWICK POTATO RESEARCH

New Brunswick is potatoes. The province's students even get a break from school during harvest season. The scope of field research is evident with the numbers from the Potato Research Centre in Fredericton. There, the development of new varieties begins with crossing two parent plants. The first generation numbers up to 75,000 plants and is greenhouse grown. It takes four or five generations to get the cultivars to the point where they can be sent out for "adaptation" trials all across the country so that they can be evaluated in a variety of conditions, from Lethbridge to P.E.I.

An array of Vanessa Currie's baby potatoes from her plot at the Elora Research Station.

Potato grower and University of Guelph grain specialist Duane Falk with a hill of the spuds he hybridized.

She then plants and nurtures them before luring industry representatives to the often steamy, dusty fields of the university's Research Station near Elora, Ontario—and to her table. She calls the occasion Potato Research Day, and it's an opportunity for growers and processors to gather and learn together. In a field filled with potato plants and piles of newly dug tubers, they slice open potatoes and talk about what's next on the horizon for the new varieties, some still unnamed. They use older varieties such as Russett Burbank and Shepody as the markers—the ones against which the others might be judged.

Currie's work continues to advance the University of Guelph's already established potato breeding legacy. It was at that university that the legendary Yukon Gold was created by the late Dr. Gary Johnston in 1966, a spud so famous both at home and globally that its name is emblazoned on menus around the world. But few know the actual story of how Yukon Gold came into being.

Right up until his death in 2002, Johnston was a true inventor. His mind worked in wonderful directions. Knowing that potatoes originated in the Andes of Peru, where there are still hundreds of varieties, he travelled there. In a market, he made it known that he wanted to buy their most expensive potato—the one they "treasured most." In fact, what they sold him was a variety whose Spanish name means "golden egg." And it was! He brought it home, bred in disease resistance, ran trials at the research station in Cambridge and eventually created one of the most successful potatoes in history.

His successor at the university, Robert Coffin, is another man who doesn't hold to convention. After moving east from Ontario to near Summerside, P.E.I., he and his wife, Joyce, began privately creating their own cultivars, including Prospect, the 2004 winner at the Royal Agricultural Winter Fair. Their latest cultivar, and one that I love, is Bijou Rouge. With its deep garnet skin and creamy interior, it is perfect for a potato salad with just the smallest bit of vinaigrette. It should never be peeled. Bijou Rouge has another interesting characteristic—it has eyebrows, perhaps indicating a connection to a primitive, lumpy Andean potato similar to the one that Johnston used to create Yukon Gold.

While the Coffins were working in P.E.I., Johnston was still creating new potatoes on his own nickel right up until the time he passed away. Since his death, Currie and her colleague, the university's barley and wheat breeder Duane Falk, have carefully maintained the basic stock of those later potatoes. One is Ruby Gold, which cannot yet be sold because of legalities around its royalties. But potatoes can surprise even the most expert breeder, and Falk, himself an organic gardener, noted a particular tuber that was different from the rest in the same hill. He cultured it and now, four years later, he has one

of the prettiest potatoes I've seen—Golden Blush. It does have a blush, and each eye is dark red. With only about 45 kilograms of seed potatoes in existence, it will still be another three to four years before Golden Blush will be market ready, because of all the hoops and regulations that every notable spud must jump through. But when it comes to market as a premium potato, the Johnston legacy will live on.

Around the world, potatoes have taken their place on the tables of dozens of cultures, and those dishes have migrated to Canada. Potatoes are mashed into filling for Eastern European perogies (page 192) and piroshki or made into dough for knishes. Whipped well, they're the basis for feathery Italian gnocchi. When cut into large chunks, they can be made into the spice-laden Indian dish Aloo Gobi (page 180). (The latter was a favourite of my sons when they were eating the results of my experiments with the products of shop-owner Bharti Vibhakar, a well-loved spice dealer and blender in Kitchener, Ontario.) Potatoes can be simply sliced and stir-fried with the requisite ginger, garlic and soy in a style reminiscent of northern China or they can be grated to make crisp-bottomed Swiss rösti and the golden potato pancakes known by some as latkes (which I love with maple syrup), Sometimes I make bite-sized portions to hold my son Mark's line-caught Chinook, which he hot-smokes behind his home in Campbell River.

Florenceville, New Brunswick, is the home of McCain Foods, the world's largest and most successful french fry processor. McCain, a Canadian company, sells more frites *in France than any other company. It produces almost one-third of the world's supply, with 30 processing plants scattered globally.*

East Indian Potato and Cabbage Sauté (Aloo Gobi)

This spice-laden dish is a perfect example of how food traditions travel to new lands with ease. I first saw Aloo Gobi cooked by sari-clad Bharti Vibhakar at one of her cooking classes in her tiny store, The Spice of India, in Kitchener, Ontario. Seated on stacking chairs and lined up in front of her, we watched and listened intently as she mixed and chatted and stirred and chatted some more. Bharti is a dedicated vegetarian, so her sessions were peppered with gentle lectures on eating healthy non-meat-based foods. She has a talent for taking the most mundane vegetables and making them utterly irresistible.

Dolloped with chutney and mint-flavoured yogurt, this dish can be served as a main course or as a side dish. In India, it would have been made with cauliflower rather than cabbage, but in the winter, when cabbage is inexpensive and widely available, this variation is not only delicious but also frugal and very Canadian.

YIELD: 3 to 4 servings

> 3 tbsp (45 mL) canola oil
> 1 small cooking onion, minced
> 1 tsp (5 mL) cumin seeds
> ½ tsp (2 mL) black mustard seeds
> ½ tsp (2 mL) cayenne pepper or hot pepper flakes
> 1 tsp (5 mL) garam masala
> 4 cups (1 L) potato chunks
> ½ cup (125 mL) water
> 1 tbsp (15 mL) grated fresh ginger
> 3 to 4 cups (750 mL to 1 L) shredded cabbage

Heat the oil in a large skillet. Add the onion and cook, stirring, until beginning to brown. With a spatula, move the onion to the side of the pan and add the cumin and black mustard seeds, cooking until the seeds begin to pop, 15 to 20 seconds. Stir in the cayenne and garam masala; continue to cook for another 10 to 15 seconds or just enough to begin to brown the masala. Add the potatoes and toss gently to coat them with the spice mixture. Add the water, stir in the ginger and top with the cabbage. Cover and reduce heat to medium-low. Continue to cook until vegetables are tender.

* Widely available at Asian food stores

Barbecue-Roasted Baby Potatoes

This recipe comes from the kitchen and backyard of Trudy Heiss, co-owner of Gray Monk winery in British Columbia. She serves these potatoes with her Planked Okanagan Trout (page 80), but they are a terrific addition to almost any barbecued meal. Choose small potatoes or halve larger ones.

YIELD: 4 servings

2 lb (1 kg) baby potatoes
2 tbsp (30 mL) canola oil

BASTING SAUCE:
1 clove garlic, minced
1 shallot, minced
¼ cup (60 mL) canola oil
2 tbsp (30 mL) grainy Dijon mustard
½ tsp (2 mL) freshly ground pepper
1 tsp (5 mL) salt
2 tbsp (30 mL) chopped fresh rosemary

In a large pot of boiling water, partially cook the potatoes. Drain and let cool enough to handle. Cut larger ones in half. Toss with the canola oil; set aside.

Make the marinade by whisking together the garlic, shallot, oil, mustard, pepper, salt and rosemary. Place the potatoes on a preheated barbecue, brushing liberally with basting sauce. Turn and roast until tender, 7 to 10 minutes. Remove and serve immediately or hold in a warm oven.

Bijou Rouge is one of the nicest potato cultivars I've tasted. It was hybridized on P.E.I. by Robert and Joyce Coffin. This image was taken on Potato Research Day at the University of Guelph's station in Elora.

Creamy Scalloped Potatoes

"Old" potatoes, as opposed to "new" ones, are the best for this traditional recipe. Bake at the same time you're roasting your ham, and perhaps with a well-scrubbed, seeded winter squash dabbed with butter and wrapped in foil.

YIELD: 6 to 8 servings

¼ cup (60 mL) butter
¼ cup (60 mL) all-purpose flour
1 tsp (5 mL) dry mustard
1 tsp (5 mL) salt
½ tsp (2 mL) freshly ground pepper
3 cups (750 mL) milk
6 cups (1.5 L) sliced peeled potatoes
2 or 3 onions, minced
1 cup (250 mL) shredded cheddar cheese

In a heavy saucepan, melt the butter over medium heat; stir in the flour and cook, stirring, for 1 minute. Add the mustard, salt and pepper; cook for 10 to 15 seconds. Slowly whisk in the milk and cook, stirring constantly, until thickened and bubbling.

Pour one-quarter of the sauce into a buttered 8-cup (2 L) casserole. Top with alternating layers of potatoes, onions and remaining sauce, ending with the sauce on top.

Cover and bake in a preheated 375°F (190°C) oven for 15 minutes; reduce heat to 350°F (180°C) and continue baking for 1½ hours or until potatoes are tender.

Uncover, sprinkle with the cheese and continue to bake for 10 to 15 minutes or until the cheese is melted and just beginning to brown.

Potato Day is held every August at the University of Guelph's Elora Research Station. Growers and processors gather at the demonstration plot to observe how new varieties, often known only by their number, grow beside the spuds that are held up as the standards. Golden Blush is only one of the hundred-odd varieties in the field on this scorching summer afternoon.

Danish Sugar-Browned Potatoes

This Christmas side dish is great at any dinner, particularly now that small potatoes are widely available. One could imagine gardeners carefully saving the small potatoes after the harvest, especially for the festive table. In Tulle Knudsen's notes, she comments that it's "special good to Roast Pork, Turkey, Green Kale and other Things." Being a practical woman with dozens of mouths to feed at the Danish retirement home Sunset Villa, south of Guelph, Ontario, she would often resort to using well-drained canned potatoes, which she spread on a kitchen towel to dry before cooking.

YIELD: 4 servings

> **4 cups (1 L) small potatoes, peeled**
> **⅓ cup (75 mL) granulated sugar**
> **¼ cup (60 mL) salted butter**

Boil the potatoes in salted water until tender. Rinse in cold water and drain thoroughly.

In a heavy skillet, melt the sugar over medium heat, being careful not to let it burn. Stir in the butter; add potatoes and continue to stir, shaking them in the pan until browned, 10 to 12 minutes. Serve immediately.

Ruby Gold, a magnificent potato hybridized by the late Gary Johnston, the same gentleman who gave Yukon Gold to the world.

Cheese-Laced Rösti Potatoes

Chris Aerni, the chef-owner of Rossmount Inn, near St. Andrews, New Brunswick, came to Canada from Switzerland to work for the restaurant chain Mövenpick. After years based in Toronto and travelling across Canada, he jumped off the corporate ship and his wife, Graziella, purchased, one of Atlantic Canada's oldest inns, at the base of Chamcook Mountain overlooking Passamoquoddy Bay. He wrote the following about this classic Swiss dish:

When cooking rösti, it is important to have a dry potato. The potatoes are cooked with the skin on until soft. They are drained and cooled overnight or a full day without removing the skin!! While the potatoes are cooling—a little history!

A simple, regular family dinner on the farm in Switzerland would have been, or still is, a bowl of soup followed by boiled potatoes in the jacket, served steaming hot with fresh churned butter and a nice selection of cheeses. The potatoes replace the bread in this case. Since potatoes were a very inexpensive day-to-day item on the menu, one would always cook a little more than the family could eat. The leftover potatoes from dinner would then be used the next morning for a breakfast rösti with eggs sunny side up. If you were lucky, you would get some bacon with it, and if not, then at least the rösti would be cooked in pork fat.

For best results, it's important that the cooked potatoes are totally cooled. This will take away the starchiness and give you a nice dry, almost fluffy rösti that will take on the butter, pork or duck fat, or whatever is used for the frying.

Before potatoes were used, there were a lot of turnip and cabbage-like vegetables. One of the other root vegetables was a kind of yellow beet (not the kind we use today in a miniature form) that was huge; it was the size of a sugar beet. Once potatoes were introduced, the varieties were all late varieties and, of course, not as refined as they are today.

And potatoes also made good ham. A farmer's saying that I remember is "*Sauhaerdoepfu*," which is Bernese and means "pig potatoes." Potatoes were grown to feed the pigs. So the farmers had specially made large round boilers with a cover to cook the spud. On the upper side there was a small door to gain access to see if the potatoes were cooked. Once cooked, the potatoes were then smashed and often mixed with wheat.

The secret of this dish is to cook it slowly until a heavy, golden crust forms. Serve it with sour cream, some crisp endive salad and perhaps, if you can find them, strips of smoked Atlantic salmon belly. Chris likes to use Armadale Farm aged gouda from near Sussex, New Brunswick, but says any good, "local cheese with character" will work.

YIELD: 6 servings

4 large potatoes, preferably yellow fleshed
3 tbsp (45 mL) unsalted butter
½ cup (125 mL) minced onion
½ tsp (2 mL) salt
½ tsp (2 mL) freshly ground pepper
1 cup (250 mL) shredded cheese

Cook unpeeled potatoes in boiling water until nearly tender. Let cool completely and, if possible, let stand overnight. Peel and shred coarsely into a large bowl.

In a 10-inch (25 cm) skillet, melt 1 tbsp (15 mL) of the butter over medium heat; sauté the onion until tender. Add to the potatoes and season with salt and pepper.

Over medium heat, melt the remaining butter in the skillet used to sauté the onions. Pat the potato mixture evenly into the pan. Scatter the cheese on top; cover and reduce heat to low. Continue cooking until the underside is deep golden, about 20 minutes.

To serve, invert the potatoes onto a large, warmed plate and slice into wedges.

Chef Chris Aerni of Rossmount Inn shows off a wild harvest of Fundy periwinkles, on a bed of seaweed that he blanches till it's bright green.

TANZANIANS (ISMAILIS) IN CANADA

The Ismailis who live in Canada trace their heritage to South Asia, particularly to India, Pakistan and Bangladesh. They are part of the Shiite branch of Islam. The main wave of immigration was from Uganda during and after 1972.

Peach and Black Pepper Potatoes

Although his ancestral roots are in India's Punjab, Shaffeen Jamal's familial odyssey began on a farm at the foot of Mount Kilimanjaro, Tanzania, where he was born. It then took him to Birmingham, England, and finally across Canada by car to Vancouver, where he and his mother, Krishna, own and operate Tamarind Bistro. Their bistro is perfumed with the spices of India and is as fragrant a restaurant as you'll find anywhere.

Shaffeen's take on traditional dishes is decidedly avant-garde. Rather than serving typical chicken biryani, the celebratory dish from both India and Pakistan which insists on long-grain rice, he makes it into sushi rolls with the biryani as a side sauce. He also created a chocolate, nut-filled samosa, which he serves with tamarind ice cream. Awesome! From a culinary history perspective, it's interesting to note that Shaffeen's spice of choice in many of his dishes is black pepper, the authentic precursor to the fiery heat of the red peppers from the New World.

This recipe is adapted and streamlined from one Shaffeen shared with me. He uses mango purée, but because peaches have a similar flavour intensity, particularly when they're at their peak of ripeness, I blended a few into a sweet purée and stirred them into the spiced potatoes. The recipe worked perfectly—it's spectacular with roasted or grilled pork.

YIELD: 4 to 6 servings

1 lb (500 g) small potatoes
2 tbsp (30 mL) clarified butter (ghee)
1 cooking onion, minced or grated
2 tsp (30 mL) garam masala*
1 clove garlic, grated or minced
1 to 2 tsp (5 to 10 mL) grated fresh ginger
¼ tsp (1 mL) chili pepper flakes or cayenne pepper
½ tsp (2 mL) turmeric
Freshly ground pepper
1½ cups (375 mL) puréed fresh or frozen unsweetened peaches
Salt

*I like to store garam masala in the freezer to keep it fresh. Purchase it from any Indian grocery or spice merchant.

Cut the potatoes into quarters. Heat butter in a heavy skillet over medium heat and cook potatoes, partially covered to allow some of the steam to escape, until browned and tender. Remove cover, stir in the onion and cook until tender and beginning to brown. Add the garam masala, garlic, ginger, chili flakes and turmeric. Cook and stir until fragrant, 1 to 2 minutes. Add a good grinding of pepper. Sir in the peach purée and season to taste with salt. Reheat until bubbling to blend the flavours. Keep warm until ready to serve.

On a cool summer afternoon, with the clouds scudding overhead, Mom and her cousin, the late Anne Wilkinson, tramped through the Vineland orchard with peach technician Rocco Guarnaccia. They were picking some ripe fruit for me to freeze for University of Guelph Chancellor Lincoln Alexander's 80th birthday party, to be held in December 2001. Creating a feast to honour such an extraordinary gentleman was as much fun as actually eating it!

Island Potato Salad

An updated version of the traditional Irish dish champ, this recipe was adapted from one developed by Joy Shinn when she worked with the Prince Edward Island potato marketing board, FoodTrust. This salad is best served at room temperature or even a bit warm.

YIELD: 4 to 6 servings

2 lb (1 kg) P.E.I. potatoes (5 or 6)
4 slices prosciutto
3 green onions, sliced diagonally

DRESSING:
2 tbsp (30 mL) apple cider vinegar
1 tbsp (15 mL) liquid honey
1 tbsp (15 mL) grainy Dijon-style mustard
¼ cup (60 mL) canola oil
Salt and freshly ground pepper to taste

The Potato Museum at O'Leary on Prince Edward Island.

Place washed potatoes in a pot and cover with water. Cook, covered, over medium heat until fork-tender, 30 to 45 minutes, depending upon the size of the potatoes. Drain and let cool. Peel and quarter or, if large, dice coarsely. Set aside.

Arrange prosciutto on a baking tray; place under broiler and broil until crisp, about 10 minutes, turning partway through cooking. Let cool, then break into small pieces.

In a serving bowl, combine green onions, prosciutto and cooked potatoes.

DRESSING: Whisk or shake together the vinegar, honey, mustard and oil until blended. Pour over the potatoes, tossing gently. Season to taste with salt and top with a good grinding of pepper.

Gefu's Stir-Fried Potatoes

Gefu Wang-Pruski is a potato researcher at Nova Scotia Agricultural College, and she loves her spuds. She was born in Harbin, a city in northeastern China, and met her Polish husband, Kris, in Edmonton, where he was involved in saskatoon berry research long before that crop was commercialized. Like his wife, he is now "doing" potatoes. The way he likes them best? "Distilled!"

This recipe illustrates how potatoes, in many cultures, are treated like a vegetable rather than a starch.

YIELD: 4 servings

> 4 potatoes
> 2 tbsp (30 mL) canola oil
> 1 or 2 green onions, chopped
> 3 slices fresh ginger, minced
> 2 tsp (10 mL) light soy sauce
> ½ tsp (2 mL) salt
> Freshly ground pepper
> 3 tbsp (45 mL) water
> 1 clove garlic, minced

Peel and slice the potatoes thinly ("about the size of Ritz crackers," says Gefu). Place in a bowl and cover with cold water. Let stand for 1 to 2 minutes. Drain thoroughly. Set aside.

Heat the oil in a wok. Add the green onion and ginger. Stir-fry on high for 10 seconds; toss in potato slices and continue to stir-fry for 1 minute. Add the soy, salt, a generous grinding of pepper and water. Cover and simmer over medium heat for 5 minutes, stirring occasionally. Add the garlic and stir for 30 seconds. Serve with steamed rice.

Laundry dries in the river breezes on an August morning near Rivière-du-Loup.

Rural Life in Saskatchewan

This letter from Minnie Schindel paints a picture of life in northern Saskatchewan half a century ago.

We had a small dairy business on the farm and used to supply the town of Garrick with milk, cream and butter. We separated the milk with a hand separator, then Mom would let skim milk sit at room temperature till it was like jelly and hang it to drip. That was our cottage cheese.

We smoked our own bacon in the smokehouse and canned a lot of meatballs. Mom canned pork chunks with spices in quart sealers. We used to have pork roasts boiled with white beans. She rendered her own lard from the fat.

In the summer, when my uncle went fishing, he always brought us back some trout, which we dipped in flour, salt and pepper, then fried. We raised a lot of chickens, turkeys and geese, so we had a cellar full of canned chicken meat and a goose or a turkey for Christmas. The rest we would sell. We also sold eggs.

We always had a big garden that kept us in vegetables all year. The carrots, peas, beans and corn were canned. Mom bought fruit with the money from the fowl and preserved it. She saved all the down from the geese, and I am still using the pillows today. We always made sauerkraut in a 10-gallon crock topped with a plate weighted down with a stone.

We had lots of blueberries, which we picked up north in the muskeg, as well as pin cherries and chokecherries. These we made into jams and jellies. We grew our own strawberries, raspberries and lots of saskatoons. We also had a hazelnut tree and a gooseberry bush.

Mom made her own soap for washing clothes. She made lots of dill, mustard and beet pickles. Our cellar was always full of preserves made with sugar, as honey was scarce; nobody kept bees.

We ate lots of perogies, stuffed with our cottage cheese, and cabbage rolls made with ground pork, rice, onions, salt and pepper. She created all her own salad dressings and pancake syrup. The only groceries we had to buy were flour, sugar, salt, spices, tea and coffee.

In summer, we ate a lot of lettuce salads with homemade dressing and sliced cucumbers with sour cream, salt and pepper. For porridge, we ground our own wheat and flax.

(April 2, 2006)

The BEST Perogies

This classic Eastern European dish is filled with Prairie ingredients: good flour, garden potatoes, homemade cottage cheese and sometimes even wild mushrooms. The recipe comes from several sources. The first is Minnie Schindel of Medicine Hat, who has strong Ukrainian roots (see letter on page 191). The second is my Polish daughter-in-law, Magdalena, whose family arrived in Canada in 1989 after escaping the most recent wave of political upheavals. Magda's mother, Nina, still gathers wild porcini mushrooms in secret places near Calgary and sautés them in butter before stuffing the small squares of dough.

You can substitute round Asian dumpling wrappers if you don't have time to make the dough; they work perfectly.

YIELD: About 3 dozen, or 6 to 8 servings

DOUGH:
- 2 eggs
- 1 tsp (5 mL) salt
- 1 cup (250 mL) cold water
- 3 cups (750 mL) all-purpose flour

FILLING:
- 6 potatoes, peeled and coarsely chopped
- 2 onions, minced
- 2 tbsp (30 mL) butter
- 2 cups (500 mL) cottage cheese
- Salt and freshly ground pepper

GARNISH:
- 2 to 3 tbsp (30 to 45 mL) butter
- Sour cream
- Minced green onion (optional)
- Crisp bacon bits (optional)

In a medium bowl, beat the eggs; whisk in salt and water. Beat in flour to make a stiff dough. Turn out onto a floured surface and knead until smooth, 5 to 6 minutes. Cover and let rest while making the filling.

Cook the potatoes in boiling salted water until tender. Drain and mash. In a small skillet, cook the onions in the butter until browned. Meanwhile, rinse the cottage cheese under cold water; place in a colander or strainer and drain well. Stir the onions and cheese into the mashed potatoes. Season to taste with salt and pepper.

Roll out dough as thinly as possible on a floured surface. Cut into 2-inch (5 cm) squares. With floured fingers, pick up a square and stretch it slightly; spoon a small mound of filling on the centre and pinch shut. Lay on a floured baking sheet and cover. Repeat until all the squares are filled.

The perogies may be frozen prior to cooking in a single layer on the baking sheet. When frozen, package in plastic bags,

To cook, bring a pot of salted water to a boil. Reduce heat to medium and cook 6 to 8 perogies at a time until they float to the surface, about 10 minutes (12 to 14 minutes if frozen). Remove with a slotted spoon; toss with a little butter and keep warm while cooking the remaining perogies.

To serve, melt the remaining butter in a skillet and fry the perogies until golden brown. Pass a bowl of sour cream either plain or liberally laced with minced green onion and perhaps some crisp bacon bits.

Fishers arrive on North Knife Lake Lodge, Manitoba, in time for a shore lunch and an afternoon of fly-casting for northern pike.

Vanessa's Shepherd's Pie with Buttermilk Mashed Potato Topping

Vanessa Currie is a potato researcher and a fabulous cook. I remember Mom making shepherd's pie with the leftover Sunday roast beef; she'd put it through the grinder and moisten it with gravy she'd also saved. But when I told Vanessa, she observed wryly, "Who ever heard of a shepherd caring for a herd of beef? It makes no sense to use ground beef in a dish like this." So this is her recipe, and (sorry, Mom) it's fabulous!

Never one to miss an opportunity to hold forth on her favourite topic—good spuds—Vanessa writes:

A word about the potatoes—I suggest Yukon Gold where available. I would not recommend red skinned, or other yellow fleshed, especially the "low-carb" varieties. These types tend to have lower specific gravities and don't mash as nicely. Long whites and russets also work well for mashing. Round whites are highly variable, and consumers can't really be sure what they're getting. Stick with longs, russets and Yukons for mashed. It's not necessary to peel the potatoes. Most of the nutrients are in the peel. In fact, coloured flesh and skin potatoes have antioxidant activity comparable to spinach and Brussels sprouts. They also have high anthocyanins, flavonoids and carotenoids. Yellow fleshed and Yukon Gold are also high in carotenoids. In general, eating the skin is important, and if the skin is coloured, so much the better. If you chop the potatoes small enough, the peelings aren't objectionable. For this dish, I love to slice a few red Thai bird chilies (the really hot, small ones) over top of my plate. The heat from the chilies goes really well with the savoury flavours of the lamb and the mild mashed potatoes.

YIELD: 4 to 6 servings

1 lb (500 g) ground lamb
1 onion, chopped
1 clove garlic, minced
2 tbsp (30 mL) all-purpose flour
1 cup (250 mL) beef stock
1 tsp (5 mL) dried thyme
¼ cup (60 mL) chopped fresh parsley
1 tbsp (15 mL) Worcestershire sauce
Salt and pepper
1 to 1½ cups (250 to 375 mL) mixed frozen peas and carrots, or fresh peas
6 or 7 Yukon Gold potatoes
½ cup (125 mL) unsalted butter
¼ to ½ cup (60 to 125 mL) buttermilk

In a skillet, fry the lamb until starting to brown. Stir in the onion and garlic; continue cooking until the mixture is well browned. Stir in the flour and cook for 20 to 30 seconds. Whisk in the stock and cook until the mixture begins to thicken. Season with the thyme, parsley, Worcestershire sauce, and salt and pepper to taste. Stir in the frozen peas and carrots or the fresh peas. Transfer to a lightly oiled medium casserole.

Scrub the potatoes; quarter them and cook in a large pot of boiling well-salted water until tender. Drain and stir in the unsalted butter and buttermilk. Season generously with salt and pepper. Mix well and mash coarsely; spread over the meat. Run a fork over the top to make little ridges, which brown up nicely when cooked.

Bake, uncovered, at 375°F (190°C) for 1 hour or until golden on the top and bubbling around the sides.

Researcher Vanessa Currie in deep agronomic discussion with one of her guests at the annual Potato Day she organizes in August.

Braised Kale and Potatoes with Sausage (Stamppot)

Ali Kendall-Morris shared this traditional Dutch recipe, a substantial combination of well-mashed potatoes and hearty smoked sausage, with me from her home in Vancouver. She says that even Polish sausage would work, but a good, fully cooked smoked sausage is best. She and her family like it with mustard.

Kale is at its best after the first frost, and when it's served in Dutch homes, a small bowl or pitcher of vinegar is passed to dribble on top of it.

There are many variations of Stamppot. One uses fresh sausages, which are fried, and any fat that remains is added to the mashed kale and potato mixture, with the meat simply served on the side.

YIELD: 6 to 8 servings

1½ lb (750 g) kale
2 cups (500 mL) water
1 tsp (5 mL) salt
2½ lb (1.25 kg) potatoes (6 or 7), peeled and quartered
4 or 5 cooked smoked sausages
¼ cup (60 mL) butter
½ cup (125 mL) milk
White vinegar

Remove and discard the heavy stems from the kale. Slice into 1-inch (2.5 cm) pieces. In a large saucepan, bring the water and salt to a boil. Add the kale and cook until it begins to wilt. Toss in potatoes and sausage, cover, reduce the heat and cook until the potatoes are tender. Remove the sausage before mashing the vegetables thoroughly. Whip in butter and milk. Scoop into a heated serving bowl. Slice the sausage and pile it on top of the potatoes. Pass the vinegar so each diner can add it to taste.

Kale, mâche and mizuna at Cookstown
Greens in Ontario, after a rain.

Lucy Ong's Curry Chicken with Potatoes

This is another of Linda Chin's Malaysian family recipes, this time from "Aunty Lucy's" kitchen.

Galangal is a rhizome that resembles ginger in shape. It's found in Eastern Europe and Asia, where it's put to both medicinal and culinary use.

The "meat curry" powder can be found at many East Indian stores labelled as such. It's not fiery, so if you cannot find it, you can use medium curry powder instead. Lemongrass is available fresh and frozen (chopped) in many stores. If you want to try to grow it yourself, Richter's Herbs in Goodwood, Ontario (www.richters.com), has a mail-order service and will mail plants anywhere within Canada.

YIELD: 4 to 6 servings

> 1 whole chicken (4 lb/2 kg)
> 2 to 4 russet potatoes
> 1 onion
> 2 or 3 cloves garlic
> 1 tbsp (15 mL) chopped lemongrass
> 1 tsp (5 mL) galangal powder (optional) or 1-inch (2.5 cm) chunk fresh
>   galangal, peeled
> 2 tbsp (30 mL) meat curry powder
> 2 tbsp (30 mL) canola oil
> 1 cup (250 mL) water
> 1 can (398 mL) coconut milk
> Salt

Cut the chicken into serving pieces; set aside. Wash and chop the potatoes into large chunks; set aside.

In a blender or food processor, grind together the onion, garlic, lemongrass and galangal until a paste forms. Mix in the curry powder.

Heat oil in a large heavy pot over medium heat; fry ground curry paste mixture until fragrant, 1 to 2 minutes.

Add the chicken, stirring to coat it with spices. Add the water, cover and bring to a boil. Uncover and reduce heat; simmer for 8 to 10 minutes. Add the potatoes and continue cooking until both the chicken and potatoes are tender, about 30 minutes. Stir frequently, adding enough water to keep the simmering going.

When chicken and potatoes are cooked, stir in the coconut milk, salting the curry to taste. Simmer for a few more minutes and serve.

It wasn't until the 19th century that Malaysia, which includes Singapore, actually became a state. Immigration to Canada was a mere trickle in the 1970s (about 100 Malaysians came annually), but in the 1980s it jumped tenfold.

Brandade Chez Paulin

Gerard Paulin of Caraquet, New Brunswick, serves this traditional French appetizer with crusty bread and recommends serving it with pastis, the French anise-flavoured liqueur. The main ingredients—potatoes and salt cod—both come from New Brunswick.

Brandade de morue harks back to the early 1800s. Originally from the south of France, it was an emulsion of olive oil, milk and poached fish. It spread northward, and potato was added to the mix to ameliorate and blend the flavours where no olive oil was available. Grimod de la Reynière, one of the fathers of French gastronomy, wrote about a Parisian restaurateur who apparently made a fortune selling his particular version of brandade which used hake *(merluche)*.

What I find interesting is the connection to an Atlantic Canadian dish called Dutch Mess (page 87). The totally unappetizing name aside, the main components are very similar to those of *brandade de morue,* although reflective of the leaner times faced by the earlier Nova Scotia settlers.

YIELD: About 2½ cups (625 mL)

¼ lb (125 g) salt cod
1 can (385 mL) evaporated milk
1 onion, minced
½ lb (250 g) potatoes (about 2)
2 or 3 cloves garlic
3 tbsp (45 mL) lemon juice
¼ cup (60 mL) olive oil
Salt
Capers, drained, or roasted red peppers

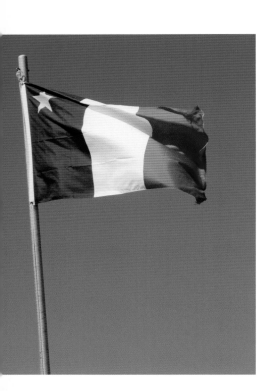

Throughout Atlantic Canada, the beautiful tri-colour Acadian flag flies proudly. But nowhere is it as prominent as on the New Brunswick coastal highways that lead to and from Caraquet.

Soak the salt cod in cold water overnight. In the morning, drain and transfer to a saucepan. Add the milk and onion; bring to a boil. Reduce heat and simmer for 20 to 30 minutes or until the fish flakes easily. Watch carefully as it can boil over.

Meanwhile, peel and cube the potatoes; cook in salted water until tender. Drain and transfer to a food processor. With a slotted spoon, add the cooked fish to the food processor along with ½ cup (125 mL) of the cooking liquid, the garlic, lemon juice and oil. Process until smooth. Add salt to taste. Continue to process until the mixture is very smooth.

Garnish with capers or roasted red peppers. Serve with hot baguettes.

Potato Buttermilk Doughnuts

At Potato World, a museum in the heart of New Brunswick's potato-growing region near Woodstock, you can taste doughnuts like these.

If you've never made doughnuts, this is a good recipe to start with. Baking powder is the leavening rather than yeast. The mashed potatoes are the secret ingredient, keeping them moist and flavourful. These doughnuts also freeze beautifully. Doughnut cutters are available at kitchen supply or hardware stores, or you can improvise with two well-washed tin cans of different sizes.

YIELD: **About 30 doughnuts and centres**

1 cup (250 mL) hot mashed potatoes
1 tbsp (15 mL) melted butter
½ cup (125 mL) buttermilk
1 cup (250 mL) granulated sugar
1 egg
1 tsp (5 mL) vanilla extract
2½ cups (625 mL) all-purpose flour
½ tsp (2 mL) salt
1 tbsp (15 mL) baking powder
Canola oil, for frying
Plain or cinnamon sugar*

In a large bowl, whip together the mashed potatoes, butter, buttermilk and sugar. Beat in the egg and vanilla.

Sift together the flour, salt and baking powder. Add to the potato mixture, combining until no dry spots remain.

In a heavy, deep saucepan or deep-fryer, begin to heat the oil to 350°F (180°C), using an accurate deep-frying thermometer.

Roll out the dough on a lightly floured board to about 1-inch (2.5 cm) thickness. Cut into round doughnuts, reserving the centres. Fry the doughnuts and the "holes" in batches in the hot oil, turning with wooden chopsticks or tongs until golden on both sides, about 3 minutes per side. The timing is approximate, depending on the frying method.

Remove, drain on paper towels and roll in cinnamon sugar or simply plain granulated or icing sugar. Store in a tightly covered container.

*To make cinnamon sugar, stir 1 tsp (5 mL) cinnamon into ½ cup (125 mL) granulated sugar.

POTATO WORLD
Potato World, located just outside Florenceville, New Brunswick, is a wonderful museum celebrating the impact the potato made on that region's earliest settlers. The museum is filled with potato memorabilia, particularly antique farm equipment, and honours the heroes of the industry. At the Harvest Café, you can buy really great hand-cut french fries or simply have a coffee with a freshly made potato doughnut.

Dairy & Eggs

Perfect inn-made yogurt swirled with Quebec's best maple syrup at Restaurant L'eau à la Bouche, in Ste. Adèle.

*m*ilk and eggs. There are few foods so basic, so absolutely elemental to the Canadian diet. They are often the ultimate comfort food and can be as simple as a perfect poached egg, its yolk soaking into a slice of warm buttered toast, or memory-laden milk pudding thickened with Irish moss, once eaten in a distant homeland. They are exquisite foods: perfectly ripened cheeses that fill our national history; rich, sour yogurt to spoon onto spicy Persian-inspired stews; silky custard-based ice cream studded with bits of maple sugar.

These foods are so ancient and were so widely distributed in the Old World that every group of settlers who came across the water brought some sort of dairy-egg culture with them. Cows were brought to New France by both Jacques Cartier in the 1540s and Samuel de Champlain in 1610. In 1611, Governor John Gray of Newfoundland wrote a flowery passage in his diary in anticipation of how well cattle would do, suggesting that the pasture was so good that a herd of 300 would manage well. In that same diary, he jotted the first record of eggs being laid plentifully in Canada by a flock on a farm near Conception Bay.

The Acadians on Prince Edward Island, like their cousins in the rest of what was to become Atlantic Canada, developed a system of "pasturing" their cows in the forest. It was almost identical to the system used in medieval Europe. Since there were no commercial feed mills and the cows barely survived the long winters, the settlers had to be savvy. In anticipation of the reduced milk supply, they made cheese to preserve the summer's abundance for the dark months that followed.

In the early 1800s, Catharine Parr Traill described the situation in *The Female Emigrant's Guide:*

> The want of succulent food during the long winter is one of the causes of a deficiency in the butter producing qualities of milk. Where roots, such as good sound turnips, cannot be had, the deficiency might be supplied by boiling oats, in a good quantity of water.

She cautioned that milking times had to be regular and "in the morning, as early as possible . . ." so that "the cow may go forth to feed while the dew is still on the herbage." She also provided methods for preserving butter for long periods of time by mixing it with salt, saltpetre and sugar, putting it into stone jars and covering the mixture with brine. She rejoiced that since more land was being cleared for real pasture, the Canadian settler was finally able to add enough cows to the herd to make cheese.

As she was writing in the early 1800s, cheesemaking had indeed become part of the culture of all regions of Canada, including British Columbia and Alberta. In the 1830s, Lydia and Hiram Ranney, farmers from Vermont, moved to Oxford County, Ontario, where Lydia started making cheese with the milk produced by five cows. She was a real innovator, much like another Oxford County woman, Elizabeth Elliott, who was also one of the pioneers. The Ranney enterprise was larger, but both of these reportedly feisty women improved the handling of cheese and the mechanics of making it. It was Lydia Ranney who introduced the technique of "cheddaring." Farms were expanding, and forage was plentiful. By the early 1850s, the Ranneys owned 550 acres and more than 100 cows and had shipped a 1,200-pound cheese (550 kilograms) to London's Great Exhibition.

By Confederation, Ontario had at least 200 cheese factories, and during 1867 the Canadian Dairyman's Association was founded in Ingersoll. Cheesemaking was big business. In 1893, the railway sheds in Perth were the nursery for the "Canadian Mite," a cheese that weighed in at 22,000 pounds (10,000 kilograms). It had taken 12 cheesemakers working at their respective factories to make the giant cheese. It was shipped to Chicago for the World's Fair, where it crashed through the floor of the exhibit hall. By 1904, Canada was exporting about 234 million pounds (160 million kilograms) of cheese annually, most of which went to Great Britain.

In tandem with eastern Canada's development, dairying was beginning to get a foothold in British Columbia. By 1847, Fort Victoria had two productive dairies. Even Fort Macleod in Alberta had milk and butter from a herd of dairy cattle that had been driven over the border from Montana. In 1888, the cheese factory in Grenfell, Saskatchewan, was producing some 60,000 pounds (27,000 kilograms) annually, and by 1889, a cooperative cheese factory had been established at Langenburg.

Together with the expansion of dairy herds, technology began to offer solutions to the arduous labour. The cream separator and, eventually, the milking machine made dairying infinitely less difficult. But when the infant son of Ontario homemaker Adelaide Hoodless died from drinking contaminated milk in 1889, Hoodless realized that education had to work hand in glove with

CHEESEMAKING IN EARLY CANADA

When Catharine Parr Traill was writing in the early 1800s, cheesemaking had indeed started to become part of the culinary culture of all regions in Canada. Her observations in *The Female Emigrant's Guide, and Hints on Canadian Housekeeping* offer some wonderful insights:

> The reason of the neglect of this valuable portion of dairy produce is evident. During the process of clearing wild land, the want of a sufficiency of pasture for cows, obliges the prudent farmer to limit this branch of his stock, according to his supply of fresh grass and dry provender for their support; consequently, for some years, he is unable to keep cows enough for the profitable manufacturing of cheese as well as butter; but now the country is opening out on every side, and there were many fine cleared farms of long standing, and under good cultivation, dairies are increasing everywhere, and the farmer's wife is beginning to see the great advantage of making good cheese, for which an excellent market can be obtained.

This book is available online in electronic format in the University of Guelph's library. Go to Collections, then to Culinary Collection.

For a detailed account of cheesemaking in Ontario, read Heather Menzies' great book, *By the Labour of Their Hands: The Story of Cheddar Cheese in Ontario* (Quarry Press, 1994).

The Elmira Produce Auction Cooperative was created in 2004 in response to the need for a system of better distribution between primarily Old Order Mennonite growers and the central Ontario public and was inspired in part by Waterloo County's innovative Foodlink program. Just-picked fruits, vegetables and flowers are sold in bulk lots mainly to restaurant owners and independent retailers. Held two or three times a week depending on the time of year, the auctions give the concept of field to fork a whole new meaning. On the day of the sale, buyers obtain a number and the auction proceeds at lightning pace.

this new industry. She campaigned mightily for the study of "domestic science" in schools and founded The Women's Institute to help educate the farm women of the day. The Women's Institute grew swiftly and is now a worldwide association of country women with links to more than 70 countries.

At the same time, educators from what is now the University of Guelph were teaching cheesemaking from a mobile classroom that travelled from farm to farm in southern Ontario. In 1893, the first on-campus course was established. In 1947, Dr. Don Irvine, a St. Catharines–born Guelph grad, returned to Guelph from Wisconsin, where he'd been teaching. He saw a huge need for instruction. "Lots of people were trying to make cheese, but they weren't doing a very good job of it," he said. It was in that context that he started the one-week short courses in making specialty cheeses like blue and Romano and Swiss. The courses are still running today, with Dr. Irvine's protégé, Dr. Art Hill, at the helm. Graduates from Dr. Hill's courses populate the cheese scene across Canada and have improved both the quality and the quantity of cheese production from coast to coast.

Cheesemaking also began to flourish in Quebec during the late 1800s. The French tradition of innovative cheeses has been rooted in Quebec since 1893, when the Trappist monks made their first rendition of Brittany's Port-Salut and named it Oka. Quebeckers even had their own special cow, the Canadienne, the breed that is said to have descended from the cows brought to Canada by both Cartier and Champlain. The Canadienne has the distinction of being the only dairy breed developed on this continent.

Yet when I first began my writing career in the early 1980s, I could count and name Canada's good specialty cheeses on my fingers. The entire industry, from coast to coast, had hiccuped, homogenized and increased production. The specialty cheeses of yore were nearly all being wiped off the culinary scene and were on their way to extinction.

Thankfully, Canada, for centuries, has had a strong underground cheese culture, one that has existed outside the traditional distribution systems. Bartered rather than sold, or simply made at home for the family, these are also the very real, secret cheeses of our nation. The influence of tradition—Italian, Portuguese, Scots, Mennonite—as well as the availability of online and on-campus training, has created a group of excellent amateur cheesemakers from coast to coast, and it's largely from these somewhat anarchistic roots that the current revolution began.

The modern-day Renaissance—and anyone who visits the specialty cheese shops that are springing up with wild abandon across the nation will see it—began in Quebec. As a province, it has encouraged this aspect of its culture more actively than any other jurisdiction in Canada. By the late 1990s, an authentic Oka was reborn: Le Migneron was created in the Charlevoix, and from the monks at Abbaye Saint-Benoit in the Eastern Townships came Bleu Bénédictin.

With all the synergy in Quebec's cheese industry, Ontarians looked east with envy. Why was it in the province that had created the Mighty Mite, the industry had faltered and choked? So little was left, save memories, of an incredibly rich history. Corporate buyouts of the myriad small factories and their subsequent closures certainly didn't help. For farmers and aspiring entrepreneurs in British Columbia and, to a lesser extent, the Prairie provinces and Atlantic Canada, the rebellious and courageous Quebec cheesemakers of the 1980s and '90s were models of activism and of cheesemaking skill.

Today, all across the nation, there are scores of producers, with many that could easily compete on the world stage. It's an extraordinary list. Sheep's milk brie from Chase, B.C., and the gorgeous David Wood creations from Saltspring Island. There are fabulous aged Goudas made by Sylvan Star and the Parmesan-style Leoni Grana from Alberta. In the southern Manitoba town of Bothwell, once renowned for its great cheddar, a new wave of cheesemakers is creating some of the most interesting cheeses around. My pick is the cheddar, which is aged in Old Vine Foch Reserve, a lush red wine from Okanagan's Quails Gate Estate Winery. Ontario is regaining renown for quintessential cheddars, from Balderson to Maple Dale to Jensen's, and produces a superb collection of sheep's and goat's milk cheeses.

There's also Quebec's full-flavoured Pied-de-Vent from Les Îles de la Madeleine, and Fritz Kaiser's Le Douanier, with the thin layer of ash running through the centre. It's hard to imagine a cheese that's creamier than Le Riopelle, named after the province's most famous artist, unless it's Upper Canada Dairy's Guernsey milk Comfort Cream! Nova Scotia's Fox Hill creates a marvellous array of products, from squeaky curds to quark to creamy havarti. And in Upper Economy, The Dutchman makes amazing black-waxed cylinders of pungent, palate-tingling Dragon's Breath. Not to be outdone, New Brunswick's artisan cheesemaker La Bergerie aux Quatres Vents is producing excellent raw milk cheeses, most notably Le Sieur de Duplessis and Oka-style Tomme de Champs Doré.

But it's a cheese from Ontario's Back Forty Artisan Cheese in Lanark County that gets my vote as one of the most delicious cheeses I've tasted anywhere on earth. Snow Road is a magnificent, albeit fragile, creation, a mixed rind soft cheese that has an extraordinary nutty flavour and points the way for the future of cheese in the nation.

Although the Romans enjoyed ices, it wasn't until the 1600s that the name "ice cream" was first written on a menu in Britain, outlining the dishes of the

Letting the whey drip from Easter cheese.

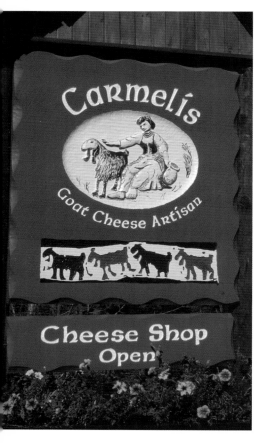

The sign for Carmelis Cheese Shop in the Okanagan Valley, B.C. (For the full story see p. 226.)

Feast of St. George. The Italians claimed *gelati,* the Indians had their *kulfi* and the Spanish took their version of ice cream to Southeast Asia.

In 1768, Alexander Menut of Quebec City wrote that making *fromage glacé à la bourgeoise* (iced cheese à la bourgeoise) was a way of creating a feast for "a reasonable price." According to historians Marc Lafrance and Yvon Deloges, authors of *A Taste of History,* the dish was a sweetened mixture of egg, milk and heavy cream, which, after cooking, was flavoured with lemon extract and frozen in a tin mould. "In the 18th century [in Quebec], water ices, ice cream and iced cheeses, as well as sherbet, were very successful. Competition to attract customers was very stiff, but the highest-quality products were found in Montreal, where the renowned Dillon sold 'Circuna Gelata,' the famous Italian ice cream."

Like cheesemaking, ice cream production in Canada was enhanced immensely by education. William Neilson (1844–1915) was the founder of the empire we know as Neilson's Dairy and, of course, Neilson's chocolate. But he was not always a brilliantly successful entrepreneur. In fact, he had a number of failures before his wife, Mary, and son, Fred, attended dairy school at the Ontario Agricultural College in Guelph in 1900. In 1903, he began to sell "bricks" of ice cream, packaging them in pints that were perfect for the households of the day, since they had limited refrigeration. In fact, most had iceboxes, requiring the delivery of ice every couple of days. Neilson's incorporated and opened a factory on Gladstone Avenue, Toronto, that had a capacity to produce 2,500 gallons of ice cream a day. By 1910, Neilson had saturated the Toronto market entirely and was sourcing milk through his own dairy in southwestern Ontario. Meanwhile, in 1914, the dairy school that Mary and Fred Neilson had attended introduced a full-fledged course in ice cream making, still the only one of its kind in Canada.

Chickens and other poultry were also a substantial part of the barnyard troop in early Canada, but were rarely noted at any length in early writings. Lescarbot mentioned them being present in Nova Scotia in 1606, and later the Recollet and Jesuit missionaries in Upper Canada mentioned them in letters home. By the 1800s, flocks of numerous species of poultry could be found throughout Canada, but it wasn't until the latter part of that century that anyone took on the research of improving egg production. In 1888, A.C. Gilbert was appointed Dominion Poultryman, reporting directly to William Saunders. His mission, above all else, was to search for high-laying strains of hens. Nineteen breeds were identified from North America and Britain. Gilbert wrote a manual on egg production before turning his efforts toward improving production during winter months and determining which hen laid the best-tasting egg, a characteristic that deserves way more attention in the labs of many modern researchers.

In 1897, Gilbert reported that a farmer who was raising 50 hens could expect 4,773 eggs during the year, and the return on them would be $78.69. Some eggs would be sold for hatching, and some birds would be sold for meat, yielding a total return of $139.19. Feed would cost $46.26 annually, for a lordly profit of $92.93.

Research in field and nest trials continued over the decades, but the most substantial new contribution is very recent: the introduction to the marketplace of the omega-3 egg, a direct response to the negative media around the link between the cholesterol in eggs and its impact on heart health. University of Guelph researcher Steve Leeson pioneered the technique of feeding chickens flaxseed to enrich the eggs they lay. The benefits of omega-3 fatty acids, particularly in fish oils, have been validated: they reduce the risk of heart attacks and strokes. When a diet rich in omega-3 was fed to both cattle and chickens to see whether fatty acids would be present in the animals' milk and the eggs, the results were positive. Eggs enriched with omega-3 are widely available. While the total fat content of the eggs remains the same, the unsaturated fat levels rise. Like fish and flax and soybeans, these eggs have become an acceptable, and delicious, part of a heart-healthy diet, ideally one that begins early in life.

Dairy products and eggs have always been more than just essential elements of what nutritionists call "a healthy diet." They are culinary stars, central to the Canadian table, be they made into Mennonite Easter Cheese (page 216) or baked into a glorious Gâteau Basque (page 219); layered in cheese-spiked Spanakopita (page 210) or oozing from the crust of a perfect butter tart (page 222).

Said to be Canada's oldest grocery store, J. A. Moisan (circa 1871) is an absolutely delightful ancient shop packed with avant-garde products, many of them made in Quebec. Some of the cheeses, like Pied-de-Vent, are often seasonal and difficult to find.

Chilled Sour Cream–Laced Cucumber Soup

In Australia, which author Bill Bryson dubbed "the sunburnt country," and from whence this recipe comes, cooks are expert at cold soups. Transplanted Aussie June Pearson shared this recipe with me when she lived in Guelph. It's unusual in that the cucumber is cooked and then simmered in chicken stock. When I made it one summer morning, I tasted it while it was still hot and, like Nettie Stanoyev's Fabulous Fresh Bean Soup (page 34), it can also be served as a prelude to a good winter meal. If you'd prefer to lighten it a bit and add extra tang, stir in buttermilk instead of sour cream.

YIELD: 6 servings

2 English cucumbers
1 tbsp (15 mL) butter
1 tbsp (15 mL) canola oil
1 small onion, minced
2 tbsp (30 mL) all-purpose flour
3 cups (750 mL) chicken or vegetable stock
Salt and white pepper
1 cup (250 mL) sour cream or buttermilk
1 clove garlic, crushed and minced
Minced green onion, chives or chive blossoms

Dice the cucumbers without peeling; set aside. Melt the butter with the oil in a saucepan over medium heat; cook the onion and cucumber, stirring occasionally, until softened, about 15 minutes. Stir in flour; continue to cook for 1 to 2 minutes. Add stock and bring to a boil. Cover, reduce heat and simmer for 20 minutes. Remove from the heat; purée using a hand blender. Stir in salt and white pepper to taste.

Refrigerate for at least 6 hours to chill or preferably overnight. Before serving, stir in the sour cream; add the garlic and purée with a hand blender or in a food processor until smooth. Serve in chilled bowls. Garnish with minced green onion, chives or chive blossoms.

A bouquet of chive blossoms.

Margaret's Peas and Eggs

Living in the Azores in the early 1950s was hard. There was a dictatorship, and many of Canada's Portuguese community immigrated at that time. Margaret Timmins' father, a draftsman, came in 1957, and since Canada wanted farmers at that time, that's what he said he was. He was sent to Winnipeg on the train from Montreal and was put to work on a railway crew. He was there for a mere 36 hours before he scraped together the bus fare to Toronto, where his cousin lived. He became a painter and never did get back to drafting. "It was all about hard work," says Margaret (a.k.a. Margarida Ferreira), who immigrated with her mother when she was three.

This Azorian dish is another one from the Ferreira kitchen in Cambridge, Ontario (see Peppery Portuguese Fish Stew, page 86, and Azorian Rice Pudding, page 238). It's about as fast a supper meal as anyone can make. Each diner gets an egg, some sausage and some peas. Chouriço is the Portuguese version of spicy chorizo sausage; it comes from the Iberian Peninsula.

YIELD: 4 servings

2 tbsp (30 mL) olive oil
1 onion, minced
2 cloves garlic, minced
2 tbsp (30 mL) pimento sauce*
1 lb (500 g) chouriço sausage, thinly sliced*
3 cups (750 mL) frozen peas
4 eggs
Salt and white pepper

In a skillet, heat the oil over medium heat; sauté the onion and garlic until browned. Stir in pimento sauce and chouriço. Cook for 3 to 4 minutes. Add the peas and cook, stirring, until thawed and completely heated through. While this mixture is steaming hot, crack the eggs on top. Season lightly with salt and white pepper. Cover and cook until the yolks are hard, 5 to 7 minutes.

*Available at Portuguese grocery stores

HEN TRIVIA

If you ever get close enough to look, you can tell which hens lay white and which lay brown eggs by the colour of their earlobes. And, *yes*, chickens do have earlobes! White earlobes mean white eggs; red earlobes mean brown eggs.

Buttery Phyllo Filled with Spinach and Cheese (Spanakopita)

I ate my first spanakopita, a Greek dish, on a light station perched high over the Pacific and surrounded by gardens filled with chard and curly kale and spinach. The perimeter was thick with salmonberries, blackberries and leathery salal. Although I've adapted this recipe, the original was first published in *The Lighthouse Cookbook* (Harbour Publishing, 1988).

The phyllo, made with Canadian wheat, can be purchased in large supermarkets or in one of the myriad Middle Eastern shops found everywhere from North Vancouver to Halifax. In downtown Montreal with my friends Anne Desjardins, Pierre Audette and René Fortin, I saw phyllo being handmade in a large, warehouse-like factory, its air misted with flour.

YIELD: 8 to 10 generous servings

> 2 tbsp (30 mL) butter
>
> 4 minced green onions
>
> 6 to 8 cups (1.5 to 2 L) fresh spinach, chard and/or kale, chopped
>
> ⅓ cup (75 mL) chopped fresh dill
>
> 1 tsp (5 mL) salt
>
> ½ tsp (2 mL) freshly ground pepper
>
> 3 eggs, beaten
>
> ½ lb (250 g) feta cheese, crumbled
>
> 1 large clove garlic, minced or grated
>
> ½ to ⅔ cup (125 to 150 mL) unsalted butter
>
> ½ lb (250 g) phyllo pastry, thawed

Melt the 2 tbsp (30 mL) butter in a large saucepan over medium heat; cook the green onions until tender and wilted. Stir in the spinach, chard and/or kale. Add the dill, salt and pepper. Cover and cook until the greens are almost tender, 4 to 6 minutes. Drain off excess liquid and let cool for 10 to 15 minutes. Chop vegetables finely.

Combine the eggs with the cheese and garlic; stir into the spinach mixture.

Melt the remaining butter and brush the bottom and sides of an 8- x 12-inch (3 L) baking pan. Lay 1 sheet of phyllo across the width of the pan and brush with butter; repeat with 3 more sheets, folding and buttering each sheet lightly. Pour in the spinach mixture and spread evenly. Top with 4 more sheets of phyllo, buttering each generously. (Refrigerate the unused phyllo, tightly wrapped, for another use.) With a very sharp knife, score the top few layers into serving portions.

Bake in a 375°F (190°C) oven for 30 to 35 minutes or until deep golden brown. Let stand for 10 minutes to set a little before serving.

After touring the floury factory at Produits de Pâtisserie Orientale, my friend Pierre Audette jumped to shake off the residue. These are his footprints on the pavement.

Creamy Coleslaw

This salad is often served as a side dish for fish 'n' chips, but it took me years to find *the* recipe. Rich and creamy and absolutely delicious, it's one I've adapted from a method shared with me by a German lady at Toronto's St. Lawrence Market. You can vary the vegetables as you wish, even adding small florets of fresh broccoli or cauliflower if you like.

YIELD: 6 to 8 servings

6 cups (1.5 L) shredded cabbage
2 carrots, peeled and shredded
1 celery stalk, diced
1 cup (250 mL) diced or shredded fennel
3 green onions, finely minced

DRESSING:
½ cup (125 mL) sour cream
¾ cup (175 mL) mayonnaise
1 tbsp (15 mL) granulated sugar
1 tbsp (15 mL) cider vinegar
2 tsp (10 mL) chopped fresh dill
Salt and freshly ground pepper

In a large bowl, toss together the cabbage, carrots, celery, fennel and onions. In a separate small bowl, stir together the sour cream, mayonnaise, sugar, vinegar and dill.

Mix with the cabbage, seasoning to taste with salt and pepper. Cover and refrigerate, chilling thoroughly, before serving.

Old-Fashioned Creamy Boiled Salad Dressing

This was the only salad dressing my mother and grandmother kept on hand before the advent of vinaigrettes in Canada. It's a concentrate and can be used as is, to spread on sandwiches in place of mayonnaise, which was, in those days, another nearly unheard-of food in rural Ontario. Or this dressing was diluted with two parts milk to one part dressing to toss with the tender spring greens just harvested from the farm garden. Equal parts of light sour cream and this dressing make one of the best potato salad dressings ever invented.

YIELD: 3½ cups (875 mL)

6 tbsp (90 mL) all-purpose flour
6 tbsp (90 mL) granulated sugar
2 tbsp (30 mL) dry mustard
2 tsp (10 mL) salt
⅔ cup (150 mL) white vinegar
3 eggs, separated
2 cups (500 mL) milk

In a heavy saucepan or in the top of a double boiler, stir together the flour, sugar, mustard and salt until no lumps remain. Whisk in the vinegar, egg yolks and milk. Cook over medium heat or saucepan of rapidly boiling water, stirring constantly, until thickened and pudding-like, for 8 to 10 minutes over direct heat, or for about 15 over boiling water.

In a separate bowl, beat egg whites until foamy. Whisk in about 1 cup (250 mL) of the thickened hot dressing. Return it all to the saucepan or double boiler and continue to cook over low heat or simmering water until steaming. Pour into clean glass jars. Refrigerate for up to 10 days.

Lettuce in Don Oliver's Nova Scotia garden.

MARGARET SHERK'S HOMESTYLE COTTAGE CHEESE

This light, slightly sour cottage cheese is traditional in the Mennonite homes of Waterloo and Wellington counties, and is unlike any cheese I've ever tasted.

Margaret Sherk, who lives just north of Elora, Ontario, usually makes this cottage cheese with raw milk. However, it's possible to make a very acceptable facsimile with "boughten" milk from the supermarket. Serve the resulting piquant cheese with fresh apple butter—it's best when smeared on warm bread—or in a small bowl, anointed with the season's first-run maple syrup.

Makes about 1½ lb (750 g)

1 cup (250 mL) buttermilk
6 cups (1.5 L) milk, either 2% or homogenized

Combine the buttermilk and milk in a large glass jar. Shake to blend. Let stand at room temperature for 4 days. When it has completely separated, transfer to a cheesecloth, gathering it up so it can be hung over a bowl deep enough to ensure that the cheese is not touching the whey that drains off. Refrigerate for a few hours or overnight. Discard whey; refrigerate cheese in an airtight container.

Indian Fresh Cheese (Paneer)

This fresh cheese is a staple in Indian kitchens. But as with so many so-called easy recipes, there are a few tricks, so I enlisted my Kashmiri friend Manjit Singh Bali to show me how he makes paneer. These are his instructions.

The saucepan should be heavy and about twice the size of the volume of milk. You can use any milk—pasteurized, raw, homogenized (3.5%) or even 2% although the latter will not give you as much cheese. To make a smaller batch, use ⅓ cup (75 mL) vinegar for 6 cups (1.5 L) milk.

YIELD: 1½ lbs (750 g)

1 bag (4 L) homogenized milk
1 cup (250 mL) white vinegar

In a large heavy saucepan over medium-high heat, bring the milk to a boil uncovered and without stirring.

When the bubbles cover the surface of the milk and it looks as though it is going to begin to boil, gradually pour in the vinegar, swirling it around the entire surface. Within moments, the milk will start to break and curdle. Continue to simmer, without stirring, for 2 to 3 minutes or until a cap of solids has floated to the top. Cover and set aside for 20 minutes to cool.

Strain through a cheesecloth-lined colander. Tighten the cheesecloth to press out the extra liquid, the whey. Let drain for 30 to 40 minutes. Press gently to flatten and release more whey. Refrigerate until needed.

Basic Yogurt

Yogurt is simply milk that has been thickened with a starter. The starter can be either a plain purchased yogurt or some that's been saved from a previous batch of yogurt you've made. While yogurt makers are available at many hardware or cooking supply stores, I simply set the filled containers into a roasting pan and fill it with warm water. To incubate it, turn on the oven briefly, just long enough to warm it, set the pan on the lowest rack and turn on the oven light. This will incubate the yogurt in 3 to 4 hours.

YIELD: About 6 cups (1.5 L)

4 cups (1 L) homogenized milk (3.5%)
1 can (385 mL) evaporated milk
½ cup (125 mL) plain yogurt

In a saucepan, heat the homogenized and evaporated milk together until lukewarm.

In a small bowl, whisk the yogurt with a little of the warmed milk; add to saucepan. Mix well and pour into clean jars. Cover with a clean dishtowel and incubate at 110° to 120°F (43° to 48°C) until set, 3 to 4 hours. Refrigerate.

Anne Desjardins is unquestionably one of Canada's most talented chefs. She carries her culinary artistry far beyond the kitchen and fills both her inn, L'Eau à la Bouche, and her home with glorious, sunny paintings that reflect her joy of life and good food.

The small hamlet of Millbank, Ontario, is steeped in Mennonite tradition. There, cheesemaker Ruth Klahsen makes small batches of stellar sheep's milk cheese. Her dairy, Monforte, supplies many of the region's top restaurants and, because she believes in the concept of tithing, she donates 10 percent of all Monforte's income to Médecins sans frontières/Doctors without Borders, the Nobel Prize–winning humanitarian aid organization. Monforte cheeses are found at the Stratford Farmers Market on Saturdays.

Easter Cheese

The Mennonite community has a very strong presence in central Canada. Many Mennonites still plough their fields with horses and go to town in buggies. There are others who merely drive black cars. They believe in helping each other and depending on no one except themselves. Their larger community is one of the most socially conscious groups on earth, with Mennonite aid workers all over the globe. In Ontario, a number of "old order" families do not participate in government-offered health care, and dozens of farms have neither electricity nor telephones. In a wired nation like Canada, this takes real determination and faith.

For many Mennonites, life tends to move with the cycles of the years. Like most of our ancestors, today's Mennonites are in tune with the changing seasons. There is a time for everything, from cutting wood and planting to piecing quilts and making sauerkraut.

Late winter is a season of frozen fields and icy roads. Families and neighbours work together to restock their larders. Pigs and cattle are slaughtered in a communal effort to make farmer's sausage and summer sausage, smoked pork chops, thick, rind-on bacon, cured hams and headcheese. When the thick coils of sausage are made, some are cooked and then preserved in jars, covered in the lard rendered from the same pig.

These preserved sausages are a favourite, and essential, fast food, all that is needed for a quick Sunday dinner after church. They can be fried in just a few minutes, and served with cream, sliced potatoes and a jar of pickles. Probably a jar of whole spiced beets or a chunky cucumber pickle would be opened if it's just the family. But if there's company, one of the children will be sent to fetch a jar of baby corn.

Spring truly begins in early March, when the maple sap begins to run. The trees are tapped with metal spigots, off which pails hang. A sleigh is drawn through the forest, and the buckets are collected and taken to a small shack, where the sap is boiled down into syrup. Sometimes farmers use a network of plastic piping that links the trees with one central collection tank. For about a month, wisps of evaporating steam can be seen curling from many a hardwood forest in Wellington and Waterloo counties in central Ontario. Although some Mennonites still make maple sugar, the main product today is syrup, which is sold at the roadside or at farmers markets. The prized first-run syrup is light in colour and concentrated in flavour, and makes a magnificent dessert when poured over slices of mild, egg-filled Easter cheese.

Easter cheese is so named because it's served at Easter time. And while few outside of the Mennonite community have tasted it, it really does bring the diner closer to God. The custardy cheese is sliced into wedges and served with the season's first maple syrup, poured generously over each portion. This version comes from Nancy Wideman who has farmed with her husband, Carl, in Wellington County for decades. Although the Widemans use their own unpasteurized milk, this recipe works perfectly with homogenized milk from the grocery store.

YIELD: About 10 servings

8 cups (2 L) homogenized milk
5 eggs
1½ cups (375 mL) buttermilk
1 tsp (5 mL) white vinegar
½ tsp (2 mL) salt

In a heavy saucepan, heat the milk until simmering. In a medium bowl, whisk together the eggs, buttermilk, vinegar and salt; gradually pour into the steaming milk. Cook over medium-low heat, stirring constantly to prevent scorching, for 15 to 20 minutes or until mixture separates and forms distinct curds.

Transfer to a cheesecloth-lined colander; let drip for 1 hour, squeezing periodically to make mixture into a ball of cheese. Serve immediately or wrap and refrigerate for up to 1 week.

Over the years the Wideman family have shared their stories along with many delicious meals, such as homemade sausage fried till golden and served with just-out-of-the-oven bread slathered with home-churned butter (which Nancy would make about once a week). Before Nancy retired from the "home farm," she would spend hours weeding and hoeing her massive garden.

Madame Dufau's Gâteau Basque

This is a legendary recipe, and this is the first time it's ever been printed. There will be people who will buy this book just for this recipe.

The story begins in southwest France, near St-Jean-de-Luz, where Roger Dufau watched his Basque *amachi* (grandmother) bake gâteau Basque in the sand. She'd light a fire, heat the sand so it was evenly hot and then bake the cake slowly. When the Algerian war broke out, Roger was about to be sent into the front lines of what he felt, and still feels, was "a stupid war." His mother, Lucie, had been in the French resistance and had smuggled people out of France for much of World War II. His uncle was part of Interpol in Paris. It took a mere three days for the 20-year-old Basque to get his visa to Canada. He landed in 1962 and started to cook in Toronto. His mother followed in 1969 to help in his shop, Le Petit Gourmet. In 1971, they moved into the heart of Toronto's Rosedale neighbourhood, at 1064 Yonge Street, and opened what would become a ragingly successful store, largely based on Lucie's gâteau Basque. Two of Roger's regular customers—who loved to talk politics and eat gâteau—were expat Americans Don Green and Michael Budman, who'd come to Canada because of their love of the land. It was shortly thereafter that the pair opened their flagship Roots store within an easy walk of the café, putting a new spin on the marketing mantra "Location, location, location."

With Le Petit Gourmet doing so well, and because he was developing an allergy to flour, Roger opened Maison Basque on Temperance Street on March 27, 1973, where he served wild fresh-caught Atlantic (!) salmon and his mother's extraordinary desserts. Within the month, Joanne Kates, Toronto's most authoritative restaurant critic, glowingly reviewed his new restaurant. There was no looking back. For years, it was included in *Where to Eat in Canada.*

The decades that interceded saw Roger cooking in Australia and eventually Tasmania. But in 1997, he returned to Elora, not too far from my own home, and opened Drew House, a bed and breakfast in the renovated home and carriage house (circa 1850) of George Drew, one of Ontario's early premiers. The recipe for gâteau Basque was still intact, and Roger was still reluctant to share it. I can understand why—it's associated with so many personal memories.

But both time and friendship change things, and a year ago, I came home to find a cream envelope stuck neatly into the crack beside my front door. It was Roger's Christmas gift, and inside, in his scrawling European hand, was the basis for the recipe you read here. It is extraordinary! Simple and buttery, this gâteau is magnificent filled either with a rich pastry cream or with apples sautéed in butter and sugar. There is enough dough to make three large gateaux, but the utter beauty of this recipe is that one can divide the dough into thirds, using the first third and refrigerating the remainder, tightly wrapped, for up to a week. While Roger sometimes uses fruit sugar for the pastry, he prefers crystallized sugar or even turbinado sugar. The eggs, in total, should measure 1¼ cups (300 mL), hence the approximate measurement for egg yolks below.

YIELD: 8 to 10 servings

> 1⅓ cups (375 mL) unsalted butter, softened
> 3 cups (750 mL) crystal sugar
> 4 eggs, plus 4 or 5 egg yolks
> 4¾ cups (1.175 L) all-purpose flour
> 1 tbsp (15 mL) baking powder
> ½ tsp (2 mL) salt
> Grated rind of 1 lemon or orange
> Pastry Cream or Sautéed Apple Filling (recipes follow)
> Egg wash, as needed
> Additional sugar, for baking
> Icing sugar, for serving

In a large mixing bowl, beat the butter until fluffy. Add the sugar and gradually incorporate the eggs and egg yolks, beating constantly. Sift together the flour, baking powder and salt. Add to the creamed mixture, along with the lemon or orange rind, to make a soft, sticky dough.

Cover the dough with plastic wrap and refrigerate for at least 4 to 6 hours or until it is very firm. It can be refrigerated for up to a week and makes three cakes.

For each gâteau, you will need a 9- to 10-inch (23 to 25 cm) metal baking ring and a sheet of parchment placed on a baking sheet.

Divide the dough into three pieces. Flour one piece generously; cover remaining dough and refrigerate.

Place dough in the centre of the parchment. Roll outward into a rough circle several inches larger than the diameter of the ring. The dough should be about ¼ inch (5 mm) thick. Press the ring into the dough, using it like a cookie cutter; remove the excess dough. Gather it up and roll it into a rope, fitting it inside the ring, pressing it up the sides. With a sharp knife, trim off and reserve excess dough.

Fill it with either the Pastry Cream or Sautéed Apple Filling. Gather random bits of the dough into a ball and roll it on a well-floured surface to make a thin top crust. Brush with egg wash and sprinkle with sugar. For the Sautéed Apple Filling, simply top randomly with the reserved dough pieces, brush with egg wash and finish with a sprinkling of sugar.

Tear off a piece of foil long enough to reach around the circumference of the ring. Twist it into a tight rope and place it at the outside base of the ring, twist ends together to tighten it. Make sure it is snug. (The foil ring prevents the dough from over-baking and also prevents any leaks.)

Place gâteau into a COLD oven and set the temperature to 325°F (160°C). Bake for 60 to 65 minutes or until rich golden brown. Remove from oven and let cool for 15 to 20 minutes before loosening with a very sharp knife and removing the ring. Before serving, dust with icing sugar.

PASTRY CREAM: Roger simplifies things by using Bird's Custard Powder and enriching it with cream, rather than milk, and 2 or 3 egg yolks, but I prefer this classic pastry cream recipe provided by my son Paul, who is a chef and also, from time to time, Roger's assistant.

½ cup (125 mL) granulated sugar
⅓ cup (50 mL) cornstarch
6 egg yolks
3 cups (750 mL) homogenized milk or half-and-half cream (10%)
1 tsp (5 mL) vanilla extract

In a stainless steel bowl, combine the sugar, cornstarch and egg yolks. Whisk until well blended and light in colour, about 2 minutes. In a small saucepan, combine the milk and vanilla. Bring to a boil. Whisk the milk mixture into the egg mixture. Return to low heat, whisking constantly, until it thickens and bubbles. Be careful not to scorch the bottom. Pour the pastry cream into a small container and cover surface with plastic wrap to prevent a skin from forming on the top. Refrigerate to chill.

SAUTÉED APPLE FILLING:
4 or 5 peeled, sliced apples (about 4 to 5 cups/1 to 1.25 L)
¼ cup (60 mL) unsalted butter
½ cup (125 mL) granulated sugar

In a large skillet, melt the butter and add the apples. Sprinkle them with sugar and sauté over medium heat until nearly tender, 6 to 8 minutes. Let cool to room temperature before filling the pastry.

Peggy Morris's Amazing Butter Tarts

Butter tarts are much like pastry. The baker has to have a special touch. Peggy is so practised at it that even though she is now legally blind, she's still able to make these dynamite tarts, the ones her four sons grew up on in Peel Township in southwestern Ontario.

YIELD: 18 tarts

1 cup (250 mL) raisins
2 eggs
⅓ cup (75 mL) corn syrup
1 cup (250 mL) packed brown sugar
3 tbsp (45 mL) melted butter
½ cup (125 mL) chopped walnuts
18 Sweet Tart Pastry shells

In a small bowl, cover raisins with boiling water. Let soak for 20 minutes. Drain and set aside.

In a small mixing bowl, whisk together the eggs, corn syrup, brown sugar, melted butter and nuts. Stir in the raisins. Pour evenly into the prepared tart shells. Bake in a preheated 450°F (220°C) oven for 5 minutes. Reduce heat to 350°F (180°C) and open door slightly for 15 to 20 seconds to bring temperature down rapidly. Bake for 15 minutes or until bubbling and deep golden brown. Let cool for 10 to 15 minutes before removing from the pan.

Sweet Tart Pastry

YIELD: Two 9-inch (23 cm) pie shells or 18 to 24 tart shells

2½ cups (625 mL) sifted cake-and-pastry flour
¼ cup (60 mL) granulated sugar
½ tsp (2 mL) salt
1 cup (250 mL) chilled unsalted butter
¾ cup (175 mL) ice water

In a bowl, sift together the flour, sugar and salt. With a pastry blender, cut in the butter until the mixture resembles fine crumbs. With a fork, stir in the ice water, ¼ cup (60 mL) at a time, until the dough can be gathered up into a ball.

Turn dough out onto a lightly floured surface. Flour a rolling pin and the top of the dough. Divide dough in half.

For pie shells, roll out, one half at a time, to form a 10- to 12-inch (25 to 30 cm) circle. Lay gently onto the pie plate. Trim the edges and re-roll scraps with remaining pastry to line second pie plate.

For tart shells, roll out one piece of dough, dusting with flour if needed, to about ⅛ inch (3 mm) thick. Using a cookie cutter, cut into approximately 4-inch (10 cm) circles and press gently into tart or muffin tins. Trim the edges and re-roll scraps with remaining pastry to line remaining tins.

Cover pastry shells with plastic wrap and refrigerate until needed or freeze in an airtight container for up to 1 month.

BUTTER TARTS—ABSOLUTELY CANADIAN!

There are friendly debates amongst bakers . . . what sort of sugar . . . brown or white . . . should corn syrup be added? Is it still a butter tart when maple syrup is in the recipe? Nuts or no nuts? Should there be vinegar or a splash of lemon, which my Grandma, on the northern edge of Wellington County, wouldn't have had? Should the pastry be made with butter or lard?

But you won't find this noble country tart in the *Oxford Companion to Food*. Nor is it in the American reference book *Food Lover's Companion*. Yet, since the turn of the last century, recipes abound for it in almost every Canadian cookbook.

Historian and friend Mary Williamson is an expert on butter tarts. She's been sleuthing the story of these marvellous tarts for years. According to her, the earliest reference was in a cookbook compiled by The Women's Auxiliary of the Royal Victoria Hospital in Barrie in 1900 and it's merely named "A filling for tarts." Butter tarts were named as such in the early editions of *The Blue Ribbon Cookbook*, and as food processing technology evolved so did recipes which included corn syrup. By 1911 the tart had exploded in popularity, and in *The Canadian Farm Cookbook* there were six butter tart recipes and three called "tart fillings." It proliferated in community and published cookbooks.

For farm women, the two essential ingredients, eggs and butter, were in abundance! And Canada, when these tarts were invented, was a farming country.

Mary elaborated, saying that the butter tart may be related to the sugar pies of Quebec or a sweet called a Border Tart from the south border of Scotland which often contains dried fruit, sugar, butter and egg. This connection makes some sense since so many of our ancestors hail from that region. In fact, that's where Mary's relatives are from themselves.

Asked about whether they were related to pecan tarts and pies of the Southern States, Mary is emphatic. "In a butter tart, pecans ARE A TRAVESTY!"

Runny or not, heavy with soaked raisins or simply the sugary egg filling, this countryside creation is one of Canada's great gifts to the culinary world. YUM!

Austrian Cheese Crêpes (Topfen Palatschinken)

Whether Erika Durlacher is entertaining at her inn, Durlacher Hof, or in her own kitchen, she cooks Austrian. In the snowy Whistler winters, she makes this fabulous dessert and sometimes serves it for breakfast. Rich eggy crêpes—I use Don Oliver's recipe (page 17)—are filled and baked. I love these crêpes still slightly warm from the oven, topped with fresh and lightly sweetened Niagara peaches or simply a drizzle of maple syrup.

YIELD: 4 to 6 servings

One batch Classic Crêpes (page 17)

FILLING:
1 cup (250 mL) ricotta cheese
2 egg yolks
⅔ cup (150 mL) granulated sugar
½ cup (125 mL) raisins
Grated rind of 1 lemon
1 tsp (5 mL) vanilla extract

CUSTARD:
1½ cups (375 mL) milk
1 egg
¼ cup (60 mL) granulated sugar

Whisk the cheese with the egg yolks, sugar, raisins, lemon and vanilla. Divide filling among crêpes. Roll and place into a buttered 2-quart (2 L) square baking dish.

CUSTARD: Stir together the milk, egg and sugar. Pour over the crêpes and bake, uncovered, in a preheated 350°F (180°C) oven for 40 to 45 minutes or until the custard is set and the top is golden. Let cool slightly before serving.

Half Moon Pastries (Hálfmánar)

In Nancy Wong's family, these buttery Icelandic turnovers signal Christmas, and she also uses the filling for another seasonal dessert, Vinarterta (page 234). She insists on grinding the cardamom fresh for every use.

YIELD: About 4 dozen

2½ cups (625 mL) all-purpose flour
2 tsp (10 mL) baking powder
1 tsp (5 mL) freshly ground cardamom
⅔ cup (150 mL) granulated sugar
1 cup (250 mL) butter
1 egg, beaten
1 tbsp (15 mL) lemon juice
¼ cup (60 mL) cold water
1½ cups (375 mL) Vinarterta filling (page 234)
Icing sugar

Sift together the flour, baking powder, cardamom and sugar. Cut in the butter until the mixture resembles coarse crumbs. Stir together the egg, lemon juice and water.

Blend the egg mixture into the dry mixture just until it holds together (you may need to add a bit more water).

Gather the pastry into a ball and turn out onto a floured surface. Roll out the dough to ⅛-inch (2 mm) thickness. Cut into rounds with a 3-inch (8 cm) cookie cutter.

Fill each round with about 2 tsp (10 mL) of the Vinarterta filling. Pinch tightly to close and make into half moon shapes. Place on lightly greased or parchment-lined baking sheets. Bake in a preheated 375°F (190°C) oven until beginning to brown, 15 to 20 minutes.

Let cool. When cool, dust with sifted icing sugar.

A Tale of Perseverance

It seems that Canada has forever welcomed immigrants who have come from war- or famine-ravaged lands. My own ancestors were on the verge of starvation in Ireland. What follows is a modern-day story of tenacity.

Fearing that their country was no longer safe, Ofri and Ofra Barmor sold their home and business in Israel and began afresh in Canada in 2003, creating Carmelis Alpine Goat Cheese Artisan Inc. They wanted to start a new life in a nation perennially at peace. They built their dairy and cheesemaking facility in a forest by Okanagan Lake. It was as idyllic as any setting could be, with their property rolling down the hillside toward the deep, cerulean blue lake. But then disaster struck. In mid-August 2003, a forest fire broke out in Okanagan Mountain Park near the city of Kelowna. Mass evacuations preceded the destruction of dozens of homes. At its peak, 650 firefighters, 20 helicopters and 200 pieces of heavy equipment were working the fire, and air tanker support was enlisted. The inferno was so strong that witnesses have said it seemed that lightning bolts tore through the flames. When the fire was finally contained one month later, the size of the area affected was determined to be 64,030 acres (25,912 hectares), with a perimeter of 122 miles (197 kilometres). Along with the 283 homes, the Barmors' farm business had been consumed.

For the Barmors, this was just another obstacle to overcome: "On August 21, Timberline Road was on fire, and our goat cheese farm, which was being built and almost completed, burned to ashes, and our house was damaged. In early October, we started to rebuild our goat cheese farm. On February 21, 2004, our first batch of cheese was ready."

Today the Barmors' dairy is perched on the same hillside, open wide to the valley air. Their herd of 100 goats move freely in and out of their shelter, trotting and gallivanting up and down the slopes. The cheesemaking facility has a wonderful smell of fresh milk, and below it the aging rooms are lined with a variety of golden wheels ripening to perfection.

Their goat milk cheese is sold to the region's top chefs and gourmands. One of their most popular cheeses is the aged Lior, named after their daughter. In Hebrew, it means "my light." From Horizon, with its layer of ash, to pungent Goatgonzola to the strikingly beautiful Vintage, a hard cheese soaked in wine from the Barmors' neighbouring vineyard, Carmelis Cheeses is more than just perfectly fermented milk; it is a chronicle of great resolve and courage—a real Canadian success story.

June's Pavlova

When they came from the heat of Australia to live in Guelph, Ontario, June Pearson and her husband, Craig, brought their Aussie love of entertaining. In Australia, baking has to be fast and easy, particularly in the summer when the thermometer soars. June's Pavlova is crisp and snowy on the outside and marshmallow-like on the inside. It can be stored for a few days in an airtight container but may have to be crisped again in a slow oven. The topping is lightly sweetened whipped cream and seasonal fruits, one of which must be somewhat tart. Strawberries and kiwi are a common topping Down Under, but here you can use a mixture of fresh local berries, some sliced peaches or apricots.

YIELD: 6 to 8 servings

> 4 egg whites, at room temperature
> 1 cup (250 mL) superfine sugar
> 1 tbsp (15 mL) cornstarch
> 2 tsp (10 mL) white vinegar

FILLING:
> 1 cup (250 mL) whipping cream (35%)
> 2 tsp (10 mL) superfine sugar
> Fresh fruit

Lightly oil or butter a baking sheet and line with parchment.

Beat the egg whites until stiff enough to hold soft peaks. Slowly beat in the sugar, a few spoonfuls at a time. This will take 2 to 3 minutes. The resulting meringue will be shiny and soft. Sift the cornstarch over it and lightly fold it in along with the vinegar.

Drop the meringue onto the centre of the prepared sheet. With a spatula, spread it into an 8-inch (20 cm) circle, smoothing the top and the sides.

Bake in a preheated 250°F (120°C) oven for 1 hour and 20 minutes. Remove from the oven and let cool on the sheet. Store in an airtight container or use immediately.

FILLING: Whip the cream with the sugar until stiff. Invert the meringue onto a serving dish (the smooth bottom becomes the top of the dessert). Spoon the whipped cream over the entire surface. Mound the fresh fruit on top. Serve immediately.

Sweet and almost perfumed, Blushing Star is among the finest examples of white peaches.

My Grandfather's Favourite Bread Pudding

In all our homespun recipes, be they from the heart of Wellington County in Ontario or the highlands of Cape Breton or downtown Vancouver, the phrase "waste not, want not" rings true. Real cooks are frugal ones.

This recipe is a basic way of using up stale bread that, in the days of yore, was preservative-free and therefore wouldn't keep for long. My grandfather, Albert Ovens, adored this pudding, and I've made countless variations of it. It's so forgiving. If you prepare it in the evening and refrigerate it, you can even bake it for breakfast the next morning. The last incarnation that graced my kitchen was filled with Ontario cherries and Niagara walnuts. Serve it warm with milk or cream.

YIELD: 4 to 6 servings

> 5 or 6 slices stale white bread
> Butter
> 3 eggs, beaten
> 2 cups (500 mL) homogenized milk
> 1 tsp (5 mL) vanilla extract
> ½ tsp (2 mL) almond extract
> ½ cup (125 mL) packed brown sugar
> ½ tsp (2 mL) cinnamon
> ½ tsp (2 mL) nutmeg
> ½ cup (125 mL) sultana or golden raisins

Trim crust from bread if heavy and thick. Butter bread lightly; tear into 1- to 2-inch (2.5 to 5 cm) chunks. Set aside.

In a separate bowl, whisk together the eggs, milk, and vanilla and almond extracts; stir in the sugar, cinnamon, nutmeg and raisins.

In an 8-inch (20 cm) square glass baking dish, layer the bread and egg mixture. The egg mixture should almost cover the bread. Place baking dish in a larger pan containing 1 inch (2.5 cm) very hot water. Bake, uncovered, in a 325°F (160°C) oven for 1 hour or until the top is golden and the custard is set.

Breakfast Custard

A simple custard is something few of us consider as a breakfast dish. But high in the hills of Cape Breton, at the lovely Chanterelle Inn, owner Earlene Busch, an American who is spending more and more time in these rolling highlands, bakes this custard for her guests. She tops it with spoonfuls of blueberry compote, but any fresh or stewed summer fruit would be wonderful.

YIELD: 6 servings

3 eggs
2 tbsp (30 mL) granulated sugar
2 cups (500 mL) milk
⅛ tsp (0.5 mL) salt
½ tsp (2 mL) vanilla extract
Cinnamon and freshly grated nutmeg

Whisk together the eggs, sugar, milk, salt and vanilla. Divide among 6 lightly buttered 1-cup (250 mL) custard dishes. Sprinkle with cinnamon and nutmeg. Set in a large baking pan lined with a tea towel. Add very hot water to reach about halfway up the side of the dishes. Bake in a preheated 350°F (180°C) oven for 30 minutes or until set. Serve warm or chilled.

Custard at Chanterelle Inn, Cape Breton, Nova Scotia.

For me, butter is almost a food group.
The bakeries in Quebec City understand
that. On Rue St-Jean, a few blocks inside
the city walls, is my personal fave. It's
an utterly fragrant boulangerie named
Paillard. Until recently a grocery store,
it was transformed early in 2006 into a
brilliant, airy bakery-cum-café. The air
itself is so thick with the fragrance of
butter that after slogging through the
snow and coming in from the nostril-
freezing cold, it's intoxicating. Every time
I visit, my mouth literally begins to water.
The almond croissants are filled with
finely crushed sweet almond paste and
strewn with the slivered nuts. Spirals of
croissant dough are laced with diced bits
of orange or lemon rind. Crusty cheese
breads ooze cheddar.

Paillard serves coffee that's roasted
especially for the café; it has become
a busy gathering place. Huge images
of people licking cream off their lips or
simply swooning with gustatory pleasure
fill one wall, coaxing the rest of us to "go
ahead and indulge!" Young people buy
slim baguettes; one of the most popular
varieties is made with kamut flour. Then
they gather up butter and conserves
and create their own picnic spread in
the centre of the long, dormitory-style
tables. Later at lunch, the breads become
the basis for thick sandwiches—chipotle
chicken on Paillard's great baguettes,
rosemary-roasted beef on ciabatta or
simply more pastry. Go early, stay late—
it's Quebec artisanal baking at its best.

Peter's Brioche

Elora's Peter Skoggard is a composer and a massage therapist, and at one point in his colourful career, he operated one of Toronto's first completely vegetarian restaurants, The Cow Café. During that urban hiatus, people came from across the city every Sunday morning to consume his brioches. His food vocabulary is as complex as his musical talent—he is currently writing an opera based on the life of Teresa Stratas—and there is no doubt that when he bakes he brings a bit of magic to the kitchen.

According to Peter, brioche goes against every bread-baking tenet in the book—it uses too much butter, too many eggs. But made on a *cool* day and according to his instructions (and with a little prayer), this brioche will be the best, richest and most sensuous bread you will ever make.

Yield: 2 large or 18 small brioches

Yeast Sponge:
½ cup (125 mL) warm water
1 tsp (5 mL) liquid honey
2 tbsp (30 mL) active dry yeast
¾ cup (175 mL) all-purpose flour

Brioche Dough:
4 cups (1 L) all-purpose flour
1 tbsp (15 mL) salt
½ cup (125 mL) liquid honey
8 eggs, lightly beaten
Additional flour (about 2 cups/500 mL)
1 cup (250 mL) butter, softened

Egg Wash:
1 egg yolk, well beaten
2 tbsp (30 mL) milk

Yeast Sponge: Rinse a small bowl with hot water to warm it. In the bowl, combine the warm water, honey and yeast. Stir and set aside to puff, 7 to 10 minutes. Sprinkle with flour, stirring with fork to make a thick batter. Let rise in a warm place for 10 minutes or until sponge-like.

Brioche Dough: In a large bowl, combine the flour and salt. Make a well in the centre and pour in the honey. Add eggs and yeast sponge, mixing until sticky and well blended. Turn out onto a generously floured board and knead in additional flour until smooth.

With a fork, mash the butter roughly. Knead briefly. It should be the consistency of the dough but not melting.

On a well-floured board, flatten the dough with the heel of your hand and press (Peter says "squish") the butter into it. Fold it up and knead a few turns, gathering and folding gently. The dough will be very sticky. Add flour if it is too sticky to work with and knead gently for 1 minute, ensuring that the work surface remains floured.

Cover the dough with a kitchen towel; let rise for 1½ to 2 hours or until doubled. (The first rising will take longer because, as Peter says, "The yeasts are overcoming their environmental difficulties.") When double, punch down and let rise again until doubled, 30 minutes to 1 hour. Punch down and shape.

For classic brioche, thoroughly butter or oil 2 large or 18 individual brioche moulds (deeply fluted metal tins). Divide the dough in half or into 18 pieces. To shape the large brioche, simply tear off a golf-ball-sized chunk of dough from each half and roll each into a ball. Shape the larger pieces into rounds and place in the tins. Make a deep indentation in the top of the dough and insert the smaller balls firmly.

Or if making small brioche, tear off a marble-sized piece of dough from each of the 18 pieces. Roll each into a round. Place the larger rounds into the moulds and poke your finger into the top of each, making an indentation for inserting the marble-sized piece. Cover and let rise until doubled.

Egg Wash: Mix together the yolk and milk. Using the lightest of pastry brushes, brush onto the unbaked brioche.

For the larger brioche, remove the middle rack (to allow them to rise) and bake in the lower third of a preheated 350°F (180°C) oven until rich golden brown, about 40 minutes. For the smaller brioche, bake in the middle of the oven for 25 to 30 minutes.

Let cool for 15 to 20 minutes on a wire rack before removing from the pans.

My Amma's (Grandmother's) Vinarterta

Vinarterta is the most traditional of Icelandic desserts. "In my family's version, the icing is meant to be thick," says Vancouver's Nancy Wong.

Most of it was on the top and only some was used to cover about the top third of the sides. So the icing was like a cap on the vinarterta, rather than completely covering it. The almonds in the icing seem unique to my family; I've never seen anyone else do it. Please leave it for at least a week—that is the minimum "aging time." We normally leave it for two and sometimes three weeks. It's incredibly yummy, and those first slices after two weeks of anticipation are just amazing. By the way, you can also freeze it. Sometimes I freeze half for use at a later time. It's very rich, and the slices should be thin—this is a case where a little goes a long way. Of course, it needs to be served with a cup of very good coffee. Coffee is the life blood of Icelanders, at least the ones in Canada—I can't speak for the ones in Iceland.

Nancy also notes that she does not use pre-ground cardamom but rather crushes or grinds it just before adding it to the flour. "I remove the seeds from the pods, put them in an envelope and pound them with a hammer—more labour-intensive but better flavour."

Make the filling first. Since this is the same filling recipe used in the Half Moon Pastries (page 225), you may wish to double it. When shaping the layers, Nancy rolls the dough out right on the baking sheet and uses a plate to cut the circle so that all the layers are uniform. Serve this vinarterta with the best coffee you can buy.

YIELD: 16 to 18 servings

PRUNE FILLING:

1 lb (500 g) pitted prunes

1 cup (250 mL) packed brown sugar

2 tsp (10 mL) cinnamon

1 tsp (5 mL) brandy

COOKIE LAYERS:

1 cup (250 mL) butter, softened

1½ cups (375 mL) granulated sugar

2 eggs

2 tbsp (30 mL) whipping cream (35%)

1 tsp (5 mL) almond extract

4 cups (1 L) all-purpose flour

1 tsp (5 mL) baking powder

⅛ tsp (0.5 mL) salt

1 tsp (5 mL) ground cardamom

½ cup (125 mL) ground almonds

ICING:

6 to 8 tbsp (90 to 125 mL) butter, softened

1½ cups (375 mL) sifted icing sugar

1 egg yolk

1 tsp (5 mL) almond extract

½ cup (125 mL) ground almonds

PRUNE FILLING: Place the prunes in a saucepan with just enough water to barely cover.

Bring to a boil and simmer, partially covered, for 20 minutes or until the prunes are soft. Drain, reserving ½ cup (125 mL) of the prune water. Finely chop the prunes and return to the pot, adding the reserved prune water and the sugar. Bring the mixture to a boil and cook until thickened to the consistency of jam, 7 to 10 minutes. Remove from heat and stir in the cinnamon and brandy.

COOKIE LAYERS: Cream the butter until fluffy and gradually add the sugar.

Beat in the eggs, 1 at a time, beating well after each addition. Add the cream and almond extract.

In a separate bowl, sift or stir together the flour, baking powder, salt, cardamom and ground almonds. Stir into the butter mixture, blending well.

Knead 10 to 15 times or until smooth and pliable. If the dough is too soft, refrigerate for 15 to 20 minutes. Divide into 6 equal parts.

Roll out each circle of dough into an 8- to 9-inch (20 to 23 cm) round on an ungreased cookie sheet. Like Nancy, use a plate as a guide to create an even circle. Bake each layer in a preheated 350°F (180°C) oven for 15 to 20 minutes or until just starting to colour on the edges.

Let cool a little on the baking sheet until the layer firms up. When partially cool, transfer to a rack or let stand on a clean towel to cool completely. At this point, the layers are crisp and hard like a sugar cookie and ready for filling.

ICING: Cream the butter with the sugar. Beat in the egg yolk. Add the almond extract and almonds and continue to beat until the icing is thick and smooth.

To assemble, divide the prune filling into 5 equal portions. Spread one cookie layer with one portion of filling right to the edges. Top with another cookie layer and spread with more filling. Continue in this manner, ending with a cookie layer on the top. Spread icing over top and sides. Cover loosely with plastic wrap and store in a cool place for 2 to 3 weeks before serving. Cut into slivers to serve.

Ukrainian Cottage Cheese Dessert (Syrnyk)

This Ukrainian Easter dessert, pronounced "sear-nick," is part of Daryl Demoskoff's personal story. Having grown up in the scenic community of Fort Qu'Appelle, about 45 minutes west of Regina, Saskatchewan, and with Doukhobor roots as well as Ukrainian, he now lives and works in the city as media relations manager for Tourism Saskatchewan. "When I still lived at home," he says, "my dad would make this dessert every Easter. Now that I have moved out on my own, it has become my duty to make this dessert for my family each Easter." This recipe comes from "a scrap of paper that has been scrawled on, spilled on, and is lying among other recipes in the bottom of a drawer!"

While it is absolutely delicious just as it is, in Daryl's household this dessert is topped with a drizzle of corn syrup and some milk or cream.

YIELD: 8 to 10 servings

CRUST:
- ⅓ cup (75 mL) butter
- ¼ cup (60 mL) granulated sugar
- 1 egg
- 1 cup (250 mL) all-purpose flour
- ¼ tsp (1 mL) salt
- 1 tsp (5 mL) baking powder

FILLING:
- 1 lb (500 g) cottage cheese
- 4 eggs
- ⅔ cup (150 mL) granulated sugar
- 3 tbsp (45 mL) melted butter
- ½ tsp (2 mL) salt
- Grated rind and juice of 1 small orange
- Grated rind and juice of ½ lemon
- 1 tsp (5 mL) vanilla extract
- ½ tsp (2 mL) cinnamon
- 2 tbsp (30 mL) all-purpose flour
- ½ cup (125 mL) raisins

Cream the butter with the sugar; whip in the egg. Sift the flour with the salt and baking powder; combine with the creamed mixture to make a smooth batter. Spread over the bottom and sides of a well-buttered 9-inch (23 cm) springform pan. Bake in a preheated 350°F (180°C) oven for 12 to 15 minutes or until just tinged light brown.

FILLING: In a food processor, combine the cottage cheese and eggs and process for 30 seconds or until the curds of the cheese are fine. Add the sugar and continue processing for a few seconds.

Transfer to a mixing bowl; whisk in the butter, salt, orange rind and juice, lemon rind and juice, vanilla, cinnamon and flour. Stir in the raisins. Spoon the mixture over the partially baked crust. Reduce the oven temperature to 300°F (150°C) and continue to bake for 60 to 65 minutes or until golden. Let cool before loosening the crust by running a sharp knife around the edge of the pan. Refrigerate until serving.

Foxhill Cheese, near Port Williams, Nova Scotia, makes a wonderful array of cheeses, from the freshest curds (love 'em!) to a new creation, an excellent Parmesan-style cheese that they've named "Parmesran."

Azorian Rice Pudding

Rich in both milk and eggs, this is one of the most traditional Portuguese sweets served to guests at religious festivals like Espirito Santo. Margaret Timmins first made this dish for me one winter before we headed to the Azores to visit her family. The rice is spread onto a plate or small platter while it's warm and decorated with narrow lines of cinnamon.

YIELD: 6 servings

1 cup (250 mL) long-grain rice
1 cup (250 mL) water
1 cup (250 mL) granulated sugar
3¼ cups (810 mL) milk
Grated rind of 1 lemon
½ tsp (2 mL) salt
4 egg yolks
Cinnamon

For the dessert to be truly traditional, lines of cinnamon must be carefully sprinkled on top.

Combine rice and water in a heavy saucepan and bring to a boil. Reduce heat and cook gently until most of the liquid is absorbed. Stir in the sugar, 3 cups (750 mL) of the milk, the lemon rind and salt; simmer over low to medium heat until rice is tender, 35 to 40 minutes.

Beat the egg yolks with the remaining milk. Add some of the hot rice mixture (about 1 cup/250 mL) to the egg mixture while stirring. Slowly return the egg mixture to the pot, stirring continually. Simmer for 1 to 2 minutes to finish cooking the eggs. Pour onto a platter. Garnish with cinnamon.

The Ultimate Cheesecake

The Jewish community has produced magnificent cream cheeses and sour cream in cities like Toronto and Winnipeg for decades. This recipe is a classic version of a New York–style cheesecake. It needs no garnishes, although it might be nice to gild the lily with some fresh fruit.

YIELD: 12 to 15 servings

CRUST:
- 1½ cups (375 mL) graham cracker crumbs
- 2 tbsp (30 mL) granulated sugar
- 2 tbsp (30 mL) melted butter

FILLING:
- 1 lb (500 g) plain cream cheese, at room temperature
- 1 cup (250 mL) granulated sugar
- 5 eggs
- 1 tsp (5 mL) vanilla extract
- 2 tbsp (30 mL) lemon juice
- Grated rind of 1 lemon
- Grated rind of 1 orange
- 2 cups (500 mL) sour cream

CRUST: In a bowl, combine the crumbs, sugar and melted butter; pat evenly into a 10-inch (25 cm) springform pan that is at least 2 inches (5 cm) deep and has been lightly oiled and lined with parchment. Bake in a pre-heated 350°F (180°C) oven for 10 minutes. Remove from oven and let cool. Reduce the oven temperature to 300°F (150°C).

FILLING: In a large bowl, beat together the cream cheese and the sugar until smooth and well combined. Add the eggs, 1 at a time, beating well after each addition. Whip in the vanilla, lemon juice, and grated lemon and orange rind. Fold in the sour cream until thoroughly combined.

Pour the filling into the crust and bake for 1 hour. Turn off the oven, but leave the cheesecake in it without opening the door for 1 hour longer. Open the oven door and let the cake cool for another 30 minutes. Remove from the oven and let cool completely; refrigerate until thoroughly chilled.

Before serving, loosen the edges with a sharp knife dipped in hot water. Remove sides from springform pan and slide cheesecake onto a serving plate. Slice with the same hot knife.

Federal food safety regulations are strict and very important, but when poorly administered they can spell disaster. A case in point is that of Darrel and Anthea Archer of Fairburn Farm on Vancouver Island. The Archers are modest people. Their goal is simple: to produce good food. They are the sort of farmers Canada needs—hard-working entrepreneurs, stewards of the land who are not afraid to risk everything. Their valley is pastoral—green and rich. They farm organically. They knew how delicious real buffalo milk mozzarella could be. They did their homework, received the various approvals and used their life savings to bring a small herd of 19 water buffalo (18 cows and one bull named James Bond, because his ear tag was 007) to the Cowichan Valley.

In spite of the fact that there has never been a recorded case of BSE in water buffalo and that these animals had been in proper quarantine, the Canadian Food Inspection Agency ordered them to be destroyed. A fight ensued, and lobbying began on many fronts, but to no avail. All the adult animals were euthanized and tested for BSE. The tests were negative. But the story does not end there. The triumph of the human spirit has prevailed. The Archers kept the calves. Now mature, they have started to produce milk and the herd is growing. The Archer family has re-financed the farm and started over. Daryl, who several years ago broke his arm in five places, is building a dairy using logs he is cutting from trees on his 130-acre property and a mill that he built himself as a young man.

Water Buffalo Yogurt Panna Cotta with Fresh Raspberry Purée

A small herd of water buffalo is being raised in the lush Cowichan Valley on Vancouver Island. Mara Jernigan, who operates the Fairburn Farm Culinary Retreat and Guesthouse on the property, makes this great dessert when there is enough water buffalo milk to make some yogurt. "This variation on panna cotta is much lighter because it is partially made with yogurt," says Mara. "In this case, water buffalo yogurt is used, but it works equally well with cow's milk yogurt or, for a more interesting flavour, sheep's or goat's milk." She recommends fine organic sugar, but if it isn't available, fruit sugar or superfine sugar will work well.

Yield: 8 servings

> 3 cups (750 mL) full-fat buffalo milk, cow's milk (page 215), sheep's milk or goat's milk yogurt
> ½ vanilla pod, or 1/2 tsp (2 mL) vanilla extract
> ¾ cup (175 mL) fine organic sugar, or fruit or fine white sugar
> 4 tsp (20 mL) unflavoured gelatin
> ½ cup (125 mL) table cream (18%)
> 2 cups (500 mL) whipping cream (35%)

Raspberry Purée:
> 2 cups (500 mL) fresh or thawed frozen raspberries
> ½ cup (125 mL) fine organic sugar, fruit or fine white sugar

Garnish:
> ½ cup (125 mL) fresh summer berries, such as raspberries, strawberries, blueberries or blackberries
> Fresh mint or lemon balm sprigs or fennel fronds
> Icing sugar

Place yogurt in a cheesecloth-lined or very fine strainer. Let drain for 1 hour. Transfer to a medium mixing bowl.

Scrape out the vanilla pod with a sharp paring knife and rub the seeds into the sugar. Whisk vanilla-flavoured sugar (or simply the sugar and vanilla extract) into the drained yogurt.

In a small saucepan, sprinkle gelatin over table cream. Let stand for 5 minutes. Place over medium heat and warm slowly, stirring constantly, until gelatin dissolves completely. Stir into the yogurt mixture.

Whip the whipping cream until stiff; fold into the yogurt mixture until completely incorporated. Ladle into individual ramekins. Place on a tray or baking sheet, cover and refrigerate until set, preferably overnight.

RASPBERRY PURÉE: In a blender, combine the berries and sugar and process until thoroughly puréed. If you're using fresh raspberries, you may need to add ¼ cup (60 mL) water. Strain the seeds from the berries using the back of a ladle to push them through a fine sieve.

To serve, pour a pool of raspberry purée onto each of 8 serving plates, tilting to spread out and cover the entire centre of the plate.

Fill a casserole with hot water and place the ramekins in the water for 1 minute to loosen each panna cotta. Run a paring knife around the inner edge of the ramekins and invert each panna cotta onto your clean hand or a stainless steel spatula; transfer them to the centre of each plate.

Garnish with fresh berries, a sprig of mint, lemon balm or fennel tops and a light dusting of icing sugar.

Hôtel Paulin Sugar Pie with Wild Berries and Goat Cheese Crème Fraîche

Chef Karen Mersereau of Hôtel Paulin in Caraquet, New Brunswick, developed this recipe using the old-fashioned Acadian original as the guide. All summer long, she buys fresh wild berries from the children who pick them to sell at the roadside. Sometimes she adds local strawberries or blackberries to this dessert; ultimately she is a seasonal chef. In the winter, she serves the dessert with oranges that she has soaked in Grand Marnier or with Elderberry Syrup (page 278). She purchases hers locally from Maury Farms. As in her Acadian Meat Pies (page 117), Karen uses lard pastry for the crust; it's traditional and very good.

YIELD: 8 servings

2 cups (500 mL) packed brown sugar
2 tbsp (30 mL) all-purpose flour
3 large eggs
½ tsp (2 mL) vanilla extract
1 can (385 mL) evaporated milk
Pastry for one 9-inch (23 cm) pie crust
Grated rind of 1 orange
2 to 3 cups (500 to 750 mL) fresh seasonal berries
Granulated sugar
Goat Cheese Crème Fraîche (recipe follows)

In a large mixing bowl, combine the brown sugar, flour and eggs. Beat on medium-high speed for 4 to 6 minutes. The mixture must be very thick and creamy. Add vanilla and milk; continue beating on medium speed for 2 minutes. Pour filling into prepared pie crust. Sprinkle with orange rind and bake in a preheated 400°F (200°C) oven for 10 minutes. Reduce heat to 350° (180°) and continue to bake for 30 to 35 minutes. The centre will look slightly puffed and soft, but as it cools, it will set. Let cool on a wire rack.

Sweeten the berries with sugar to taste and fold into the Goat Cheese Crème Fraîche. Serve the pie at room temperature and spoon the creamy berry mixture over it.

Goat Cheese Crème Fraîche

This recipe can easily be doubled or tripled so that you have a supply of crème fraîche. The crème can be refrigerated for up to one week.

YIELD: 1 cup (250 mL)

½ cup (125 mL) whipping cream (35%)
¼ cup (60 mL) plain goat cheese, softened
¼ cup (60 mL) thick yogurt

In a glass bowl, mix the cream with the goat cheese until smooth. Stir in the yogurt and cover with plastic wrap. Let stand at room temperature overnight. Refrigerate before serving.

In Caraquet, New Brunswick, Hôtel Paulin is proudly Acadian!

Fruit & Nuts

Al Sullivan's strawberry plants in flower at the University of Guelph research station.

Perhaps it's because we were country people that few things give me as much pleasure as driving the back roads of Ontario's Wellington and Grey counties. Mom and I would just get into the 1959 Pontiac—a smart two-tone hardtop—with all the windows rolled down for a complete panorama of open space, and with the wind blowing through our hair, we'd head out to explore. It was like we were going on an edible treasure hunt with no particular destination. We might get waylaid by a row of elderberries hanging seductively on the other side of a watery ditch in Proton Township, or by a hedgerow of chokecherries that we'd pick quickly and pile into the weathered wooden baskets that were made in our town of Mount Forest. We would make it all the way to Beaver Valley at least once in the autumn for apples and cider. It wasn't until I moved to Elora with a young family that I started picking the wild grapes that grow in profusion around this part of the county. One year, I made so much of the tart, purple jelly that I was able to sell it and buy all our Christmas presents with the profits. Today, I have an elderberry bush in my backyard (for the birds) and a huge old black walnut that drops its tennis-ball-size nuts every autumn to the delight of squirrels and the utter peril of anyone walking below.

From intensely flavoured indigenous berries to the huge array of tree fruits that immigrated with the early settlers, Canada overflows with summer fruit. Historically, berries were treasured by the Aboriginals, who intuitively understood the nutritional and medicinal value of fruits like blueberries and cranberries, something our scientific community is just now confirming.

The lowbush blueberry was harvested from Manitoba to Labrador. The Ojibwa cooked them with corn and baked them into a sweet bread. They were essential to many Naskapi dishes in Labrador, including a dried blueberry cake that would have been ideal sustenance for travelling across the barrens. Four species of cranberries flourish across Canada. They were often eaten fresh to quench thirst or simply as a snack in the East. The various indigenous peoples inhabiting what is now British Columbia cooked them to serve with deer meat. Cranberries grew widely in the Fraser Valley. Salal, a

West Coast plant, produces a dry, dark blue berry, which was the most important of all berries in the Northwest. The berries would be mashed and cooked in bentwood boxes using hot rocks. When the mixture was jamlike, it was turned out onto racks to dry in front of the fire. Easily dried into blocks, it was stored for winter. The saskatoon berry, or serviceberry, grows across Canada and as far north as eastern James Bay. It was, and still is, a very important wild fruit. Dried and mixed with fat and dried meat (bison or caribou), the berries made pemmican, while in the Interior of British Columbia, they were cooked with salmon pieces and chunks of venison.

The strawberry, one of the world's favourite fruits, is native to Canada, but according to berry specialist Dr. Al Sullivan of the Ontario Agricultural College, the large berries we now grow were likely hybridized by accident in the 1760s in a royal garden in France, when the tiny sweet varieties from the New World were being grown beside the less flavourful European strain. There are two wild species in Canada: the Woodland Strawberry, which grows in southern Canada, and the Blueleaf Strawberry, which spreads up into the Yukon.

The wild raspberry family is another indigenous fruit that spread from coast to coast. Cloudberries, known as bakeapples when picked in the bogs of Newfoundland, sweep across the northern regions of Canada. Red and black raspberries, thimbleberries, thorn-clad blackberries and peach-coloured salmonberries provide ready food—to be picked and eaten on the move or gathered, crushed and dried into storable chunks. Some are kept in water or, on the West Coast, in fermented fish oil.

As our First Nations peoples were harvesting and preserving summer berries, another fruit collection was being created around the Mediterranean and across Europe, one that would eventually journey to the New World. Peaches, which originated in the north of Persia, arrived on that menu in roughly 300 BC. Apricots came from China in about 100 BC. Plums, which have roots in both Eastern Europe (European plum) and Western Asia (damson plum), began to be treasured in early Rome. Pears, cultivated in China for four millennia, were added to the table. Cherries were taken from the wild in the Balkans. Apples, which have become the most important fruit in Canada, were transported across the Caucasus, to grace the tables of the ancients.

When New World exploration and settlement began, these fruits were well established and understood in Europe, and they would, as a matter of course, become part of the cargo of the ships crossing the Atlantic. Champlain recorded the planting of apple trees in Quebec City in his journal dated 1616. Starting an apple orchard was critical so that cider, a traditional French beverage, could be produced. His trees bore fruit for 25 years. We know there was

P.E.I. Preserves

Prince Edward Island is full to overflowing with entrepreneurial spirit, and for as long as I've known Bruce MacNaughton, he's been held up as an icon of Maritime ingenuity. He's combined the mantra "location, location, location" with an understanding of what it takes to create an authentic experience. He built an internationally recognized jam and preserve business in an old butter factory (circa 1913) right on the Clyde River near New Glasgow, now famous all over the globe for its lobster suppers and within striking distance of Charlottetown. Bruce's Prince Edward Island Preserves is one of Canada's finest culinary tourism destinations. And it's not by chance. He's thought about it—a lot—and poured his heart and soul into it.

Bruce is, first and foremost, an islander. He loves his province and is not afraid to show that pride. Often kilt-clad, all summer long he meets busloads of tourists who come to see the jam being produced and have a bite to eat in his light-filled Café on the Clyde, all the while listening to Maritime music, including Bruce's supremely talented friend Lennie Gallant. Bruce's first jar of jam was given to the late Joe Ghiz in 1985. His millionth was given to then Premier Pat Binns. Both were Strawberry–Grand Marnier.

Ray Kaczmarski, the hands-on manager of the Vineland Research Station, believes that these soon-to-be-named clingstone peaches are the finest to have been bred in decades.

Huge and sweet, these still-to-be named cherries are identified at their home at the Vineland Research Station as only Van x V69068. I preserve them in Kittling Ridge brandy.

another orchard of both apples and pears in Port Royal in 1635, as this was noted by a Recollet priest who'd brought them from France the previous year.

One of the best accounts of early agriculture in that newly settled region was written in the mid-1700s by Governor Villebon, who called Port Royal "a little Normandy for apples." He criticized the populace for their laziness, but then went on to list the varieties they'd already planted. "Calvilles, Rambours, Reinettes and three or more varieties are found at Port Royal, and russet pears. There were other varieties of pears and cherries, including Bigarotiers which they allowed to go to ruin," he griped.

In spite of Villebon's pessimism, the Annapolis Valley flourished. Its climate was, and still is, ideal. Sheltered, and blessed with sun for much longer than other locations in the Maritimes, the region produces a large and luscious crop of apples. When Nova Scotians wax lyrical about apples, it's usually about their Gravenstein, called the quintessential all-round apple by the Nova Scotia Fruit Growers Association. The Gravenstein apple's heritage dates back to before 1669 in Germany, but it came to Nova Scotia from the London Horticultural Society in the mid-1800s. Charles Prescott was the region's Johnny Appleseed, almost single-handedly establishing the Gravenstein as the apple of choice. He gave away cuttings to all and sundry. It was such a superior early apple that, with Prescott's help, by 1859 virtually every farm had a tree. This marvellous old apple, with its defined striping, now officially called the Old-Fashioned Gravenstein, is grown only by a handful of Nova Scotian orchardists.

Fate stepped in with another twist. In the 1870s, the apple trees of France were damaged by a serious blight and people in eastern Canada were encouraged to grow apples. By 1884, Nova Scotia was exporting apple trees back to the continent. At Mabou on Cape Breton, three small nurseries alone shipped over 4,000 seedlings.

Fruit travelled farther west with the fur trade. Apples, grapes and stone fruits were planted at the St. Charles Mission in the Peace River Valley in the 1880s. In British Columbia, the early fruit tree plantings by the Hudson's Bay Company, along the Old Yale Road in the lower Fraser River Valley and east toward Ashcroft, are dated 1843. By the end of the following century, apples had spread to British Columbia, where Fort Langley's orchard was hailed as a huge success. On Vancouver Island, apple varieties called Fallawater, Bellflower, Astrachan and Lemon Pippin were planted in orchards near Victoria. As the industry thrived and more growers came on stream, so did a vibrant research community. William Saunders brought many apple seedlings to his new position as the first director of Ottawa's Central Experimental Farm. His successor, W.T. Macoun, eventually named some 174 new cultivars. Kentville, Nova

Scotia, Morden, Manitoba, and Summerland, British Columbia, all bred fruit trees, with the Spartan apple coming from the B.C. station.

The Vineland Research Station in southern Ontario, which celebrated its centennial in 2006, has a substantial library of heritage apples and an enormous collection of peaches, pears and plums, numbering several thousand cultivars each. It's one of my favourite places on earth in late summer. I wander through the ongoing trials of various new and older peach, plum, cherry and pear cultivars, tasting and comparing with a tissue under my chin to catch the juice. Although some of these varieties never find their way through the regular grocery distribution system, they can sometimes be found in farmers markets across the province and at the numerous roadside stands that spring up along Lake Erie's north shore route during growing season, from Niagara to Leamington.

Transparents are among the earliest of apple varieties. They're sold by the bushel at Guelph's Farmers Market and make spectacular applesauce.

Summer and early autumn are the times when it's a bit easy to go wild and purchase all the produce in sight. But if we are collectively serious about eating locally, it is one of the best, most delicious and economical ways of shopping. Freezing fruit is so simple and often requires only the freezer containers. Cut plums in half, remove the pits and, bingo, they're done. Strawberries can be sweetened or not. The same is true of all the other berry varieties. The bonus is that, particularly for home cooks, fruit is often transferable from one recipe to another. Dried or fresh cranberries go so well with apples that they can be tossed into Clay-Baked Pork with Apples (page 252) or strewn on top of the Apple Custard Torte (page 270). Cherries or even plums can be substituted for apples in Apple Clafoutis (page 260). Rhubarb Cobbler (page 267) and Four-Generation Rhubarb Pie (page 266) are great with a handful of strawberries or raspberries gently stirred in. Peach and Apricot Platz (page 268) can become Apple, Pear and Blackberry Platz if the season or the spirit moves you.

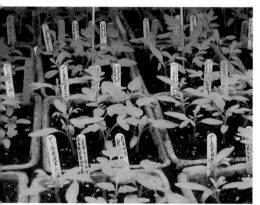

Chilled Fresh Tomato Soup (Gazpacho)

Although it's possible to make a decent cold tomato soup at other times of the year, the very best—and most authentic—is prepared when tomatoes are at the very peak of their season in late August. Never peel them—just remove any blemishes. At that same time of year, cucumbers are sold by the bushel. The small ones can also be used, scrubbed well but without peeling. Large ones should be peeled and seeded.

In the summer of 2007, I discovered an incredible cider vinegar from Domaine Levasseur in Quebec. Unfiltered and unpasteurized, it is perfect for this classic cold soup. Instead of the more commonly used olive oil, I substituted Jason Persall's cold-pressed soybean oil in one batch and Highwood Crossings organic cold-pressed canola in another. Spectacular!

YIELD: 6 to 8 servings

> 8 to 12 tomatoes, unpeeled
> 3 to 6 small garden cucumbers
> 2 or 3 green onions
> 2 cloves garlic
> 1 sweet red pepper, seeded
> ½ sweet green pepper, seeded
> ¼ cup (60 mL) high-quality apple cider vinegar
> ½ cup (125 mL) cold-pressed canola or soybean oil
> Salt and freshly ground pepper
> Condiments: Sour cream or yogurt, chopped chives or green onions, additional chopped tomatoes and cucumbers and toasted croutons

Prepare the soup in the traditional fashion by chopping the tomatoes, cucumbers, green onions, garlic and red and green peppers by hand. Or simply chop them coarsely and place in a food processor and pulse to make a rough soup. Some cooks continue to process the vegetables to make them into a smooth purée.

Transfer to a glass or ceramic bowl; stir in the vinegar and oil. Season to taste with salt and pepper. Cover and refrigerate for at least 4 hours or until thoroughly chilled, or overnight. Serve in chilled bowls, passing the remaining condiments separately.

Tulle's Red Cabbage (Ródkål)

This is the other recipe sought after by Tulle Knudstrup's niece, Alessandra (see page 129 for the whole story). It is a quintessential version of sweet 'n' sour red cabbage. Tulle suggested that apples could also be added to this dish, which is often an accompaniment for frikadeller (page 128), fresh ham with the skin on, or poultry, the preferences being duck or goose. If you don't have quite enough room for all the cabbage at the beginning, be patient; it will cook down and eventually it will all fit in the pot. Slow cooking and stirring allows the colour to infuse the white parts of the leaves.

YIELD: 6 to 8 servings

1 red cabbage (about 3 lb/1.5 kg)
⅓ cup (75 mL) butter
½ cup (125 mL) granulated sugar
2 tbsp (30 mL) white vinegar
Juice of ½ lemon
1 tsp (5 mL) salt
1 cup (250 mL) red currants
1 cup (250 mL) pitted prunes

Peel the outside leaves off the cabbage and discard. Cut cabbage into quarters, removing the core. Slice thinly; set aside.

In a large saucepan, heat the butter, sugar, vinegar, lemon juice, salt and red currants over medium heat. Add the cabbage and prunes. Cover and steam for 1 to 1 ½ hours, stirring often at the beginning to allow the juices to seep from the cabbage and to prevent burning. Taste to adjust the seasonings by adding more salt, vinegar and/or sugar as needed.

Clay-Baked Pork with Apples

Clay baking is an ancient and supremely simple cooking method, resulting in foods that rival any braised dish a cook can serve. The only prerequisite is that the clay pot has to be soaked for a few hours. Immerse it in cold water in the sink for a day or overnight. Once the pot is soaked, cooking food in it is fast and it's the easiest way I've found to create a perfect winter meal.

This is free-form cooking. Depending on the size of your baker, you can add a few potato chunks, some celery, a few pieces of squash or a chopped, unpeeled tomato. After the baker is full of meat, vegetables and apples, add enough cider and stock so that it's visible just below the surface. My clay baker takes about 2 to 2½ cups (500 to 625 mL) liquid.

YIELD: 4 to 6 servings

> 2 to 3 lb (1 to 1.5 kg) lean pork
> 1 large onion, coarsely chopped
> 3 carrots, peeled and cut into 1-inch (2.5 cm) chunks
> 1 large cooking apple, cored and chopped
> 1½ cups (375 mL) apple cider
> 1½ cups (375 mL) chicken stock
> 1 tsp (5 mL) salt
> ½ tsp (2 mL) hot paprika
> ½ tsp (2 mL) freshly ground pepper
> 2 tbsp (30 mL) cornstarch

Soak the clay baker in cold water for 4 to 6 hours. Set the baker on a towel and add the pork, onion, carrots, apple, apple cider, 1 cup (250 mL) of the chicken stock, salt, paprika and pepper. Cover and place in a cold oven. Bake at 350°F (180°C) for 3 hours. Stir the cornstarch into the remaining stock until smooth; set aside.

About 30 minutes before the baking time is up, carefully remove the baker from the oven, loosening the lid with a sharp knife if necessary. Stir in the stock mixture; re-cover and return to the oven to thicken and finish baking.

Chefs Brian Schmeler and Stacey Kanelos gave my grandson Ayden an apple tree on his arrival into this world. (Chefs love to give food gifts!) Planted in the Elora backyard of my friends Eleanor and John Morris, this apple, the first one to be picked, travelled across Canada in Great-Grandma Anne's luggage to Victoria, B.C., where Ayden clearly enjoyed eating it.

Spiced Summer Berry Sauce

As the berries come into season, the texture and flavour of this relish changes. Trudi Heiss serves this with Planked Okanagan Trout (page 80), but it's amazing with any other grilled fish or even barbecued pork.

Yield: About 1 cup (250 mL)

1 cup (250 mL) berries, such as blueberries, cranberries, blackberries or raspberries

6 tbsp (90 mL) granulated sugar

1 sprig summer savory or tarragon

½ tsp (2 mL) crushed pink peppercorns (optional but recommended)

⅛ tsp (0.5 mL) each cinnamon and nutmeg

1 tbsp (15 mL) water

1 tbsp (15 mL) lemon juice

Salt and freshly ground pepper

In a small heavy saucepan over medium heat, combine the berries, sugar, savory, pink peppercorns, cinnamon, nutmeg, water and lemon juice; bring to a boil. Cover, reduce heat and simmer for 4 to 6 minutes or until the berries are soft. Remove from heat and let cool. When cool, season, cover and refrigerate.

A few boxes of Al Sullivan's summer raspberry crop, harvested at the Elora Research Station.

New Brunswick Berry and Rhubarb Compote

At Hôtel Paulin (circa 1891) in Caraquet, New Brunswick, Karen Mersereau and Gerard Paulin serve this compote with his Acadian Meat Pie (page 117) or with a silky cod liver pâté. Usually made in a terrine, the pâté is soft and sea flavoured, made with the fresh cod livers Gerard sources from local fishermen who call him on their way to the docks. The compote will store for a few weeks in the refrigerator.

YIELD: 4 cups (1 L)

> 2 cups (500 mL) blueberries
> 2 cups (500 mL) chopped rhubarb
> 2 cups (500 mL) cranberries
> 1½ cups (375 mL) granulated sugar
> ⅛ tsp (0.5 mL) ground ginger
> ⅛ tsp (0.5 mL) ground allspice
> ⅛ tsp (0.5 mL) ground cloves
> Orange juice

In a heavy saucepan, combine the blueberries, rhubarb, cranberries and sugar. Crush gently to release the juices. Stir in the ginger, allspice and cloves and cook over medium heat until the mixture comes to a boil. Reduce heat and simmer for 10 to 15 minutes or until thickened, adding orange juice if the mixture becomes too thick before the berries are fully cooked.
Pour into clean glass jars and seal. Let cool. Refrigerate.

A tree on Tancook Island, near Chester, Nova Scotia, is decorated with fishing floats, making it look a bit like Christmas all year round.

Whipped Wild Berry Pudding

This easy recipe is a perfect example of the resilience of the Finnish people, who are noted for their *sisu,* or "fortitude." In 1901, a group of Finns settled on Malcolm Island, on the northwest coast of British Columbia, in their quest to create Utopia. Looking at the map of the coast, one might think that the climate would be horrendous. But when I arrived there in late June, Tuula Lewis's garden was more advanced than my own in southern Ontario. A huge sour cherry tree towered over the backyard, laden with fruit. She picks wild blackberries for much of the summer and cooks them to extract the juice in a multi-layered juicer from Finland. Then she makes this delicious dessert. The recipe's simplicity makes it almost unbelievable when one first reads it. The pudding is best made on the day you plan to serve it. In Finland it was made with lingonberries, which we know in some parts of Canada as partridgeberries. But any tart fruit like cranberries or even strawberries will work well. A reminder: farina is commercially known as Cream of Wheat or wheat hearts.

YIELD: 4 servings

> 2 cups (500 mL) fruit juice
> ½ cup (125 mL) granulated sugar
> ¼ cup (60 mL) farina

In a saucepan over medium heat, bring the juice and sugar to a boil. Stir in the farina and cook over medium heat until thickened, 4 to 6 minutes. Remove from the heat and transfer to a mixing bowl. With an electric mixer on high speed, beat the hot pudding for 10 to 15 minutes or until fluffy and much lighter in colour. Serve with whipped cream or simply as is, garnished with some fruit.

The sweeping cobble beach at Sointula on a moody B.C. day.

Brazilian Strawberry Mousse

Brazilians love fluffy desserts. At home they use guava, papaya and mango. Here, expat Brazilian Karen Baxter says that the freshest, ripest summer berries are the best.

YIELD: 8 to 10 servings

2 tbsp (30 mL) unflavoured gelatin
½ cup (125 mL) cold water
½ cup (125 mL) boiling water
2 lb (1 kg) fresh strawberries, stemmed and sliced
1 can (300 mL) sweetened condensed milk
1¼ cups (300 mL) whipping cream (35%)
Fresh whole or sliced berries

Sprinkle the gelatin over the cold water in a heatproof measuring cup. Let soften for 5 minutes. Add boiling water and stir until the gelatin melts. Set aside.

In a food processor or blender, process the strawberries until well puréed. With the motor running, pour in the sweetened condensed milk; process for a few seconds. Add the softened gelatin; process for a few seconds longer. Pour the mixture into a large bowl. Cover and refrigerate for 45 to 60 minutes or until just beginning to thicken slightly.

Whip the cream until stiff. Fold into the strawberry mixture and refrigerate until chilled and set, 2 to 3 hours. Serve garnished with fresh berries.

Strawberries at the Trout Lake Farmers Market in downtown Vancouver.

THE E.D. SMITH STORY

The House that Jam Built by Llewellyn S. Smith (1995) chronicles the eight generations of his family and their many contributions to Canada. Ernest D'Israeli Smith was born in 1853 into a Loyalist farming family. Because of poor eyesight, he was unable to continue his education and stayed on the farm near Winona, Ontario. Roads in that region are still named by the number of miles from the American border. Today's wineries often allude to them: On the Twenty, a fine inn and restaurant that is also the home of Cave Springs Winery; Thirty Bench, another great winery just a little farther away; and, finally, The Fifty, where E.D. Smith's grandparents settled. He later lived on a property through which Fifty Mile Creek flowed.

E.D. Smith was a savvy man. He watched his accounts studiously. Fortunately, he was also a diarist. Truisms are spread throughout his writings. "Grapes will pay here I believe," he wrote in 1879. In September of that year, he shipped his first harvest to Guelph, Ontario. In November of 1880, he penned, "I intend to go into fruit now extensively as I believe that there will be an almost unlimited market for the next generations."

With that, he planned the next decade of farming operations, which included the planting of peaches, apples and plums. He also budgeted for bees because every orchard of the day had its own pollinating hives. In 1883, he decided he'd had enough of wholesalers, so he began his own distribution system. When prices fell and sales weren't up to his predictions, he decided to make jam, the first such operation in Canada. By 1905, his factory was in full operation. E.D. Smith Pure Fruit Jam became an icon of Canadian food manufacturing.

B.C. Apple Clafoutis with Fluffy Soured-Cream Topping (Battu)

Pierre Dubrulle has been on the vanguard of British Columbia's food scene since he arrived from France in October 1971. He always understood "local," and his classic book, *The Canadian Chef from France* (Centax, 1986), is one of the earliest examples of how classic techniques can be applied to local ingredients.

Pierre was born in France "under heavy Allied bombardment" after his parents had already lost two children. "My mother was so frightened that she could not nurse me, so my father bought a goat and I was raised on goat's milk," says Pierre. He grew up in a family that truly lived food. "My dad introduced me to hunting and fishing, so my mum would cook all kinds of game and river fish. We had an extensive garden with 200 fruit trees. Butter and milk came from the farm nearby."

This recipe was his mother's and may also be made with almost any seasonal fruit—pitted cherries, pitted and halved plums or pears. Top with Pierre's *battu,* his rendition of crème fraîche.

From his current home, a B & B in Mission, B.C., Pierre reminisces:

My mother used to serve her clafoutis aux pommes using apples from our orchard back in Sailly-sur-la-Lys in Northern France. She would make it and there was never any left over, as we would eat it all on the same day. It was so good. The battu recipe is from my chef and mentor, Armando Invernizzi, the man to whom I owe so much and with whom I did my apprenticeship in my hometown of Lille, also in Northern France. He would combine equal parts of plain yogurt and crème fraîche. When I came to Canada, crème fraîche was not available, so I thought of replacing it with sour cream. A touch of kirsch is recommended and a bit of icing sugar for sweetener.

Pierre tells the story of a visit to Toronto in 1986 to promote his cookbook: "Peter Gzowski invited me to be on his *Morningside* show, and I brought him the apple clafoutis, which he raved about on air after indulging in a large slice."

Today, Pierre buys his apples from Silverhill Orchards, a local orchard that also grows heirloom tomatoes and makes its own apple cider vinegar.

YIELD: 6 to 8 servings

3 lb (1.5 kg) apples

6 eggs

⅔ cup (150 mL) granulated sugar

⅔ cup (150 mL) all-purpose flour

⅔ cup (150 mL) cornstarch

2 tbsp (30 mL) baking powder

⅛ tsp (0.5 mL) salt

⅞ cup (200 mL) hot melted butter

6 tbsp (90 mL) granulated sugar

Battu (recipe follows)

Butter and generously flour two 9-inch (23 cm) shallow tart pans.

Peel and core the apples; cut into small cubes. Beat the eggs with ⅔ cup (150 mL) sugar.

Sift in the flour, cornstarch, baking powder and salt, stirring until evenly combined. Gently whisk in the hot melted butter. Divide the batter between the pans; spread with apples and sprinkle with 6 tbsp (90 mL) sugar.

Bake in a preheated 350°F (180°C) oven for 40 minutes or until beginning to brown. Serve while still warm, topped with battu.

Battu

Yield: 2½ cups (625 mL)

½ cup (125 mL) whipping cream (35%)

1 cup (250 mL) plain yogurt

1 cup (250 mL) sour cream

½ cup (125 mL) icing sugar

1 tbsp (15 mL) kirsch

Whip the cream until stiff; stir in the yogurt, sour cream, sugar and kirsch.

Cover and refrigerate until serving. Spoon over fresh clafoutis or other fruit tart.

Evaluating apples is part of the task of men like Dr. Peter Rideout and his colleagues Andrew Jamieson and Doug Nichols, shown here with Nova Scotian-grown Honeycrisp, a variety that flourishes in the cool Maritime nights. Based at Kentville, Dr. Rideout and his colleagues are developing newer strains of fruit (the KRSO2 strawberry will be great for the jam industry) and perfecting older ones (sea buckthorn for its essential oils and thorn-less blackberries) for the specific climate conditions of Atlantic Canada. The 10 (which was the mark out of 10) on the apple was the evaluation by Kentville Station staff ... they loved it.

Island Blueberry Buckle

The red dust of Prince Edward Island swirled behind John and Flossie MacDonald's truck as we ripped down the back roads near Souris. We were hunting for a field of blueberries. We emerged onto a sunny knoll above the field, where huge harvesters were coming directly toward us in the summer sun. In front of us were stacks of boxes, most full of richly flavoured berries.

There are many island variations on this dessert, but this is Flossie's. It showcases the old-fashioned spices of the Maritimes. Serve the blueberry buckle warm with whipped cream or ice cream.

YIELD: 6 servings

TOPPING:
⅓ cup (75 mL) granulated sugar
⅓ cup (75 mL) all-purpose flour
½ tsp (2 mL) cinnamon
¼ cup (60 mL) chilled butter

BATTER:
½ cup (125 mL) butter, softened
½ cup (125 mL) granulated sugar
3 eggs, beaten
½ cup (125 mL) milk
1½ cups (375 mL) all-purpose flour
2 tsp (10 mL) baking powder
¼ tsp (1 mL) salt
1 tsp (5 mL) nutmeg
¼ tsp (1 mL) cloves
2 cups (500 mL) blueberries

In 2005, John and Flossie MacDonald took me on a drive on eastern P.E.I. to show me how blueberries were harvested mechanically. We climbed into their big rumbling truck and took off along the red earth roads near Souris. Finally, down what was more of a dirt track than a road, we came upon a large acreage of ripe berries. There the harvest was in full swing. These were some of the berries picked that day.

TOPPING: Combine the sugar, flour and cinnamon; cut in the butter until crumbly with the consistency of cornmeal. Set aside.

BATTER: Beat butter until light in colour; whip in the sugar, eggs and milk. Sift together the flour, baking powder, salt, nutmeg and cloves. Spread in a lightly oiled 9- x 13-inch (3.5 L) baking pan. Spread the blueberries evenly over the base.

Sprinkle the topping evenly over the blueberries. Bake in a preheated 350°F (180°C) oven for 45 minutes or until golden and crusted.

Butter-Honey Blueberry Muffins

Jo Marie Powers, my friend and co-author of *The Farmers Market Cookbook* (Stoddart, 1984), has a rambling old cottage in the Moon River basin in the middle of Ontario's prime blueberry country. She freezes bags of berries and uses this recipe all year long.

YIELD: 12 muffins

> ¼ cup (60 mL) butter, softened
> ½ cup (125 mL) granulated sugar
> ¼ cup (60 mL) liquid honey
> 1 egg
> 1½ cups (375 mL) cake-and-pastry flour
> 2 tsp (10 mL) baking powder
> ½ tsp (2 mL) salt
> ½ cup (125 mL) buttermilk
> 1½ cups (375 mL) wild blueberries

Whip the butter, sugar and honey until well blended. Add the egg and beat until light in colour. In a separate bowl, sift together the flour, baking powder and salt. Add to the creamed ingredients alternately with the buttermilk. Gently fold in the blueberries.

Spoon into well-oiled or paper-lined muffin tins. Place in a preheated 400°F (200°C) oven; reduce heat to 375°F (190°C) and bake for 25 to 30 minutes or until golden.

Harvesting P.E.I. blueberries near Souris and selling them at the Charlottetown Farmers Market.

Great-Grandma's Sour Cream Apple Pie

"We always called this Dutch apple pie," writes my mother. She adds:

> It was quite a favourite in my growing-up years. I recall vividly my grand-mother making it. She was from Prussia. The sour cream came, of course, from the cream can in the cellar. That cream can held the makings of our home-churned butter, sour cream for mother's biscuits, et cetera. What was left over was picked up by the creamery truck to be made into butter, which eventually found its way into our local grocery stores.

Northern Spys are often huge, so if you use another, smaller variety like Cortland or Gala, you will likely have to increase the number of apples.

YIELD: 6 to 8 servings

    One unbaked 9-inch (23 cm) pie shell (page 222)
    3 or 4 large tart apples, such as Northern Spy
    1 cup (250 mL) granulated sugar
    3 tbsp (45 mL) all-purpose flour
    ½ tsp (2 mL) salt
    1 cup (250 mL) sour cream
    1 tsp (5 mL) cinnamon

Peel and slice the apples into the unbaked pie shell. Reserve 1 tbsp (15 mL) of the sugar. Stir the remaining sugar with the flour, salt and sour cream until smooth. Spread over the apples. Sprinkle with cinnamon and reserved sugar. Bake in a preheated 425°F (210°C) oven for 10 minutes. Reduce heat to 350°F (180°C) and continue baking until bubbling and lightly browned, 35 to 40 minutes. Let cool for 30 minutes to set before serving.

The old apple tree at Margaret Sherk and Elmer Wideman's farm bends under the weight of fruit.

Four-Generation Rhubarb Pie

This recipe, from Fred Gordon of Elora, Ontario, spans his family's culinary history. "This recipe is quite old," he says. "My Grandmother Sanderson, my mom's mom, had it in her recipe file, written in her mother's hand, and my mom has it written in her mother's hand, and mine is in my mom's hand." Fred harvests his own rhubarb for this superb pie, the most delicious version I've tasted.

YIELD: 6 to 8 servings

   1¼ cups (300 mL) granulated sugar
   ¼ cup (60 mL) all-purpose flour
   ¼ tsp (1 mL) salt
   3 tbsp (45 mL) orange juice
   Grated rind of 1 orange (optional)
   ¼ cup (60 mL) melted butter
   3 eggs, separated
   2½ cups (625 mL) diced rhubarb
   9-inch (23 cm) deep pie shell (page 222)

In a large bowl, combine 1 cup (250 mL) of the granulated sugar with the flour and the salt. Stir in the orange juice, rind (if using) and the melted butter to make a paste-like consistency.

In a small bowl, gently beat the egg yolks and stir into the orange juice mixture. Add the diced rhubarb and stir to coat thoroughly.

In a separate bowl, beat the egg whites until soft peaks form. Gradually beat in ¼ cup (60 mL) sugar until stiff peaks form. Gently fold into the rhubarb mixture, taking care to incorporate thoroughly but not to deflate the egg whites.

Pour into the pie shell and bake for 25 minutes in a preheated 375°F (190°C) oven. Reduce heat to 325°F (160°C) and bake for 25 to 30 minutes longer or until golden brown and the centre is set.

Nova Scotian Rhubarb Cobbler

The classic recipes are often the finest. This one is Marie Nightingale's favourite springtime dessert. It first appeared in her groundbreaking volume, *Out of Old Nova Scotia Kitchens,* in 1970. If there is one Maritime cookbook that should be on every bookshelf, this is it. Marie worked at the *Halifax Chronicle,* and she was the first journalist in Canada to research and write about regional food traditions, filling in the stories with homestyle, often homespun, recipes. This is what she wrote about this dessert: "Until not too many years ago, rhubarb was used in a spring tonic and given to every member of the household whether he was sick or not. The following recipe is a pleasant way of serving rhubarb." I enjoy it served warm with cream and maple syrup drizzled over top.

YIELD: 9 servings

BASE:
   ½ cup (125 mL) granulated sugar
   ½ tsp (2 mL) salt
   2 tbsp (30 mL) cornstarch
   4 cups (1 L) rhubarb pieces (1 inch/2.5 cm)
   1 cup (250 mL) water

COBBLER TOPPING:
   2 cups (500 mL) all-purpose flour
   ½ tsp (2 mL) salt
   1 tbsp (15 mL) baking powder
   3 tbsp (45 mL) granulated sugar
   ¼ cup (60 mL) chilled butter
   1 cup (250 mL) milk (approximately)

BASE: Mix together the sugar, salt and cornstarch. Add the rhubarb and water, mixing well, and pour into a greased 9-inch (23 cm) square pan. Place in a preheated 425°F (210°C) oven and bring to a boil.

TOPPING: Meanwhile, combine the flour, salt, baking powder and 2 tbsp (30 mL) of the sugar. Cut in the butter until the consistency of cornmeal. Add the milk, stirring lightly, to make a batter that will drop from your spoon. Drop by tablespoons onto the bubbling fruit mixture and sprinkle with the remaining sugar. Return to the oven, sliding a foil-covered baking sheet onto the rack below to catch any drips. Bake for 20 to 25 minutes longer or until deep golden.

ICE CIDER

Ice cider (*cidre de glace*) begins, like icewine, with frozen fruit. The producers seem to be moving toward regulation that would prevent them from merely freezing apple cider and removing the ice cap before fermentation to a more traditional method, similar to that of icewine, whereby the frozen fruit is harvested from the tree. Ice cider is sweeter and less expensive than icewine, with about 12 percent alcohol. The best place to purchase ice cider is at the Société des Alcools (SAQ) outlets around Quebec.

Peach and Apricot Platz

In Ontario, peaches, apricots, cherries and pears all flourish, from Niagara to Leamington. This is likely the lushest drive one can take during the harvest. Mile after mile of fruit trees hang heavy with the sweetest harvest. Near Windsor, there is a substantial Russian Mennonite community, which has tenaciously maintained its culinary traditions, both at home and in the large religious community.

I first heard of *platz* from a vendor at the Windsor Farmers Market. He knew it as "pie by the yard." The word "pie" belies its lovely cake-like base, studded with seasonal or home-frozen fruit and sprinkled with a buttery crumb topping. You'll note that the instructions don't require that the fruit be peeled. It's a personal decision.

I often make this dessert with plums, which are among the easiest summer fruits to freeze. Simply wash them, pat dry and halve them, removing the stones. Fill whatever size freezer bag you wish, pushing out as much air as possible before tying the bag tightly and popping it into the freezer.

YIELD: 8 to 10 servings

CRUMB TOPPING:
½ cup (125 mL) all-purpose flour
½ cup (125 mL) granulated sugar
½ cup (125 mL) butter, softened

BASE:
½ cup (125 mL) granulated sugar
½ cup (125 mL) butter, softened
2 eggs
1 tsp (5 mL) vanilla extract
1½ cups (375 mL) all-purpose flour
2 tsp (10 mL) baking powder
¼ cup (60 mL) milk

1½ cups (375 mL) sliced peaches
1 cup (250 mL) halved pitted apricots

CRUMB TOPPING: Combine the flour and sugar; cut in the butter until crumbly. Set aside.

BASE: In a medium bowl, thoroughly cream together the sugar, butter, eggs and vanilla. In a separate bowl, sift together the flour and baking powder. Add to the creamed mixture alternately with the milk, forming a smooth, thick batter. Spread evenly on the base of a well-oiled or parchment-lined 9- x 13-inch (3.5 L) baking pan.

Arrange fruit in rows or simply strew it on top of the batter. Scatter evenly with the crumb topping and bake in a preheated 350°F (180°C) oven for 45 to 50 minutes or until golden brown around the edges. Cut into squares. Serve warm with milk, cream or ice cream.

Bins of perfectly ripe clingstone peaches await processing and freezing at Cherry Lane Frozen Foods near Vineland, Ontario.

The Kelowna Land and Orchard Company was founded by the Bullock family in 1904, and has been a working orchard ever since. Apples from their 104 acres are shipped around North America, but their main specialty is the precious Fuji apples they ship to Japan. Fuji apples are painstaking to produce. Each specimen is covered with a paper bag as it matures to prevent coloration. When the bag is removed, a sticky emblem is applied depending upon the intended destination. It may be a heart for a wedding party or a good luck wish. As the apple's skin darkens, the inscription remains creamy white, and when the decal is removed, the logo or greeting remains. KLO has the North American rights to produce Fuji apples—it's worth a trip to the orchard just to see the production.

Apple Custard Torte

Recipes, like ingredients, travel. My mother adapted this torte from one that superstar pastry chef Joanne Yolles of Toronto learned from the late Lillian Kaplun, the lady who, for at least one generation, taught Jewish ladies in that city to bake.

YIELD: 10 to 12 servings

BASE:
- ½ cup (125 mL) butter, softened
- ¾ cup (175 mL) granulated sugar
- 2 eggs
- 1½ cups (375 mL) all-purpose flour
- 2 tsp (10 mL) baking powder
- ½ tsp (2 mL) salt
- 6 Idared or other medium-sized, firm cooking apple, peeled and cut into eighths
- ½ tsp (2 mL) cinnamon

CUSTARD:
- ⅓ cup (75 mL) whipping cream (35%)
- ¾ cup (175 mL) granulated sugar
- 4 eggs
- 1 tsp (5 mL) vanilla extract

Lightly oil a 10-inch (25 cm) springform pan.

BASE: Cream together the butter, sugar and eggs until fluffy and light in colour. Sift the flour with the baking powder and salt. Carefully fold into the creamed mixture just until no dry spots remain. Spread evenly in the prepared pan. Stand the apple wedges upright until the entire surface is covered thickly with apples. Sprinkle with cinnamon. Bake in a preheated 350°F (180°C) oven for 55 to 60 minutes or until apples are tender.

CUSTARD: Whisk the cream with the sugar and eggs, stir in vanilla; pour over the baked base. Reduce oven temperature to 325°F (160°C) and bake torte for 30 to 35 minutes or until custard is set. Let cool for 10 to 15 minutes before loosening from pan and sliding onto a serving plate. Serve warm.

Date and Nut Loaf

The sweets offerings of the homemakers in my family always included Date and Nut Loaf. The loaves were wrapped and donated to bake sales or sliced and lightly buttered to serve with tea at baby and bridal showers, and, of course, at funerals.

This recipe is my mother's. She often doubles it and freezes the second loaf. While she uses walnuts, I like the heart nuts from the Niagara region of Ontario.

YIELD: 1 loaf

1½ cups (375 mL) chopped dates
1 cup (250 mL) boiling water
1 tsp (5 mL) baking soda
½ cup (125 mL) butter, softened
1 cup (250 mL) granulated sugar
1 egg
1 tsp (5 mL) vanilla extract
1¾ cups (425 mL) all-purpose flour
½ tsp (2 mL) baking powder
½ cup (125 mL) chopped walnuts, hazelnuts or heart nuts

In a small bowl, combine the dates, boiling water and baking soda. Set aside to cool completely.

Cream the butter with the sugar, egg and vanilla, beating until fluffy and light.

Sift or stir together the flour and baking powder. Add to the creamed mixture alternately with the date mixture; mix until no dry spots remain. Stir in the nuts. Transfer the batter to a well-oiled and parchment-lined 9- x 5-inch (2 L) loaf pan. Bake in a preheated 325°F (160°C) oven for 1 hour or until a tester inserted into the centre comes out clean.

NUT HARVESTING IN CANADA

Every autumn, with buckets and smiles, nut harvesters troop through the long, wet grass of the Gellatly Nut Farm near Kelowna, B.C., to collect a winter's supply. It speaks of well over a century of Canadian culinary history. "There is a distinct sense of magic in the air when you walk under those ancient and unusual trees," says local writer Judy Steeves.

Just as in some of the centuries-old cathedrals in England, or among the monstrous toppled blocks of rock at Glastonbury or Stonehenge, there is an eerie feeling of the past among those towering, cultivated trees along the lakeshore in Westbank.

The Gellatly Nut Farm is Canada's oldest nut orchard. In 1905, David Gellatly began to plant and nurture tree nuts that he believed would be suitable for the climate of British Columbia and the temperate parts of Canada. With his brother Jack, he built a thriving business. A great deal of their success had to do with Jack's skill at hybridization. His new nut varieties were exported to Europe and all over North America. From heart nuts to butternuts, from chestnuts to walnuts, the Gellatlys planted over 1,000 trees on their 9.8 acres. Many of the cultivars that Jack hybridized were given the suffix "oka" for easy identification. Chinoka is a "trazelnut," a cross between a Turkish hazelnut and a filbert. Right up until his death in 1969, Jack pruned and tended his nut grove, which is now a regional park.

Classic Baklava

The Greeks are known for these sticky pastries that are sliced and served still dripping with sweetness. There's nothing like having them baked fresh—they perfume the house. Baklava has an ancient history dating from Assyria in about the 8th century BC; it likely included nuts and honey. One thing that seems to have been understood then is the relationship between the spicing and the aphrodisiac qualities of the dessert. Cinnamon was the choice for women, while cardamom was considered good for men.

This baklava was adapted from a Stroutzas family recipe.

YIELD: About 24 servings

SOAKING SYRUP:
> 2 cups (500 mL) granulated sugar
> 1½ cups (375 mL) water
> 1 cinnamon stick
> 1 tbsp (15 mL) lemon juice

BAKLAVA:
> 3 cups (750 mL) ground or finely chopped almonds or walnuts
> ¼ cup (60 mL) granulated sugar
> ½ tsp (2 mL) cinnamon
> 1 pkg (16 oz/454 g) phyllo pastry, thawed if frozen
> ¾ cup (175 mL) melted unsalted butter

SOAKING SYRUP: In a heavy saucepan, combine the sugar, water and cinnamon. Heat gently to boiling and when boiling, add the lemon juice. Simmer for 5 minutes. Remove from heat and set aside to cool.

BAKLAVA: Stir together the nuts, sugar and cinnamon. Lay a sheet of phyllo in the bottom of each of 2 buttered 9 x 13-inch (3.5 L) cake pans, folding the sheet of dough back onto itself. Brush with melted butter and add 2 more sheets, without buttering them. Divide half of the nut mixture between the pans, spreading it evenly. Layer another 3 sheets of phyllo on each pan, buttering them generously. Spread with the remaining nut mixture. Layer the remaining phyllo pastry onto the baklava, buttering each sheet.

With an extremely sharp knife, cut the top layer of the baklava into diamonds or squares.

Bake in a preheated 350°F (180°C) oven until golden brown, 30 to 35 minutes. Remove from oven and immediately pour soaking syrup over both pans. Let cool completely before serving.

Nuts arranged on the cracking stump at Gellatly Nut Farm, clockwise from the top: shiny sweet chestnuts are at the top in the centre; the green heart nut and its brown nut are to the right. Below them are two giant Manoka walnuts developed on the farm in the 1940s and regular English Broadview walnuts. To the left are Fioka heartnuts, some as they come from the tree and the other brown and wrinkly. This heartnut is also called "Buartnut." The letters "oka" in any of the nut names indicate that that variety was developed in the Okanagan at that farm.

Margaret's Spiced Plum Butter

Apple butter is a long-standing tradition in central Ontario, so when Margaret Sherk, a Mennonite lady who is not only a dentist but also farms in Wellington County, found this recipe, she tackled it. Margaret and her husband, Elmer Wideman, have an orchard with their own purple plums. "Because I have made this in very large quantities, each batch is a little different," says Margaret. "Elmer likes not too much spice and more sugar than I do. Keeps it interesting!"

The original recipe came from a fabulous preserving book, *Put a Lid on It* (Macmillan Canada, 1997), by Ellie Topp and Margaret Howard, but Margaret Sherk began playing with her own variations. I love this butter! It's wonderful on breakfast toast, which merely serves as a vehicle to get the butter to one's mouth. And like the quince paste I've tasted in Australia, it's also great with soft goat's milk cheese.

Either fresh or frozen plums can be used. If you boil the plum butter until it's very thick, this recipe will make about 1 cup (250 mL), but it's possible to stop the cooking process a little earlier to obtain a slightly larger yield. That's really at the cook's discretion.

A profusion of crabapple blossoms on a very old tree in Margaret Sherk and Elmer Wideman's Wellington County yard.

YIELD: **About 1 cup (250 mL)**

> 4 cups (1 L) halved, pitted purple plums
> ½ cup (125 mL) water
> ¾ cup (175 mL) granulated sugar
> 2 sticks (2 inches/5 cm) cinnamon
> 2 or 3 whole star anise

In a large heavy saucepan, simmer the plums in the water until very soft, 20 to 30 minutes. Remove from heat and let cool for 15 to 20 minutes. Purée in a blender or food processor until very smooth.

Return to saucepan and add the sugar, cinnamon and star anise; return to a boil. Reduce heat and simmer, uncovered, until desired thickness, about 30 minutes. Stir often to prevent burning. Discard spices and pour into a sterilized jar. Seal and refrigerate.

Blackcurrant Preserve

My mother made dozens of jars of this preserve when she managed a small market garden in addition to teaching elementary school in the small hamlet of Milliken, a place that is now merely a name on the sprawling map of Metropolitan Toronto. She sold the excess currants, along with cucumbers, beans, raspberries and lettuce, at a small roadside stand.

Because blackcurrants have their own pectin, this recipe is about as easy as any can get. The preserve will never be thick and jammy, but it will be perfect on toast or as a drink when boiling water is added. This recipe, as my mom has proven, is easily multiplied. (Pictured with Peter's Brioche, page 232.)

YIELD: 1½ cups (375 mL)

2 cups (500 mL) granulated sugar
1 cup (250 mL) water
1 cup (250 mL) blackcurrants

In a medium saucepan over medium heat, combine the sugar, water and currants. Cook, uncovered and stirring, until the currants are very soft, 15 to 20 minutes.

Spoon into hot, sterilized jars and seal. Store in a cool, dark place.

Wild Elderberry Syrup

My late stepfather, Glenn MacDonald, remembered his mother making this syrup from the plentiful elderberries that used to flourish along the back roads of central Ontario. As all those who settled in that region were aware, it was important to use every opportunity to supplement the family meal with such foraged foods.

This syrup is delicious on pancakes, poured over ice cream or simply added to a glass of cold milk.

YIELD: 10 cups (2.5 L) or enough to fill five 2-cup (500 mL) jars

> 6 cups (1.5 L) stemmed elderberries
> 6 cups (1.5 L) water
> 12 cups (3 L) granulated sugar
> ¼ cup (60 mL) lemon juice

In a large saucepan, combine the elderberries and water; cover and bring to a boil over medium heat. Reduce heat and simmer, crushing fruit from time to time with the back of a wooden spoon, for 20 to 30 minutes or until fruit is very soft.

With a ladle, transfer to a dampened jelly bag or a colander lined with cheesecloth. Let drain into a basin or a bowl overnight.

Measure 6 cups (1.5 L) of the drained juice into a large heavy saucepan. Stir in the sugar and lemon juice. Cook over low heat, uncovered and stirring, until sugar has dissolved. Increase heat to high and bring to a boil. Cook, stirring, for 5 minutes or until syrupy.

Pour into hot, sterilized jars and seal.

Peach Chutney

When those of us here in Canada wanted to make terrific chutney but simply didn't have access to mangoes, a fruit that has only recently been widely available in markets outside of urban centres, we chose the perfect peaches that Canadian farmers are so expert at growing. Freestone peaches are the best for this chutney, and of those my personal choice is Loring, a big, sweet, late-harvested fruit.

YIELD: About 8 cups (2 L) or enough to fill four 2-cup (500 mL) jars

8 cups (2 L) sliced peeled fresh peaches
2 tbsp (30 mL) coarse pickling salt
3 cups (750 mL) granulated sugar
1½ cups (375 mL) cider vinegar
4 cloves garlic, minced
1½ cups (375 mL) finely chopped onion
2 tsp (10 mL) ground ginger
½ to 1 tsp (2 to 5 mL) red pepper flakes
¾ cup (175 mL) lemon juice
1 cup (250 mL) golden raisins
⅔ cup (150 mL) chopped candied ginger

In a large bowl, cover peaches with a brine made of the coarse salt and 4 cups (1 L) cold water. Cover and let stand for 8 hours or overnight. Drain thoroughly.

In a large saucepan over medium heat, combine the sugar, vinegar, garlic, onion, ginger, red pepper flakes, lemon juice and raisins. Add the peaches and bring to a boil. Reduce heat until the chutney is barely bubbling. Simmer until the peaches are translucent and the mixture is beginning to thicken, 35 to 40 minutes. Add the candied ginger and continue to cook for 10 minutes, stirring often to prevent sticking. At this point, it's possible to create an even thicker chutney, if desired, by simply boiling it longer.

Ladle into hot, sterilized jars. Seal tightly and store in a cool, dark place.

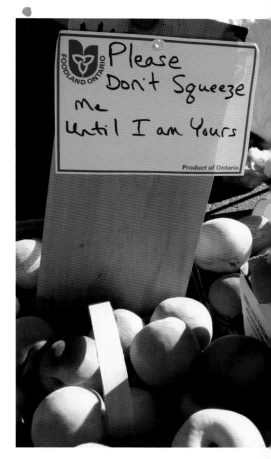

The ripest peaches for sale at the Guelph Farmers Market.

Green Tomato Pickle (Flossie's Chow)

There are many names for this recipe: chow chow or ketchup *vert* or governor's sauce. In the Maritimes, it's a must-serve with salt cod. In Quebec, it goes with tourtière, and in Ontario and farther west, it's essential with cold roast beef. Some versions call for whole pickling spice, which may be tied in a bag—or not. Others call for a series of spices, which usually include mustard and celery seeds and a bit of cinnamon. They all take turmeric. Most versions are not thickened with flour or cornstarch but are simmered, concentrating the flavours to a pungent intensity, whereas this Green Tomato Pickle, from Prince Edward Islander Flossie MacDonald, is milder and faster to make.

YIELD: 6 cups (1.5 L) or enough to fill three 2-cup (500 mL) jars

> 6 cups (1.5 L) thinly sliced green tomatoes
> 2 cups (500 mL) thinly sliced cooking onions
> 2½ tbsp (40 mL) coarse pickling salt
> 1½ cups (375 mL) granulated sugar
> 1½ cups (375 mL) white vinegar
> 2 tsp (10 mL) whole pickling spice
> 2 tbsp (30 mL) cornstarch
> ½ tsp (2 mL) turmeric
> ½ tsp (2 mL) dry mustard

In a bowl, combine the green tomatoes and onions; sprinkle with the salt, stir lightly and cover. Let stand overnight.

In the morning, drain and rinse with cold water. Drain thoroughly and transfer to a heavy saucepan. Stir in the sugar, 1 cup (250 mL) of the vinegar and the whole pickling spice; cover and bring to a boil over medium heat. Reduce heat and simmer for 20 to 25 minutes or until the vegetables are tender.

In a small bowl, stir together the cornstarch, turmeric, dry mustard and remaining vinegar. When smooth, add to the saucepan and continue to cook, stirring, for 10 to 15 minutes or until thickened and bubbling.

Ladle into hot, sterilized jars and seal tightly. Store in a cool, dark place.

Grown by David Cohlmeyer of Cookstown, Ontario, these tomatoes are definitely green in colour but they are fully ripe, not the unripe ones required for Flossie's Chow.

Hot Dog Relish

No one—and I mean *no one*—in my childhood ever bought that yucky green relish that we now seem to assume is what "goes with" hot dogs, sausages and burgers. This recipe is from my sister-in-law Kay Fettes' kitchen. Making it every autumn is a family tradition. If you're using an old-fashioned grinder, spread newspapers on the floor to catch the drips or move the entire operation outside.

YIELD: 16 cups (4 L) or enough to fill eight 2-cup (500 mL) jars

4 large cucumbers
9 green tomatoes
2 sweet red peppers, seeded
2 sweet green peppers, seeded
1 or 2 hot red peppers, seeded
3 large cooking onions, peeled
¼ cup (60 mL) coarse pickling salt
4 cups (1 L) white vinegar
½ cup (125 mL) finely diced celery
3½ cups (875 mL) granulated sugar
¼ cup (60 mL) all-purpose flour
1 tbsp (15 mL) dry mustard or finely ground yellow mustard seeds
½ tsp (2 mL) turmeric

Trim the ends off the cucumbers and the tomatoes. Coarsely grind them and place them into a large bowl. Either mince or grind the red, green and hot peppers and onions. Add to the cucumbers and tomatoes. Sprinkle with salt, stir lightly, cover and let stand overnight.

In the morning, drain thoroughly and transfer to a large saucepan. Add the vinegar, celery and 3 cups (750 mL) of the sugar; bring to a boil over medium heat. Reduce heat and boil gently for 20 minutes, stirring often to prevent sticking. Meanwhile, combine the remaining sugar with the flour, mustard and turmeric. When the relish is cooked, add the flour mixture; cook, stirring, for 3 to 4 minutes or until bubbling and thickened.

Ladle into hot, sterilized jars, seal and store in a cool, dark place.

LYCOPENE

It wasn't till 1987 that a University of Toronto researcher, Dr. Venket Rao, pushed tomatoes onto the list of super foods with his analysis of lycopene. A powerful antioxidant found in tomato skins, lycopene is now credited with a raft of health benefits including the prevention of prostate cancer, among other cancers, osteoporosis and heart disease. It's bioavailability—the rate at which the body absorbs it—is greatly enhanced when the tomato skins are cooked as in tomato paste. Now I never have to peel another tomato again, and once again, I feel virtuous opening a tin of tomatoes as a side dish for supper.

Mustard Pickle

To make a great mustard pickle is not difficult. However, it does take patience, which is something Elaine Mayne of Arthur, Ontario, developed over the years as she raised nine children on a shoestring budget. The secret to making this pickle is in the careful chopping of the cucumbers and the onions—they should be in ½-inch (1 cm) chunks. This relish is phenomenal on scrambled eggs.

YIELD: Enough to fill 12 1-cup (250 mL) jars

If the cucumbers are large, peel and seed them with a spoon. If they're small, simply chop them without peeling.

8 cups (2 L) chopped cucumbers
4 cups (1 L) chopped cooking onions
2 tbsp (30 mL) coarse pickling salt
1 large green pepper, seeded and finely chopped
1 large sweet red pepper, seeded and finely chopped
2 celery stalks, finely diced
4 cups (1 L) white vinegar
5 cups (1.25 L) granulated sugar
¾ cup (175 mL) all-purpose flour
1 tbsp (15 mL) dry mustard
1 tsp (5 mL) turmeric

In a large glass or crockery bowl, combine the cucumbers and onions; sprinkle with the salt, stir lightly, cover and let stand overnight at room temperature.

In the morning, drain well and place in a heavy saucepan. Stir in the green and red pepper, celery, vinegar and 4 cups (1 L) of the sugar; cover and bring to a boil. Reduce heat and simmer for 10 minutes. Meanwhile, stir together the remaining sugar, flour, mustard and turmeric. Add to the cooked pickle, stirring and cooking constantly until thickened.

Ladle it into hot, sterilized jars and seal. Store in a cool, dark place.

Winter Tomato Relish
(Chili Sauce/Ketchup *Rouge*)

With late summer being such a busy time, I rarely make chili sauce with fresh tomatoes. I find it much easier to freeze whole or chopped well-washed plum tomatoes and then use them over the winter in soups or for this excellent relish. I do not peel them. I begin the relish with a large tin of tomatoes or an equal amount of home-canned tomatoes.

YIELD: About 16 cups (4 L) or enough to fill eight 2-cup (500 mL) jars

1 can (2.84 L/100 oz) whole or diced tomatoes, or 12½ cups (3.125 L) home-
    canned tomatoes
2½ lb (1.2 kg) frozen tomatoes, either diced or whole
3 large onions, minced
3 cups (750 mL) diced celery
2 large sweet red peppers, seeded and diced
2 tbsp (30 mL) coarse pickling salt
½ cup (125 mL) whole pickling spice
2 tbsp (30 mL) whole allspice
1 tbsp (15 mL) coriander seed
1 tbsp (15 mL) mustard seed
1 tsp (5 mL) whole black peppercorns
1 tsp (5 mL) red pepper flakes, or 1 whole dried chili
2 cups (500 mL) apple cider vinegar
3½ cups (875 mL) brown sugar

Combine canned and frozen tomatoes in a heavy saucepans; stir in onions, celery, diced peppers and salt.

Make a spice bag by measuring pickling spice, allspice, coriander seed, mustard seed, black peppercorns and red pepper flakes onto a piece of cheesecloth. Tie tightly with a bit of string and immerse in the tomato mixture.

Add the vinegar, cover and bring to a boil over medium heat.

Reduce heat, uncover and simmer for 90 minutes or until starting to thicken, stirring often to prevent sticking.

Stir in the brown sugar, return to a boil and simmer for an additional 20 to 25 minutes or until thickened once again.

Remove cheesecloth bag. Ladle into hot, sterilized jars and seal tightly. Store in a cool, dark place.

These plum-style tomatoes are an old Heinz canning variety. I grew them from seeds that orbited the earth 171 times in a space shuttle mission, as part of a germination experiment conducted by University of Guelph's Dr. Mike Dixon. They germinated all right . . . so well that I had to enlist the help of my friend Margaret Sherk, who donated a large piece of her garden to their cultivation and care.

The Contemporary Palate

In the heritage grain field at the Wellington County Museum.

*T*he spring day I visited Joan Heath and Corey Loessin and their children, Audra and Aiden, on their 5,500-acre farm near Radisson, Saskatchewan, Joan was preparing a tailgate lunch of the finest order. It was a feast, similar to all the others she's made twice a day over the many years of her marriage. The kitchen was filled with the smell of freshly baked Nana's (Utterly Fabulous) Multi-Grain Rolls (page 149) and simmering Spicy Saskatchewan-Braised Beef (page 107) to be served with garlic mashed potatoes. She'd whipped up a fabulous Wheat Berry Salad (page 296), a spinach salad with strawberries and a canola dressing, an utterly delicious Prairie Lentil and Grain Cake (page 309), and her spectacular Prairie Grain Cookies (page 165). She packed the truck and we headed out.

Saskatchewan is a land of grand scale, a province where, perhaps because of the sky, things seem larger. Farms are enormous. Equipment to work them is gigantic and costs hundreds of thousands of dollars. It's a hard, rich life. Those who work the land are experts at multi-tasking. It seems to be part of the psyche. They are on the front lines of Canada's agricultural community.

As we drove, a big golden coyote trotted along in the ditch, unafraid and proud of it. Above a hawk wheeled, kittling on the updrafts of spring. On the 360-degree horizon, small dust clouds spiralled from the seeders of their neighbours. The land wasn't green yet. We parked behind a pile of brush, out of the chilling May wind, and waited. Just after noon, Corey arrived. He'd been working since 6 a.m. and wasn't going to stop till after 10 p.m. The crops had to go in when the earth was dry and warm enough. They'd just invested in a $200,000 air drill so that they could seed more and faster, sweeping the fields in graceful GPS-guided arcs with the long arms of the seeder extending like giant wings behind a multi-thousand-dollar tractor.

The sacks of seeds on the edge of the field provided an additional wind break. The following year, those seeds would provide the raw materials, the ingredients, for Joan and countless others to use for similar lunches and a multitude of dinners.

Safe out of the cold gusts, we needed the hot meal. That day Corey was seeding Blaze lentils, a variety developed at Pulse Crop Research Lab in Saskatoon, on part of his acreage. Had he run into a problem with the variety, he could call up the guy who developed it. This is the beauty of what is currently unfolding in food production in Canada. Not only are we privy to the indigenous foods of Canada, with origins we can only guess, there are men and women who are quietly, and frequently without fanfare, setting the future tables of our land with new foods. With them we complete the cycle of Canada's food life. While some of these researchers have retired, their stories are still very much with us, something that older food cultures cannot claim.

Corey is typical of thousands of western farmers. He plans his planting in order: peas first, then lentils, canola, barley and wheat. It's a massive task, and he is cultivating today's superfoods, ones with demonstrated health benefits. Most were well known to ancient cultures. Lentils date from 9500 BC, grown in the Fertile Crescent around the Mediterranean, while chickpeas were first cultivated in about 6000 BC. Soybeans are actually the oldest superfood, having been domesticated in northeastern China around the 11th century BC. Rapeseed, flax, safflower and broad beans were all domesticated very early.

Where these extraordinary crops dropped off the ship on the voyage to the New World is anyone's guess. Perhaps, with the available supply of meat and fish, the settlers simply turned their back on this traditional knowledge and buried it with the memories of starvation. Broad beans—the *gourganes* of old Quebec—were grown in gardens across the region and saved from year to year. Of the other old crops, only flax seems to have been cultivated, for making linen. In 1752, the *Halifax Gazette* printed a notice from the governor, who, in an attempt to wrest arable land from the forest, offered 20 shillings per acre that was cleared and planted with flax or hemp. By the end of that century, there were settlers who would insist on wearing only linen made with the flax they grew themselves. Little or no attention was paid to the pulse family, and the cooking fats of choice were lard and butter.

Thankfully, these incredible old crops are new again. They are among the healthiest on earth, and Canada grows them to perfection. These crops reflect the stories and the expansive dreams of the modern-day researchers who brought them to fruition. It's not a flight of fancy to say that what they perceived was an almost blank slate of possibilities. Armed with knowledge and determination and with large brushstrokes of imagination, they drew pulses and oil seeds on the Prairies and soybeans across central Canada.

Long before writer Michael Pollan's dictum "Eat food. Not too much. Mostly plants," was published in the *New York Times Magazine* in 2007, Canadian researchers and growers had been setting the stage for the shift he encourages and creating an array of healthy plant foods with fabulous flavours.

FROM ANCIENT GREECE AND ROME TO TODAY

Hippocrates, the father of modern medicine and a contemporary of Plato, wrote about how important chickpeas, lentils and flax were for the Greek diet. In ancient Rome, lentil stew, or *puls*, was a staple of the poor, who ironically had a far more wholesome diet than the elite who tended to dine on exotica. Roasted chickpeas were served in the *tavernae* (taverns), where the plebeian men went to drink. By the early Middle Ages, the production of pulses of all sorts—broad beans, chickpeas and yellow peas—increased to feed the masses. Eaten fresh or dried for storage, they were also ground into flour to be added to bread. They were part of the collective culture in Indian, Persian and Jewish/Mediterranean cuisine.

By the late Middle Ages, lentils, faba beans, peas and chickpeas had completely infiltrated the food ways of the poor across Europe and the Middle East. Although quantities were meagre, the scope of their diet also included cabbage, spinach, garlic, leeks, turnips and potatoes, many of the healthiest ingredients on today's modern shopping list.

After he'd established Canada as a pulse-growing nation, Dr. Al Slinkard turned his creativity to another product used the world over: spices. With the generally sunny, dry climate of the southern Prairies, Slinkard determined that the province was ideal for growing crops like fenugreek, cumin and coriander. He has released a number of new, more pungent varieties, so when East Indian cooks want the very best, they shop Saskatchewan.

Not only have our researchers given the world new varieties across many plant varieties, one team gave the world its finest oil, canola. Standing in a flowering canola field in the July sunshine is one of the most exquisite and quintessentially Canadian experiences. Canola is *the* Canadian oil, and the healthiest edible oil on the planet. As the world's only Made in Canada crop, it is often the nation's most valuable one, with annual exports of canola seed, oil and meal that are valued at over $3 billion.

Canola began as rapeseed, first planted at the Central Experimental Farm by William Saunders in 1899. By the 1940s, rapeseed was being grown under contract for the government because it was recognized for its ability to produce oil that would better cling to water- and steam-washed metals and as an additive for marine oils that would prevent salt damage. However, it was not edible because of the erucic acid it contained. In 1958, two professors, Keith Downey and the late Baldur Stefansson, took this on as a challenge, and in two different locations, they set about to improve the qualities of rapeseed by lowering the erucic acid and another component, glucosinolate. In other words, they wanted to make it into food. It took a decade, but in 1968, Downey released Oro with low erucic acid. Then in 1974, Stefansson released Tower, the first "double low" variety with reduced erucic acid and glucosinolate levels. Tower became the first registered variety of the new plant they called "canola." This was the beginning!

Another agricultural researcher who specializes in turning dreams into reality is Dr. Al Slinkard of the University of Saskatchewan. Because of him, Canada is now the world's leading exporter of lentils and peas, and one of the top global producers of chickpeas. His Laird lentil is to the culinary world what Marquis wheat was and Yukon Gold potatoes are—a true, unmitigated star! Laird is the most recognized lentil in the world. It is brilliantly easy to cook, inexpensive, high in protein and it makes amazing stews and soups and spreads, absorbing flavours easily.

Slinkard grew up in a family of four kids on a small quarter-section farm at the base of a mountain in northern Idaho. He labels himself a "hillbilly." He was invited to join the University of Saskatchewan in 1972 to be in charge of "peas and special crops." Was it for the money? The prestige? It was neither. He accepted because of the colossal challenge that the work presented. At that time, "it was a very small department trying to do research for 45 million acres of cropland," Slinkard says. The main crop was durum wheat, and fewer than a dozen farmers in the province had tried to grow lentils. He looked around the province and determined that there was potential for pulse crops like those he'd seen growing in Washington State, next to where he'd grown up. He released the large-seeded green lentil, Laird, in 1978, and in 1980, another one he named Eston, which was also green but decidedly smaller. Both have become standards for the crop—they are the Kleenex or Tim's of the "aggie" community. Another cultivar Slinkard developed is a white lentil he named CDC Gold. It has a gorgeous golden hue when cooked, and Slinkard, who loves to eat, serves it in a salad. Someday it will find its way to the tables of Canada. As the late Gary Johnston of Yukon Gold potato fame used to say, "Plant breeders must be patient."

The beauty of lentils, as opposed to any other pulse crop, is that they take so little fuel to cook. A pot of split Eston lentils cooks perfectly in less than 15 minutes, without the pre-soaking that beans need. For wealthy North America, this may not mean a lot, but for much of the world, which suffers from a lack of available fuel, it means a meal.

Now professor emeritus at the same university's Crop Development Centre, Dr. Slinkard effectively laid the foundation for the Canadian pulse industry, releasing 19 new varieties. He had, and still has, a vision. Some hillbilly!

During his time at the Crop Development Centre in the University of Saskatchewan, Slinkard advised and coached a number of graduate students. One of them is the man who has taken over as the Pulse Crop Research Chair, the supercharged Dr. Bert Vandenberg. Like Slinkard, he also grew up on farmland, but his home was in southern Ontario's fruit country. Vandenberg's cultivars are taking the pulse industry to still another level. The Blaze lentil, the variety that Corey Loessin plants, is a Vandenburg release, and the lentil cake that Joan baked that spring day near Radisson used this delicious pulse.

In addition to supervising tens of thousands of botanic experiments, Vandenberg coaches Masters-level soccer. He has seen how his players need to have a long stretch of energy rather than a short burst. So he's developed what he calls The Soccer Diet, which consists of a mild curried dhal that he serves a few hours before the game. His theory that soccer players excel at their game after a meal of lentils may be a case of wishful thinking, but it is currently being scientifically evaluated. He also loves to eat good food, so within the confines of his own lab, he runs recipe contests and holds potlucks. The 2005 lentil recipe winner was Devini DeSilva's Delicious Lentil Curry (page 306).

Another plant food that has had huge culinary success is the soybean. Yet when it first arrived in Canada, it was only used as a forage crop to feed to livestock. Charles Zavitz, the renowned plant breeder from the Ontario Agricultural College, planted it in his experimental plot in 1893 as a mere novelty. But not content to leave well enough alone, Zavitz worked with the beans for several decades, paying special attention to some he had imported from Japan. Eventually, the list was whittled down to a manageable 22 plants

Flax in bloom at Kings Landing Historical Settlement.

from some 10,000 plants, and the one with the highest yield was chosen to be released in 1923 as OAC 211. Zavitz did for soybeans what he'd done for barley (see page 147), and rather than being a conversation crop in a farmer's field, the soybean began to take its place as an important piece of the Canadian agricultural puzzle. Soybeans have become the number one cash crop in Ontario. Around the province and across the nation, soy-based food businesses have spun up, and soy milk, tofu, ice cream, miso and tempeh are being produced.

Flax migrated from Atlantic Canada to Quebec and Ontario before finally reaching western Canada by 1875. It wasn't until half a century later, though, that the icon of the Canadian breakfast table was created: Red River Cereal. It seems that humans have known intuitively that flaxseed is good for health but only recently has it been proven to be a major source of omega-3, an essential nutrient to the human body, with over 50 percent alpha-linoleic acid. Even adding 10 to 20 percent to the feed ration of chickens translates into heart-healthy omega-3-enriched eggs (page 207), and similar strides are being made in other foods, such as pork, milk and cheese. Canada continues to be the world's largest producer and exporter of flaxseed, representing about 80 percent of world trade. As a result, Canadian supply conditions have a major impact on the global flaxseed market. Canada has exported an average of almost $250 million per year in flaxseed for the past five years. As the world population becomes more and more health conscious, production is expected to skyrocket.

There could be no clearer demonstration of the importance of agricultural research to the creation of good food, particularly when harnessed with our creative, often tenacious farming community on the same culinary team. The resulting synergy spills over the brim of our well-filled national glass and soaks into every other aspect of the food life of Canada. Wendell Berry's axiom "Eating is an agricultural act" rings loud and clear. From a lab in Saskatoon, with its thousands of seedlings, to an orchard bearing new cultivars in the Annapolis Valley, from a culinary studio in Niagara overlooking an exquisitely groomed vineyard to an avant-garde kitchen garden on southern Vancouver Island, researchers, chefs and historians, enthnobotanists, conservationists and food writers are laying the foundation for what is potentially the richest food culture on earth. From the ancient harvests of the original palate to old crops made new again, this is the real food of Canada. The circle is complete. We are preparing to feed the world. The future can be ours if we claim it. This is our Canada—strong, proud and absolutely *delicious!*

Canola in flower near Meota, Saskatchewan.

The Canola Industry

Today the canola industry has some 60,000 farmers, working 11.3 million acres. There are 13 processing plants in five provinces. Annual primary crushing capacity for all plants totals about four million tons of canola seed. Four million tons of canola seed produces approximately 1.6 million tons of canola oil and 2.4 million tons of canola meal, which is used as feed for all sorts of livestock and even as a supplement to fish food in the aquaculture industry. The canola industry contributes more than $6 billion annually to the Canadian economy.

Why Is Canola Oil Healthy?

Research has shown a link between saturated fat and increased serum cholesterol that, in turn, is associated with increased coronary heart disease risk. Canola oil has the lowest level of saturated fat (7 percent) of all oils on the market today. It's also high (61 percent) in the monounsaturated fatty acid oleic acid. Oleic acid has been shown to reduce serum cholesterol levels and "bad" (LDL) cholesterol levels. Oleic acid does not affect levels of "good" (HDL) cholesterol.

Two classes of polyunsaturated fatty acids (omega-3 and omega-6) are essential for humans, since they cannot be synthesized in the body and must be supplied through diet. Canola oil contains a moderate level (22 percent) of omega-6 (polyunsaturated fatty acid linoleic acid) and an appreciable amount (11 percent) of omega-3 (alpha-linoleic acid).

Omega-3 has been shown to be effective in lowering serum triglyceride levels, as well as in reducing platelet aggregation and increasing blood clotting time. These anti-blood-clotting effects play an important role in the reduction of coronary heart disease.

Keiko's Miso Soup

Keiko Yakimo, whose story appears earlier in this book (page 62), was born in Canada, and her miso soup is a great example of the evolution recipes go through when specific traditional ingredients may not be available. There's no seaweed, in this soup but the unmistakeable flavour of dashi is there. If you wish, add some dry *wakame,* the seaweed my Japanese daughter-in-law, Kaori, uses.

YIELD: 3 to 4 servings

2 tofu puffs (aburage)
4 to 6 cups (1 to 1.5 L) water
½ cup (125 mL) shiro miso
1 tbsp (15 mL) dashi powder
1 pkg (approximately 500 g) tofu, drained and cut into 1-inch (2.5 cm) cubes
2 cups (500 mL) snap peas, strings removed

Soak the tofu puffs in cold water for 5 to 10 minutes; drain and slice. Set aside.

In a large saucepan, bring the water to a boil and stir in the miso and dashi powder. When the miso has dissolved, add the tofu puffs, diced tofu and snap peas. Reheat and simmer for 2 to 3 minutes.

Hearty Split Pea Soup with Smoked Sausage

Before they retired, Mary and Jack Klein were two of the finest bakers in my village. Coming from Holland, they brought their food ways with them. This is a great winter soup, the kind that Mary's mother would have served during the foggy days on the Atlantic coast, and now one that Mary herself serves as winter closes in in southern Ontario. This recipe is almost identical to one that Saskatchewan's Joan Heath shared with me last spring. She and her husband, Corey, grow peas for drying.

YIELD: 8 to 10 servings

1 lean pork hock
8 cups (2 L) chicken stock
1¼ cups (300 mL) split peas
2 bay leaves
Salt and freshly ground pepper
½ lb (250 g) mild smoked sausage, diced
2 leeks, well washed and chopped
2 or 3 carrots, peeled and diced

In a large soup kettle, combine the pork hock and stock; bring to a boil. Cover and simmer gently for 1 hour. Add split peas and bay leaves. Cook until meat is very tender and vegetables are cooked, about 1 hour longer, adding additional water or stock if needed.

Remove hock and set aside until cool enough to handle. Remove the lean meat from the bones and chop. Discard the rest. Skim the fat from the soup. Season the soup to taste with salt and lots of pepper. Add the pork, smoked sausage, leeks and carrots; simmer until sausage is thoroughly cooked and vegetables are tender, 20 to 30 minutes. Ladle into heated soup bowls.

Annapolis Cider Vinegar and Poppy Seed Dressing

Across Canada, apple cider vinegar is being made in small, artisanal batches. In Cambridge, Nova Scotia, Boates Farm (www.boatvin.com) produces what they call a "balsamic-style apple cider vinegar." When I picked up a bottle at their great roadside stand, I immediately thought of a recipe that came from The Garrison House Inn, a small lovely country inn that I'd visited in Annapolis Royal well over two decades before. This is my version of the recipe, which has been a standby in my own kitchen since 1987. I use this dressing on all sorts of salads, and it's even better when you have some fresh sliced fruit, such as local strawberries or blackberries, strewn on top of the greens.

YIELD: 1½ cups (375 mL)

1 egg

2 tbsp (30 mL) granulated sugar

1 tbsp (15 mL) grainy or plain Dijon mustard

⅓ cup (75 mL) Boates Balsamic-Style Apple Cider Vinegar or any other fine apple cider vinegar

½ tsp (2 mL) salt

½ tsp (2 mL) coarse black pepper

¼ cup (60 mL) finely chopped green onion or garlic chives

1 cup (250 mL) canola oil

1 tbsp (15 mL) poppy seeds

In a food processor, combine the egg, sugar, mustard, vinegar, salt, pepper and green onion. Process until smooth. With the motor running, pour in the oil slowly in a steady stream. Stir in the poppy seeds and refrigerate until ready to use.

New Age Caesar Dressing

Alison Bell teaches chef training at David Thompson Secondary School in Invermere, B.C. She writes that it "can be both extremely rewarding and, at times, quite challenging." The students learn culinary skills and then put them into practice at the school's cafeteria, The Rocky Mountain Café. "We developed this recipe to give students a healthier version of the ubiquitous teen salad favourite, the caesar—it's always the biggest seller," says Alison. "With a little innovation, we can provide a healthy alternative to this less-than-healthy salad choice. Funny thing, if you ask students if they like tofu, they usually grimace, but when you turn it into a delicious salad dressing, it's another story entirely."

She notes that "if the dressing is a little too acidic for your taste, add a pinch of salt. If you prefer to make a vegan caesar dressing, replace the anchovy paste with 2 tsp (10 mL) tamari and omit the cheese."

Toss it with greens and croutons, and more Parmesan if you wish. It's very, very good!

YIELD: 1½ cups (375 mL)

¼ cup (60 mL) lemon juice
2 tsp (10 mL) grated lemon rind
2 or 3 cloves garlic, minced
½ tsp (2 mL) red pepper flakes
2 tbsp (30 mL) anchovy paste
2 tsp (10 mL) Dijon mustard
8 oz (250 g) silken tofu, preferably organic
½ cup (125 mL) cold-pressed soybean oil, local sunflower oil or canola oil
⅓ cup (75 mL) freshly grated Parmesan cheese
2 tbsp (30 mL) minced Italian parsley
Salt and freshly ground pepper

In a food processor, blend the lemon juice, rind, garlic, red pepper flakes, anchovy paste, mustard and tofu until smooth. With motor running, slowly add the soybean oil. Fold in the Parmesan cheese, minced parsley, and salt and pepper to taste.

SUNFLOWER OIL

Sunflower oil (*Helianthus annuus* var.) is native to North America. Because sunflower seeds are so rich in oil, they were a special food of the Aboriginal populace across much of the continent. However, sunflowers weren't grown commercially in Canada until 1920. Most sunflower seed is sold as either confectionery product or as birdseed. Although there is no large crushing facility in Canada, the seed is often pressed to order in small quantities. NuSun sunflower oil is processed in Mitchell, Ontario, and Ferme Champy in Upton, Quebec, produces Champy huile de tournesol biologique.

SAFFLOWER OIL

Safflower oil *(Carthamus tinctorium)* hails from the Near East, from where it travelled east to China along the Silk Road sometime between the first and seventh centuries AD. In Canada, it was first experimented with in Ottawa in 1936, and although it has never reached the production levels of soy or canola, it is very healthy, with a high unsaturated fat (linoleic) content. Canadian safflower seed is harvested in Manitoba, Saskatchewan and Alberta.

Saskatchewan Wheat Berry and Wild Rice Salad

This is another one of Joan Heath's excellent recipes, and she says the salad can be made ahead, without the nuts and sunflower seeds, and refrigerated for up to three days. While the cooking of the various grains may seem a bit fussy, the results are worth it. Serve the salad on a bed of spinach or baby salad greens.

YIELD: 8 to 10 servings

1 cup (250 mL) wheat berries
¾ cup (175 mL) wild rice
1 cup (250 mL) pot barley
4 green onions, thinly sliced
1 sweet red pepper, seeded and diced
⅓ cup (75 mL) raisins
½ cup (125 mL) roasted hazelnuts, chopped
½ cup (125 mL) toasted sunflower seeds

DRESSING:
¼ cup (60 mL) canola oil
¼ cup (60 mL) soy sauce
¼ cup (60 mL) lemon juice
1 tbsp (15 mL) Dijon mustard
2 cloves garlic, minced
½ tsp (2 mL) salt
¼ tsp (1 mL) freshly ground pepper

In a saucepan, cover wheat berries with water and bring to a boil. Salt lightly, reduce heat, cover and simmer until tender but firm, about 1¼ hours. Drain.

Meanwhile, in a separate saucepan, do the same with the wild rice, simmering until tender and most of the grains have split, about 45 minutes. Drain.

In a third saucepan, do the same with the barley, stirring occasionally and simmering until tender, about 20 minutes. Drain.

DRESSING: In a large bowl, whisk together the oil, soy sauce, lemon juice, mustard, garlic, salt and pepper. Add the wheat berries, wild rice, barley, green onions, red pepper and raisins. Toss to combine. Stir in the hazelnuts and sunflower seeds.

Spiced Soybean Hummus

A staple in the Middle East, traditional hummus is made from well-cooked chickpeas. This updated recipe uses canned soybeans, which are softer, easy to purée and higher in protein. Serve the hummus with vegetables and/or pita chips.

YIELD: About 3½ cups (875 mL)

1 can (19 oz/540 mL) soybeans, well rinsed and thoroughly drained
2 large cloves garlic, coarsely chopped
½ cup (125 mL) chopped green onion
½ cup (125 mL) chopped fresh parsley
½ cup (125 mL) tahini
¼ cup (60 mL) fresh lemon juice
¼ cup (60 mL) water
¼ cup (60 mL) canola or olive oil
1 tsp (5 mL) salt
¼ tsp (1 mL) red pepper flakes
Freshly ground pepper

In a food processor, combine the soybeans, garlic, green onions, parsley, tahini, lemon juice, water, oil, salt and red pepper flakes. Process until very smooth. Transfer to a serving bowl or spread on a plate. Generously grind pepper over top.

In Quebec and in Acadian regions salted herbs (*herbes salées*) are often used to flavour foods. They date back to the earliest French settlement. They were cheap, available and could be stored all winter long. The following technique can be found in *La Cuisinière Canadienne*.

Pick over parsley, chervil and chives that have been well washed. Alternate layers of salt with layers of herbs in a large container, and leave them to be used for thin soups.

Golden Vegetable Chickpea Fritters (Pakoras)

It's so great to see a bag of chickpea flour with Product of Canada emblazoned proudly on it rather than hidden quietly under a UPC code. Even a decade ago, this flour would not have reached the mainstream, but today one can find it not only in the specialty stores of Southeast Asia but also in many of the major grocery chains.

Canada makes excellent chickpea (besan) flour and exports a lot of it to India, where these fritters are served in many variations, this being only one of them, and my own version at that. While I like cauliflower and carrots and onion slices, it's worth experimenting. If I have leftover cauliflower stems, I slice them the same thickness as the carrot and include them in my veggie mix. Some cooks even coat small chunks of potato with the batter before deep-frying. Use a yogurt-based dip like the Kashmiri Mint Chutney (page 79) or simply plain yogurt.

YIELD: 4 to 6 servings

> 1 cup (250 mL) chickpea flour
> 1 tsp (5 mL) salt
> ½ tsp (2 mL) turmeric
> ½ tsp (2 mL) ground cumin
> ½ tsp (2 mL) baking powder
> ¼ tsp (1 mL) cayenne pepper
> ¾ cup (175 mL) water
> 3 to 4 cups (750 mL to 1 L) small pieces of vegetables, such as cauliflower florets and thinly sliced carrots
> Canola oil, for frying

In a medium bowl, whisk together the flour, salt, turmeric, cumin, baking powder and cayenne. Gradually mix in the water, mixing well so that there are no lumps. Toss the vegetables with the batter. Set aside.

Add enough oil to a heavy, deep saucepan or deep-fryer to come about 2 inches (5 cm) up the side. Using a frying thermometer, heat to 350°F (180°C). With tongs, remove some of the batter-covered vegetables from the bowl and carefully transfer to the hot oil.

Fry in batches until golden, 4 to 5 minutes. Remove with a slotted spoon and let drain on a baking sheet lined with paper towels. Keep warm in a 250°F (120°C) oven until all the fritters are cooked.

Nettie Cronish's Tofu Neatballs

Nettie Cronish is a vegetarian chef and cookbook author. Her recipes have also been published in magazines like *Homemakers* and *Alive*. Her cooking classes at Toronto's Big Carrot are sold out months in advance.

These delicious tofu "neatballs" are a great example of cross-cultural cooking. Nettie makes them into rounds and serves them in pita bread with a variety of greens—lettuce, shredded kale, minced green onions—and/or tomatoes. The fresh sage is the clincher here. It's a great addition!

I like the mixture shaped into patties, which I find easier to brown. Handle the patties or neatballs gently; as they cook, they become firmer. They're great instead of meatballs on top of pasta with sauce poured over them.

If you don't use the entire mixture, refrigerate it, tightly covered, for up to two days. Nettie says that she bakes the neatballs before freezing them, so she can quickly pan-fry some when she needs them.

YIELD: 18 to 24 neatballs or patties

1 pkg (350 g) extra-firm tofu, well crumbled

2 tbsp (30 mL) soy sauce

1 tsp (5 mL) mirin (optional)

3 cloves garlic, minced

2 tbsp (30 mL) ground flaxseed

6 tbsp (90 mL) water

1 cup (250 mL) fresh whole-grain bread crumbs

⅓ cup (75 mL) freshly grated Parmesan cheese

¼ cup (60 mL) chopped fresh sage

1 tsp (5 mL) dried oregano

1 tsp (5 mL) dried basil

2 eggs, lightly beaten

Olive or canola oil, for frying

In a large bowl, combine crumbled tofu, soy sauce, mirin (if using) and garlic. Set aside for at least 5 minutes.

Stir together the ground flax and water; let stand for 2 minutes before adding to the tofu mixture. Stir in the bread crumbs, cheese, sage, oregano, basil and eggs, mixing thoroughly.

Shape heaping tablespoons into tightly packed balls or patties, handling gently.

In a large, well-seasoned cast-iron or high-quality non-stick skillet, heat 2 tbsp (30 mL) oil over medium-high heat; brown balls or patties in batches on all sides, about 8 to 10 minutes, adding oil as needed to keep them from sticking. Keep warm until serving.

SOY SCIENCE

Project Soy, a competition and challenge to students at the University of Guelph to find innovative new uses for soybeans, was created in 1996. Entrepreneur, philanthropist and grower Peter Hannam has helped immensely by creating the Hannam Soybean Utilization Fund, a $1 million gift to the University of Guelph, his alma mater. Over the years, the students have risen to the occasion, dreaming up and creating everything from heart-healthy bagels to edible and biodegradable food packaging trays. Here are a few of the creations from the past several years.

Bouggie was designed for people on the move by Sylvie Dandurand. It's a dry soup base with a good source of protein, iron and phosphates. Bouggie is made without GMOs, and is certified organic. Soybeans were mixed with other vegetables to create the base, making it a low-cost production.

ProbiSoy is a soy-based health drink developed by College d'Alfred student Leontily Cordeiro. It's ideal for individuals looking to increase their soy intake who may have lactose intolerance or allergies to milk products. It's made organically and helps promote proper digestion and nutrition levels in the body.

Sweetened Condensed Soy by Leslie Edwardson is a soy-based condensed milk that could be used as an alternative to regular dairy-based sweetened condensed milk. The product can be used to make dairy-free desserts for vegetarians, people with milk allergies, and those that are lactose intolerant. Soy adds a nutritional punch to the condensed product as well, giving another bonus to this alternative product.

JAYS Pancakes, or "Sunshine Solutions Pancakes," developed by Jessica Warnock, Yvonne Yung, Sarah Ong and Anangelina Archile, are microwavable pancakes combining nutrition, taste and convenience in one package. The pancakes are made with soy milk instead of cow's milk, and a blend of different flours (soy, whole wheat and potato), which boosts the nutritional content.

Decadence Doughnuts were created by Sayward Fetterly, Jessica Speziale and Sandra Kolaczek as a healthier doughnut that would appeal to adults, sparing them the guilt of eating an unhealthy snack. Soy flour and soy milk were used as alternatives in the ingredients, and soy-based oil was used for the cooking.

Green Bean Café, by Jennifer Prine, Lee Weiss and Andrea Kocmarek, is a unique line of soy coffee blends and flavoured soy mixes. The students' goal in developing them was to enjoy the goodness of soy by providing healthy alternative beverages that don't taste like they are alternative. Flavours include chocolate raspberry, amaretto and Irish cream, and the drinks are high in natural protein and soy isoflavones.

Chocsoylate, by Helle Thomsen, Qian Guo and Lei Ma, combines soy protein and chocolate to create an easy and convenient way to incorporate more soy protein in the diet while also enjoying the health benefits of both soy and chocolate. Each serving provides 7 g of high-quality soy protein, good-for-you antioxidants and the delicious taste and texture of traditional chocolate with no soy taste.

Soy Smart Enriched Soy Protein Bread was developed by Adrienne Legris and Julie Charman, whose goal was to produce a multi-grain bread that could be effectively manufactured on the industrial scale, while meeting the needs of consumers in promoting healthy living. The bread is low fat, high protein, a high source of fibre, and a source of 10 essential nutrients.

Soy and Lentil Burritos

This recipe is from Marilyn Crowley, one of the most respected food writers in Canada. She has a golden palate and understands flavour to such an extent that I can usually identify her recipies even if she doesn't sign her name.

Marilyn writes from her home in Kingston:

Freezing changes the texture of tofu dramatically, making it more meat-like and familiar. The mild smoky flavour of the chipotle pepper is subtle, and the spice is hot. A fresh jalapeño pepper can be substituted; however, there will be no smoky flavour and less spicy heat. Offer additional burrito filling garnishes, such as hot rice, guacamole, diced tomatoes, sliced green onions, grated Monterey Jack or cheddar cheese, shredded lettuce and cooling sour cream.

A chipotle pepper is a jalapeño pepper that has been smoked. They're often packed in dark red adobo sauce, which is made from ground chilies, herbs and vinegar, and are fiery enough that usually only one is needed in a recipe. Individually wrap the other chilies along with a bit of sauce and freeze to use in soups and Mexican-inspired dishes such as chili con carne.

My great friend Eleanor Morris has used this recipe for years and makes a stew-like variation by adding a full 28-oz (796 mL) can of tomatoes, then serving the mixture on top of steamed barley.

YIELD: 6 burritos

1 pkg (1 lb/500 g) regular or firm tofu

1 tbsp (15 mL) olive or canola oil

¾ cup (175 mL) chopped onion

1 large or 2 small cloves garlic, minced

2 tsp (10 mL) chili powder

1 tsp (5 mL) ground cumin

1 can (19 oz/540 mL) lentils (undrained)

1 cup (250 mL) fresh plum tomatoes, seeded and diced, or drained canned diced tomatoes

1 chipotle pepper in adobo sauce, seeded and chopped, plus 2 tsp (10 mL) adobo sauce (or 1 large jalapeño pepper, seeded and diced)

2 tbsp (30 mL) chopped fresh coriander

6 large flour tortillas (approx 10 inches/25 cm)

GARNISHES: guacamole, diced tomatoes, chopped green onions, more minced coriander, shredded cheeses, shredded lettuce and/or sour cream, tomato salsa or hot sauce

Freeze tofu package until solid. In a saucepan, bring 1 inch (2.5 cm) water to a boil. Remove tofu from package; place frozen block in boiling water. Cover when bubbling; reduce heat and simmer for 20 minutes. Drain in colander; let cool to lukewarm. Cut into quarters. Squeeze tofu firmly using hands; discard liquid. Pull tofu apart into small crumbled pieces.

Heat oil in large saucepan over medium heat. Add onion and garlic; cook for 1 to 2 minutes. Add chili powder and cumin; cook for 1 minute. Stir in tofu; cook for 3 minutes, stirring often. Add lentils, including liquid, tomatoes, chipotle and adobo sauce; mash lentils lightly. Heat until bubbling, stirring often. Reduce heat and simmer, stirring occasionally, for 20 minutes. Uncover and simmer for 5 minutes or until thickened. Stir in coriander.

Warm tortillas individually in a large dry skillet over medium heat, turning once. Spoon about ⅔ cup (150 mL) of the lentil mixture in centre of each tortilla. Add garnishes as desired. Tuck in edges while rolling into cigar shape. Serve with tomato salsa or hot sauce.

Warm Balsamic Lentils

This is another one of Mark Mitchell's terrific and flexible recipes. He uses the lentils under his grilled salmon fillets (page 56). They're great with Boates balsamic-style cider vinegar from Kings County, Nova Scotia; maple vinegar from Quebec; an off-dry wine vinegar from Niagara, like Minus 8; the authentically made balsamic from Venturi-Schultz on Vancouver Island or Spinnaker's Pale Ale Malt Vinegar from Victoria.

Lentils are very easy to cook but canned lentils are the ultimate in convenience.

YIELD: 3 to 4 servings

3 tbsp (45 mL) canola oil
1 small onion, minced
2 cloves garlic, crushed and minced
1 carrot, peeled and finely diced
⅓ cup (75 mL) finely chopped celery
¼ cup (60 mL) diced sweet red pepper
1 tsp (5 mL) salt
¼ tsp (1 mL) crushed chili peppers (optional)
1 can (19 oz/540 mL) lentils, drained, or 2 cups (500 mL) cooked lentils
2 tbsp (30 mL) high-quality local vinegar

Heat the oil in a skillet over medium heat; sauté the onion, garlic, carrot, celery, pepper and salt for 3 to 4 minutes or until beginning to soften and brown. Stir in the chili peppers and drained lentils and heat through. Add the vinegar, mixing to combine. Cover and keep warm until serving.

Devini DeSilva's Delicious Lentil Curry (Dhal)

Devini is a research associate in the pulse crop breeding program at the Crop Development Centre, University of Saskatchewan. She came to Canada in 1995 to do her master's degree with Dr. Al Slinkard at the university. She lives in Saskatoon with her husband and two grown children.

Split lentil curry is an essential part of everyday meals in Sri Lanka. It's simple and delicious. Because no soaking is necessary, it takes less than 15 minutes to prepare. They often have potlucks at the Pulse Research Centre, and according to Dr. Burt Vandenberg, Devini's dhal was voted "the best one in our lab."

Like most home cooks, Devini often adds to, subtracts from and varies the recipe. Below is the basic dhal, but included are a number of options. The variation she calls Limited Edition adds many additional layers of flavour. "If you think more spice is nice," she says, "add 1 tsp (5 mL) crushed chili flakes when making the curry, and for variety, add a handful of one of the following: fresh spinach leaves, freshly picked lamb's quarters, Swiss chard, beet greens or chopped cauliflower."

YIELD: 6 to 8 servings

1 cup (250 mL) split red lentils
1 cup (250 mL) water
½ tsp (2 mL) turmeric
1 tsp (5 mL) roasted fenugreek powder
1 tsp (5 mL) curry powder
1 hot green pepper or other chili, seeded and thinly sliced
1 small onion, diced
4 cloves garlic, sliced
6 curry leaves (optional) *
2 inches (5 cm) pandan leaf (optional) *
1½ cups (375 mL) soy milk or half-and-half cream (10%), or 1 can (398 mL) coconut milk
1 tsp (5 mL) salt
2 tsp (10 mL) lime juice

*Available in Indian and Asian food stores.

Wash the lentils; drain well. Transfer to a medium saucepan and add water. Stir in turmeric, fenugreek powder and curry powder; add hot pepper, onion, garlic and curry leaves and pandan leaf (if using). Cover and bring to a boil; reduce heat to very low and steam for 7 minutes or until most of the liquid is absorbed and lentils are beginning to soften. Add milk and salt, stirring to combine. Cover and return to a boil over high heat. Cook, stirring, until the mixture is bubbling and thickened, about 10 minutes. Remove from heat and discard pandan leaf (if using). Stir in lime juice. Serve immediately with Coconut Roti (page 308), rice or even French bread. Or stir into the even spicier mixture that Devini calls Limited Edition (see below).

Limited Edition

2 dried chilies
½ tsp (2 mL) black mustard seeds
1 tbsp (15 mL) canola oil
1 small onion, thinly sliced
1 small green chili, seeded and thinly sliced
½ tsp (2 mL) curry powder
2 or 3 curry leaves
1 clove garlic, crushed

Chop the dried chilies and place in a bowl; cover with boiling salted water. Soak for 10 minutes. Drain and mince.

Roast the mustard seeds in a dry skillet over medium heat until they begin to pop, 1 to 2 minutes. Add the oil, then stir in the onion, green chili, curry powder, curry leaves and crushed garlic. Stir well and cook for 1 minute. Add the cooked lentil curry to the saucepan. Reheat for 1 minute before serving.

Coconut Roti

Devini dictated this recipe to me over the phone during a mid-winter storm. With the wind howling, it felt so good to bake flatbread on my old cast-iron griddle, brush it with butter and use it as a vehicle to get the delicious, tummy-warming dhal to my mouth. I've streamlined her recipe slightly in order to speed up the process. Using a food processor, it's quite possible to make the roti during the time the lentils are cooking.

YIELD: 8 roti

¾ cup (175 mL) desiccated unsweetened coconut
½ cup (125 mL) boiling water
2½ cups (625 mL) all-purpose flour
1 tbsp (15 mL) active dry yeast
1 tsp (5 mL) salt
1 cup (250 mL) very hot water
2 tbsp (30 mL) canola oil
Additional flour, as needed
Soft or clarified butter, as needed

In a small bowl, combine the coconut and boiling water. Set aside to cool slightly.

In a food processor, combine the flour, yeast and salt. Pulse to combine.

Add the oil to the hot water. With the motor running, pour it into the food processor and process till the dough comes away from the sides of the bowl, 15 to 20 seconds. Add the coconut mixture and continue to process briefly. Turn out onto a generously floured board and let rest for 5 to 10 minutes.

Meanwhile, heat a cast-iron skillet or griddle over medium-high heat.

Divide the dough into 8 pieces and roll one at a time into a 6- to 8-inch (15 to 20 cm) length, dusting with flour as often as required to keep from sticking. Place on the hot dry pan and cook till the underside is lightly browned, 1 to 2 minutes. Flip and bake till puffy and browned, 1 to 2 minutes longer. Brush each roti with butter and transfer to a warm oven or wrap in a kitchen towel until ready to serve.

Prairie Lentil and Grain Cake with Buttery Broiler Icing

This is one of the most unusual and utterly delicious cakes I've ever tasted. Created by Joan Heath of Radisson, Saskatchewan, it stays fresh for ages. Filled with grains, the special ingredient is puréed lentils, one of the crops she and her husband harvest. To make the purée, she measures the lentils and then adds twice the amount of water, then brings the lentils to a boil and simmers them until they're soft, 35 to 40 minutes, before blending them in a food processor or mashing them until smooth. She freezes any leftover lentils to extend meat loaf or enrich muffins.

YIELD: 10 to 12 servings

½ cup (125 mL) rolled oats

1½ cups (375 mL) whole wheat flour or multi-grain flour

¼ cup (60 mL) barley flour or buckwheat flour

½ tsp (2 mL) salt

1 tsp (5 mL) cinnamon

1 tsp (5 mL) baking soda

¼ cup (60 mL) whole flaxseed

¼ cup (60 mL) ground flaxseed

2 tsp (10 mL) baking powder

½ cup (125 mL) raisins

½ cup (125 mL) chopped dates

½ cup (125 mL) canola oil

2 eggs

1 tsp (5 mL) vanilla extract

⅔ cup (150 mL) liquid honey

1½ cups (375 mL) lentil purée

Broiler Icing (recipe follows)

In a bowl, combine the rolled oats, whole wheat flour, barley flour, salt, cinnamon, baking soda, flax, ground flax and baking powder. Stir in the raisins and dates.

In another bowl, whisk together the canola oil, eggs, vanilla, honey and 1 cup (250 mL) of the lentil purée.

Stir in the remaining lentil purée. Add the flour mixture, stirring to combine thoroughly until no wet spots remain. Spread batter in a well-oiled 9- x 13-inch (3.5 L) cake pan; bake in a preheated 350°F (180°C) oven for 25 to 30 minutes or until a cake tester comes out clean.

Let cool before icing with Broiler Icing.

Broiler Icing

⅔ cup (150 mL) packed brown sugar

¼ cup (60 mL) butter

2 tbsp (30 mL) cream or milk

¼ cup (60 mL) shredded coconut

¼ cup (60 mL) chopped walnuts

In a small saucepan, combine the sugar, butter, cream, coconut and walnuts. Heat, stirring, until hot and sugar is dissolved. Spread over cake. Place in the oven under the broiler and broil until the surface is covered with bubbles and beginning to brown, 3 to 5 minutes.

The delicate almost-waxen blossoms of the rare native clove currant (Ribes odoratum), a large bush that yields somewhat seedy, mild-flavoured fruit. This particular shrub flourishes in the middle of the well-tilled earth of Margaret Sherk's garden in Wellington County.

During the hiatus between books there has been a considerable evolution of Anita Stewart, Culinary Activist. When I first used this moniker, it was because I felt that it was possible to make things happen. Little did I know that this was precisely what Carême, Fourier, Balzac, Grimod de la Reynière and Brillat-Savarin had done in 18th- and 19th-century France. But they assumed a different title, that of "gastronomer." They were working in their many genres—chef, utopian philosopher, playwright, traveller, social commentator—to illustrate that their national culinary culture was worth honouring; in fact it was worth celebrating with every ounce of their strength. They delighted in their new-found cuisine, as I have. This book has come out of 25 years of joy-filled exploration. But I did not do it alone. The help I've had over the years has been astounding.

First and foremost, I extend my deepest appreciation to His Excellency Jean-Daniel Lafond for honouring my ideas and my work with his praise. When we met in 2006, we talked gastronomy and we talked Canada. This is a gentleman who, when he believes in something, acts. Creating an award for the culinary arts is extraordinarily important. He recognizes that Canadians must begin to make some culinary heroes. With the endorsement of Her Excellency, the Governor General of Canada, he has seen to it that men and women who put good food and wine onto our personal tables and who also have the agronomic skill sets to feed the world will be lauded and honoured. My most sincere thanks to those who introduced us—Janet Dorozynski of the Department of Foreign Affairs, Melanie Kwong of Parks Canada, and Christine MacIntyre and Cidália Gaspar of Rideau Hall. The conversation continues.

Thank you so much to Jo Marie Powers, who challenged me to write my first cookbook; expert culinary historians Dr. Mary Williamson and Elizabeth Driver; ethno-botanist Dr. Nancy Turner; educator and writer Dr. Barbara Santich, and Slow Food journal editor John Irving, who allowed me to write freely for that international journal and the website. To anthropologists Hilary Stewart and Joy Inglis who, over the years, with the help of our friend Eric Peterson, have facilitated my understanding of the customs and lives of the coastal First Nations. We ate so well!

Thanks to my dear, too-distant friends Frederique and Sinclair Philip; Edith and Victor Newman; Anne Desjardins and Pierre Audette. And to my friend Carol Ferguson, who stated flatly that no magazine would ever send a photographer to the places I wanted to explore so "Get a decent camera!"; to Julia Aitken, whose sense of humour is always an encouragement to continue; and to Marie Nightingale, whose knowledge of Nova Scotia cooking transcends all others'.

My deepest appreciation to the team at the Canola Council of Canada—Robert Hunter, Diane Wreford, Dorothy Long and Ellen Pruden of CanolaInfo, and above all to Dr. Terry Downey and the late Baldur Steffanson, who created the healthiest oil on earth.

In this business of agriculture, thanks to Dr. Robert McLaughlin, whose influence is woven invisibly throughout this book, and to Dr. Alan Wildeman, Sue Bennett, Carolynne Griffiths, David Cohlmeyer and Deborah Whale—you are committed, brilliant people and always an inspiration.

To the researchers and educators who put food (and some great beer) on our collective tables: David Hume, Duane Falk, Art Hill and Doug Goff, Mary Buhr, Peter Pauls, Terry Daynard, Al Sullivan, Rick Upfold, Steve Leeson and Rickey Yada, Rich Moccia, Mike Burke and David Bevan of the Alma Research Station; botanist Derek Bewley; Neil Miles, Peter Kevan and bee lab manager Paul Kelly; Vineland's Bill Lay and Rocco Guarnaccia, pear researcher extraordinaire David Hunter, and bean and peanut expert Tom Michaels. Many thanks to both Simon Lachance and OMAFRA's Dave Chapeskie for their help with the maple research. All of Canada should join with me to thank Bruce Holub, the determined researcher who spent years campaigning against trans-fats and trumpeting the merits of omega-3.

Thanks to the University of Guelph's Owen Roberts, Michael Ridley and Judy Wanner, who've been so helpful in my research endeavours.

It's always fun to hang around the Simcoe Research Station with Al McKeown, John Cline, Adam Dale and the most enthusiastic promoter of things local I've met in ages, Mike Columbus, not to mention the former director, Arthur Loughton.

Meeting pulse researcher Bert Vandenberg at the University of Saskatchewan was inspiring and a tad daunting. Not only did he take the time to show off his lab and brag about those working there with him, he put me in touch with one of Canada's great agricultural thinkers, Al Slinkard, who, like his protégé, knows the meaning of the word "action" intimately.

And to the many researchers at the Nova Scotia Agricultural College in

ORIGINS OF THE FEAST

L'Ordre de bon temps, or The Order of Good Cheer, was North America's first feasting society. Founded by Samuel de Champlain at the Habitation, Port Royal, Nova Scotia, it was specifically created to prevent "land sickness" or scurvy. Men were commissioned to go out hunting for the day and bring back the finest game. Although there are no written records of the menus, we can surmise that they would consist of indigenous ingredients, such as Jerusalem artichokes, shellfish, butternuts and possibly grapes, all embellished with imported items from France, such as prunes and Armagnac. Because the French invited the powerful Mi'kmaq chief (sagamore) Membertou and his band to the feasts, these gatherings also became very important politically, cementing a friendship between the French and Mi'kmaq that lasted over a century and through a variety of conflicts.

Janice Beaton, who now lives in Calgary but whose roots run deep in her beloved Cape Breton Island, salutes a summer sunset looking west to Prince Edward Island from high atop an island hill.

Truro: Jill Rogers; Raj Lada; Dave Percival and his assistant, Gloria Thyssen; Gefu Wang-Pruski and Kris Pruski; and retired NSAC professor Don Crober.

At Kentville, Nova Scotia, Peter Rideout, Doug Nichols and Andrew Jamieson gave me an incredible guided tour.

Many thanks to Maria McGowan at Pier 21 in Halifax and particularly to Pier 21's communications manager Carrie-Ann Smith, who shared her love of the history of Canada with me and referred me to the work of Paul Robert Magosci, the Chair of Ukrainian Studies at the University of Toronto. We all owe a huge debt of gratitude Dr. Magosci for his extraordinary work on the origins of Canada's peoples.

Hitting the road was intense and rewarding, particularly when the journey included meetings and visits and meals with some extraordinary Canadians: Janice Beaton and her family, Elizabeth and Angus Beaton; Jim St. Clair, *the* historian of Cape Breton Island; Kevin MacLeod and his generous Cape Breton family of great cooks; Vancouver Island's chef/mycologist Bill Jones and entrepreneur/publican Paul Hadfield; Sandra Kochan and Dave Gamble who, for years, have been my guides to the Okanagan; Michael and Carrie Chong, who, with their wee family, are profoundly committed to Canadian agriculture; Ontario's Deputy Minister of Agriculture, Dr. Bruce Archibald, and his tenacious team at that ministry both in Guelph and Toronto; Tomas Nimmo, who generously shared his soy contacts; Margaret Thibeault, when she was at the Beef Information Centre, and Charles Bruce Thompson of Ontario Pork; and Montreal bread guru, baker James MacGuire. Strident advocates for northern Ontario came in the form of Stig Puschel, Maurice Landriault and John Rowsell.

In the Maritimes I owe so much to people like proud Canadian business hero Archie MacLean of New Brunswick; Flossie and John MacDonald in Souris, P.E.I.; Brian Kienapple, the head of Slow Food's convivium in Nova Scotia; and Frances Brogan and David O'Brien, who gave me the late Ron Nickerson's fabulous Maritime cookbook and took me paddling. Nova Scotia's wise gourmande, Senator Donald Oliver, proudly shared his sharply honed kitchen skills, showed off his deer-proof garden and prepared a fabulous lunch. Margaret Weeks of Charlottetown and Joy Shinn were a huge help in the early days of my research there. Thanks so much to inveterate Colville Bay oysterman Johnny Flynn and the crew of the venerable *Owen Mor*.

The team of tasters that I turned to were truly the best sort of friends any aspiring cookbook author could have. First, they liked to eat; secondly they gave very, sometimes too, honest opinions, and finally, they helped to do the dishes (I hate doing dishes). Huge thanks to Gar, Sarah, Eric, Scott, Carolyn, Donna, Dave and Lillian, John and Eleanor, Rob and Kendra. On Prince Edward Island, where I spent several weeks working on the manuscript, my tasting team comprised Ann and Sheila Wilmer, and the late Ned and Bruce Wilmer, two generous, gentle friends who loved to share a kitchen and great wine with me. Mike Smith helped a lot, too!

And thanks and hugs to all the fabulous cooks . . . Mark and Kaori Stewart, Paul Stewart, Magdalena and Nina Ciechanowska, Mark Mitchell, June Pearson, Alison Bell, Marie Nightingale, Karen Mersereau and Gerard Paulin, Earlene Busch, Margaret Timmins, Mara Jernigan, Keiko Yakimo and Ray Girard, Candice Stanoyev and Shaffeen Jamal, Stephen Wong, Meeru and Vikram Vij, Michael Allemeier, Pierre and Bonnie Dubrulle, Erika and Peter Durlacher, Holly Rowland, Roswitha Rosswog, Wendy Abram, George Koyionis, Laurice de Gale, Trudy Heiss, Michael and Nobuyo Stadtländer, Jean-Francis and Alessandra Quaglia, Linda Chin and her "aunty" Lucy Ong, Nancy Wong, Eve Johnson and Stephen Wong,

Warmest thanks to Tuula Lewis from Sointula, and to Jayne Lloyd-Jones, who expedited the trip. Thanks to Edmonton's Gail Hall and Saskatchewan's

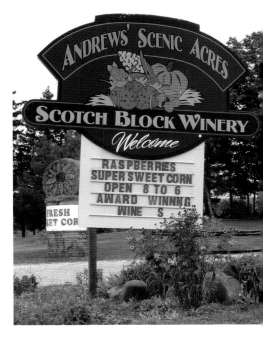

Andrews' Scenic Acres is a great example of diversification. Not content to limit himself to a pick-your-own operation, Bert Andrews has a great fruit winery, processes his own berries from blackcurrants to blueberries, and is now even bottling his own delicious blackcurrant juice. It's one of the few places I know where you can buy local frozen fruit throughout the year.

Joan Heath and Corey Loessin and to Ali Kendall-Morris, the Olson family of Manitoba fishing fame, Abi and Farouk Dadashi, Nettie Cronish and Marilyn Crowley, Kay Fettes and Lynda McGowan.

Closer to home, my deep appreciation goes to a group of top-notch local cooks: Peter Skoggard, Fred Gordon, Manjit Singh Bali, the Knudstrup family, and in particular Nancy and her late husband, Peter, Margaret Sherk and Elmer Wideman; Peggy and Eleanor Morris, Elaine Mayne and Karen Baxter, Tony Garaffa, Vanessa Currie, Roger Dufau and Alex Sgroi.

Thanks also to Joanne Yolles, now at the pastry kitchen of the Toronto restaurant Pangaea; the Stroutzas family of Alex Farms cheese fame; and from the north, Caryn Colman and Frances Boyes; and the Foire Gourmande cooks, Debbie Demers and Sanaa El Asfi and cheesemakers Hélène Lessard and Christian Barrette of Lorrainville, Quebec.

Although it's clear when I'm on air that I love holding forth, I have expert help. Thanks to my great CBC producers—Sandy Mowat and Mariel Borelli—along with my buddy Jeff Goodes, host of *Fresh Air*, Ontario's best weekend morning show.

My most sincere appreciation must also go to a huge variety of tourism folks, including many of my colleagues at the Society of American Travel Writers who've helped over the past decade. Carol Horne of Tourism P.E.I.; Randy Brooks and Sue Jeffries from Nova Scotia; Saskatchewan's Daryl Demoskoff, who has also turned out to be a great cook; Montreal's inimitable Gilles Bengle and Isabel Gil of Quebec; Colette Fontaine and Cathy Senecal from Manitoba; Kristine George of Victoria and a host of others from British Columbia—Mika Ryan, Cindy Burr, Janice Greenwood and Lana Kingston; Monica Campbell-Hoppé, Yvonne Nichie, Laura Fairweather; and Susan Iris and Heather Dolan from the Canadian Tourism Commission. And last but absolutely not least, Paul Raynor, Malcolm Andrews and Catherine Kaloutsky of VIA Rail, who stepped up to the plate to help with travel. What a way to go!

A huge thanks to my literary agent, Ashton Westwood, and the great team from HarperCollins, including my superb editor Kirsten Hanson, designer Sharon Kish, and, of course, longtime colleague and friend David Kent. This has been an extraordinary publishing experience!

Once again I had the great pleasure to work with photographer Robert Wigington and super food stylist, Olga Truchan.

And I would also like to thank the other publishers who've been part of this long, convoluted, exciting story. They mentored me. To Scott McIntyre of Douglas & McIntyre; Allan MacDougall from Raincoast; former book packager Denise Schon; and Howard White of Harbour Publishing—I hope you'll agree that we really have made a difference!

Herring from the Gulf of St. Lawrence is netted and processed on the Magdalen Islands before being shipped around the globe as "bloaters" or whole smoked herring.

18 LBS 8.2 KG NET
CHOICE BLOATERS
LE FUMOIR D'ANTAN
ILE DE LA MADELEINE
PRODUCT OF CANADA

INDEX